Confrontation

Confrontation

The Destruction of a College President

by Ken Metzler

University of Oregon Press

Eugene, Oregon

University of Oregon Press
5283 University of Oregon
Eugene, OR 97403-5283

ISBN   0-87114-103-5

Preface

The University of Oregon never ceases to astonish me. It is reissuing this book, which has been out of print for two decades.

Why the astonishment? Because professors from other universities warned that writing about the administration of your own campus is a splendid way to commit career suicide. It could ruin your academic career because Somebody Important might take offense at your portrayal of truth and blackball any future bids for promotion up the academic ladder to the exalted rank of "full professor." Forget about "academic freedom"—that essentially applies to research and publication on topics outside the confines of your own institution.

Confrontation came out in 1973. My bid for full professor was never blackballed, and, indeed, I learned eventually that *Confrontation* had become one of the major exhibits in my file to earn the ultimate academic promotion. Astonishing.

So the University of Oregon, I claim with pride, is my kind of university. It believes, in administrative echelons as well as the teaching faculty, in the classic pronouncements of academic and literary freedom, such as—*we do not fear to tolerate error so long as reason is left free to combat it* (Jefferson 1820), or *where there is much desire to learn there will be much arguing, many opinions, for opinion in good men is but learning in the making* (Milton 1644), or *the ultimate societal good is reached by a free trade of ideas* (Holmes, Jr. 1919).

Charles E. Johnson, the ill-fated protagonist in this factual account of his year as president of the University of Oregon (1968-1969), believed in those concepts with his heart and soul. This University tends not to hire presidents who believe otherwise. Johnson now emerges in my mind as almost a Christ-like figure, condemned brutally for his belief that reason and logic would prevail over the dark forces of evil, violence and intellectual corruption.

And he was right—but only in the long run. Unfortunately, his was a short run. He failed in his bid for the permanent presidency. The political forces arrayed against him were too formidable, too unreasonable. Students behaving as thugs, roughed up a military recruiting table one day, and Johnson tried to reason with them. If the Communist party had a right to visit the campus and make a presentation, he said, then why must we deny—by force—military recruiters the same right?

It was not a good year for reason to combat error. Dr. Johnson paid a horrible price for his belief in the power of reason and logic.

This was not an easy book to write. From the beginning, I could sense a few administrative stones being tentatively tossed in my direction. But I also sensed an overwhelming move within the University community for me to proceed with the research and writing, and damn the torpedoes. The move was accompanied by offers of assistance from every quarter, including the Johnson family, the new president, Robert Clark, and the Oregon governor, Tom McCall. It became a community effort.

The book was well-received by college administrators around the country. Clark Kerr, the embattled president of the University of California, wrote to say that *Confrontation* "rings true on every page."

S. I. Hayakawa, the equally embattled president of San Francisco State University (later a U. S. senator), wrote two reviews, suggesting that the book "creates a vivid sense of the kind of person Johnson was. The book rings true from beginning to end. And since I was a participant in similar events in the same academic year, I could not help reading it with intense interest and sympathy."

An editorial in the *Oregon Statesman*, said, "The 'Charles Johnson' tragedy is an all-too-relevant illustration of the need for consideration and understanding the problems faced by government administrators and elected officials. Johnson stuck to his principles. The campus weathered the year and the era of confrontation. But the price was too high."

"He literally gave his life to a public responsibility the stresses of which were not realized by the people he served," wrote Malcolm Bauer in *The Oregonian*.

And so it went. I compiled a folder of book reviews—all favorable— most written by prominent educators and journalists. I guess they made a favorable impression on the faculty committee for promotion and tenure.

Though it eventually went out of print, *Confrontation* never really died. Almost every year over the ensuing two decades brought comments about what I had written or requests for permission to make copies of the book for use in libraries and or higher education seminars.

And now the University of Oregon is reissuing this book as part of a new publishing program. *Confrontation*, an editor said, depicts an important chapter in the history of the University of Oregon.

I am honored to have this book included in the new publications list. The University of Oregon is a great institution, and I appreciated its encouragement of my own search for truth, imperfect as it may have been, in exploring the "Chuck Johnson Tragedy."

—Ken Metzler, July 2001

Contents

Tables

Confrontation

One:
Questions

In Oregon, a university president is dead. He died at 8:20 the morning of Tuesday, June 17, 1969, at milepost 25.64 on U.S. Highway 126, 280 feet east of the intersection with Goodpasture Road, approximately seventeen miles east of Springfield, Oregon.

It was an elegant setting for death. Death touched by the warmth of the morning sun. Death amid the trees, the towering, deep-green Douglas firs, the cedars, the maples, the alders. Death beside the clear, swift, waters of the McKenzie River, roaring through the boulders, refracting the sunlight into a shower of diamonds. Death within view of the Goodpasture Bridge with its rustic wooden enclosure, its roof, its slatted windows.

It was not an elegant death. Death, the autopsy report said, came as a result of "multiple, severe, total-body-crushing injuries." The injuries included explosive ruptures of the liver, spleen, and right ventricle . . . multiple ruptures of the bowels . . . ruptures of the stomach and the pericardial sac . . . tears and rips in the lungs and the interventricular septum . . . multiple fractures of the spine, pelvis, legs, and arms . . . posterior fractures of ribs 2 through 10 . . . a crushed head. . . .

All injuries occurred when the Volkswagen he was driving crashed head-on into a Mack B-61 Diesel log truck and Peerless log trailer loaded with thirteen logs. He died instantly.

His name: Charles E. Johnson. Age: forty-eight. Occupation: acting president of the University of Oregon.

On the day of the death, James Jensen, the president of a sister institution, Oregon State University, bitterly told a journalist, "This is a terrible tragedy. I hope now the people of Oregon will understand—"

He paused.

"Well, perhaps I'd just better not say what I hope the people of Oregon will understand."

What was there to say? Only two weeks earlier the news media had reported that President Johnson had disappeared from his home for several hours after he'd failed to show for a faculty reception in his honor. The papers said he'd collapsed from "fatigue and exhaustion." Some faculty colleagues suspected that the phrase might be euphemistic for more bizarre manifestations of stress. Rumor suggested that the president had been depressed for weeks, that he'd suffered mysterious mental "blackouts," that he'd been consulting a psychiatrist, that, indeed, he'd suffered a complete nervous breakdown.

At the very least it was possible to say that he was a casualty of the times. The times had taken the life of another college president, Courtney Smith of Swarthmore who, in January 1969, collapsed and died of a heart attack in the middle of a crisis over demands from black students. And the times had caused other presidents to quit their jobs, their sudden resignations often accompanied by petulant remarks about the sheer impossibility and the "savage demands" (as one phrased it) of their work.

Throughout Oregon the death of Charles Johnson elicited feelings of guilt and remorse. Even the state's governor confided the feeling that he might with justification be accused of "murder." A coed who had been a vociferous member of militant student groups felt such pangs of remorse that she wanted to write the president's widow a letter.

4

But she didn't know what to say.

What was there to say? A president was dead. Could anybody see, at the outset of the year, the great wave of social protest that, colliding with the great wave of reaction, might rip to shreds any man caught in the maelstrom?

Oregonians could only shake their heads and call it a "terrible tragedy"—and wonder privately if he'd committed suicide. They wondered, too, what the college presidency was coming to that it could prematurely kill a gentle man like Chuck Johnson. They called it the "Tragedy of Charles E. Johnson."

But tragedy, by one definition, must have meaning and purpose. Was there meaning in the death of Charles Ellicott Johnson, PhD, acting president of the University of Oregon in the academic year 1968-69? Did his death contain a message for the living?

He was the only university president literally driven to his death during an era of nationwide campus turmoil. College students had been struck down by bullets and bombs; a college president had been stricken by a heart attack. But only one president, Charles E. Johnson, was literally driven to a point of mental breakdown and, subsequently, to his death by the stresses of his job. What meaning indeed?

Two:
A Fork in the Career Road

To understand something about death, it is sometimes necessary to understand something about life. The life of Charles Johnson was surrounded by a surface kind of gaiety and by a rural, ragging humor of the kind evident at the party attended by Johnson and his wife on June 3, 1968, a little more than a year before his death.

It was a memorable social event. Glenn Starlin, a professor of speech, and his wife planned a small dinner party for that date, inviting two faculty colleagues and their wives, John and Betty Jean Hulteng and Charles and Jeanne Johnson.

An item in that evening's newspaper had prompted John Hulteng, a professor of journalism, to buy a bottle of champagne en route to the party.

"Clearly," said Hulteng amiably, "this calls for a celebration."

Page one of the local daily, the *Eugene Register-Guard*, showed a bespectacled man peering out from a photograph. It was Charles Johnson, his long, oval face creased by a wide grin that exposed a slightly crooked front tooth, chipped at the bottom. The photo portrayed a man of seeming goodwill, of self-confidence without arrogance. The accompanying story tended to confirm that impression.

INTERIM PRESIDENT NAMED BY U OF O

"President Flemming leaves a mighty large pair of shoes to fill. The university has taken long strides in recent years and he leaves a record of real achievement.

"But a university seldom stands still for long. It either moves ahead or it moves backward. I see my job as keeping it moving ahead."

Those words were offered Monday by the man who will temporarily replace University of Oregon President Arthur Flemming when the 62-year-old former Secretary of Health, Education, and Welfare leaves the U of O Aug. 1 to become president of Macalester College in St. Paul, Minn.

He is Charles Johnson, 47-year-old professor of accounting and dean of the university's College of Liberal Arts since the summer of 1963.

Johnson was named acting U of O president Sunday by the State Board of Higher Education. . . .

As acting president, Johnson will take over Flemming's duties upon his departure and will serve in that capacity until the state board names a permanent replacement.

A presidential "search" committee composed of U of O faculty, administrators, students, alumni and state board members recently began a nationwide search for a new president that is expected to take several months to a year to complete. . . .

The story also cited Johnson's academic background (CPA, PhD from Minnesota), the sabbatical leave he had postponed to accept the appointment, his brief teaching job at Berkeley before coming to Oregon in 1952, his coauthorship of three textbooks on accounting, and his salary as president: $32,500 a year plus $2,000 for expenses, the same as Flemming had been getting.

They were ready that evening at the Starlin's house for the arrival of President-designate and Mrs. Johnson. The hosts had already foreseen the suddenly auspicious nature of the occasion. Quickly, they had erected a WELCOME MR. PRESIDENT banner and from it had pointedly hung several aspirin tins and a sympathy card on strings. They knew it was precisely the kind of mildly ironic gesture the "Guest of Honor" would enjoy.

8

Applause greeted his entry. "Speech! Speech!"

He grinned. "No speeches," he said. That was one of the advantages of being an interim president: you didn't have to give an inaugural address. And there were other benefits, he said, accepting a proffered glass of champagne. The position would give him a reserved parking spot on the campus, no small advantage on a campus overcrowded with cars. But, come to think of it, there *must* be an easier way to get a reserved spot.

Well, he said, glancing at the sympathy card, a "get-well" card might have been more appropriate. Not that he didn't appreciate sympathy; he needed all he could get. But a man would have to be sick or have a hole in the head to accept a university presidency in this turbulent era. However, since the job was temporary, with the end clearly in view, no one would have to mount a campaign to "throw the bastard out."

Johnson greeted the mock seriousness of his colleagues—the deferential repartee, the "Yes sir, Mr. President . . . No sir, Mr. President . . ."—the way he greeted most situations and most people: with a wide, toothy grin accented by the crooked tooth chipped at the bottom. The big grin, the chipped tooth, the spectacles—all these seemed to soften the awesome impact of the man that resulted from his height and his voice.

He towered to six feet, four inches, and most of it was in his legs. He was an ungainly figure, constantly stumbling over chairs and crashing into desk corners. He was slightly hunch-shouldered, his neck protruding forward as though continually in position to duck low-hanging obstacles.

And his voice. His voice was deep-timbred. It was the Voice of Authority. His friends and family said he never raised it above a conversational level. He didn't have to. It easily over-rode most group conversation, rendering it, by contrast, to the status of gossipy chatter; but he seldom used it in an authoritarian way. Now, as ever, he enjoyed telling jokes on himself, anecdotes touching on his own ineptitudes. He had, for example, been appointed the acting president of the university for one simple reason: "No one else was dumb enough to take it."

9

He had become the dean of the College of Liberal Arts almost six years earlier—a *business* professor chosen to lead the conflicting cultures of science and the humanities—for an equally simple reason: "If the dean is a scientist," he explained, "the humanists claim he doesn't understand their problems. If the dean is a humanist, the scientists claim he doesn't understand *their* problems. They chose me because I have the advantage of not understanding *anybody's* problems."

And, of course, the reason for his original entry into the academic profession was just as easily explained: absentmindedness. He cited the time he'd driven to work one morning, parking his car in its usual spot. He rushed to his office. Returning to his car some eight hours later, he was surprised to find the engine still running. He'd forgotten to turn it off.

He was that way with machinery: completely inept. He was so hopelessly clumsy with power lawn mowers, for example, that he decided to buy *two* of them, fully convinced that at any given time at least one wouldn't start.

And then he related the most foolish act of all: the time he tried to learn to fly an airplane. He had taken lessons for weeks, and finally soloed. Flying alone one day he overshot the runway at the Eugene airport and flipped the tiny two-seat Cessna over on its back. He climbed out unhurt but feeling very foolish. "The runway wasn't long enough," he replied to the solicitous inquiries of his friends. Then he admitted with a wry grin that a DC-9 jet airliner had no trouble making a safe, routine landing on the same runway a day or two later to inaugurate jet service to Eugene.

That was Chuck Johnson, ever the clown, laughing at himself. To be able to laugh at yourself, he once said, was a sign of emotional stability.

Everybody called him Chuck.

"In looking ahead to the interim presidency," said Chuck Johnson, "I'm reminded of a Satchel Paige story I once heard. Satch is called in to relieve Bob Feller in a scoreless game between Cleveland and the Yankees. Satch takes his time getting to the mound. He stops to tie his shoelace. He adjusts his belt. He mops his brow. 'Come on, Paige,' says the ump, 'you're holding up the game.' 'How many Yankees are out?' asks Paige. No outs. 'How many Yankees on base?' Bases loaded. 'Who's at bat?' DiMaggio. 'Well,' says Paige, 'you want me to rush into *that* kind of trouble?' "

Yes, Johnson saw trouble ahead. "From my vantage point," he said, turning serious, "all the insuperable problems of the university appear to be spelled b-u-d-g-e-t. The further I dig in this area the more frightening the situation looks."

Johnson said that he had obtained a "clear understanding" from the chancellor of the Oregon State System of Higher Education that his interim role would *not* be that of a mere caretaker, however. He would perform like a president, make decisions like a president, and defer no problems to his successor. The institution could not afford otherwise. The days when a do-nothing interim president might coast along on the momentum of his predecessor were gone. It was crucial to keep the institution moving ahead full steam, as Arthur Flemming had done.

Yet the prospect for the future made him apprehensive. He said he felt like the man who had just arrived at a dude ranch and was asked, "Have you ever ridden a horse before?" When he replied, "No," he was told, "Well, here's a horse that's never been ridden before, either. You can just start out together."

Perhaps his humor contributed to people's view of him as "unflappable." It was a term commonly used to describe him. It was a word used by members of the Advisory Council, an influential group of professors elected by their colleagues to serve as advisers and confidants to the university president. Their recommendation had been sought for candidates for the interim presidency when Arthur Flemming announced his resignation. Try the unflappable Chuck Johnson first, came the unanimous reply. The endorsement was a strong one: Johnson was the kind of administrator who could take two warring factions and, after two hours of deliberations, send them away, if not smiling, at least satisfied that the dispute had been

11

painstakingly adjudicated and equitably resolved. Johnson, said the Advisory Council, was the man best able to cope with the diverse and crushing problems and the many warring factions of higher education in 1968. If Johnson turned down the job then the council would try to find others.

Yet for all his humor, perhaps partly because of it, Johnson was considered a loner—ever the tall stranger from Wyoming. Perhaps his humor appeared to be used too flippantly; it tended to keep people at arm's length. That was the way he seemed to prefer it. He kept his personal feelings to himself. He did not confide in people. If others ventured uncomfortably close to the inner Charles Johnson, he put them off with a diffident remark: The inner Charles Johnson was a clown. Look at all the dumb things he'd done.

But when the news about himself was good, the recognition of a superior accomplishment, for example, he seemed reticent about discussing it. "Oh, by the way—" he would often say, in a tone almost apologetic for having brought it up.

"Oh, by the way," he told his secretary at the end of a conversation about office details, "they've asked me to take the acting presidency." He had slipped in the message so unobtrusively that the secretary could only stare at him uncomprehendingly. "They've asked you *what?*"

Smooth and articulate as he might have been in business conversations, Johnson was uncommonly shy in talking about himself on any level other than one of self-effacement. He seldom expressed his personal feelings in conversation. When he did, it was more often apt to be in writing. He'd been that way since childhood, his notes and letters often more expressive of his inner feelings than his spoken words. His Mother's Day letter to his stepmother, Cora Johnson, written when he was seventeen and a cadet at a military academy in New Mexico, was an early example.

. . . I believe this Mother's Day has meant more to me than any other. I've been away from home for almost nine months now, and as I see things from a distance I begin to realize how much you've meant to me as a mother. I know that in the past I may not have seemed appreciative of all the things you've done for me, nor maybe cooperated very well, but it wasn't that I didn't appreciate it. In most cases I didn't understand at the time how much it would mean to me later, and when I did want to express my gratitude I couldn't seem to find the words. This is just a note to try to express my thoughts on Mother's Day and to tell you from the bottom of my heart I love you.

He had been a quiet, thoughtful youngster, and he had a talent for writing. He had even considered journalism as a career. At thirteen, with the aid of some fellow junior high school students in Great Falls, Montana, he published a little neighborhood newspaper, *Dew Telle*. At eighteen he had seen his first words published in a "real" newspaper, a weekly in Browning, Montana, where he worked for a year as a bookkeeper to earn money for college. Getting published was a heady experience. He wrote home about it.

> . . . This week I found on the editorial page, my column, complete and word for word as I had written it. Monday, he, the editor, came in and asked if I would write a column like that every week. Of course I was tickled to death, but I managed to gulp and nonchalantly say that I might be able to find the time between other pressing duties to run off a few lines for his paper. When the New York Times calls, I think I'll hold out for $300 a month. . . .

And in 1964, twenty-six years later, the explanation of why he had recently turned down a lucrative offer to leave academic life and become a vice-president and treasurer for an insurance company in Portland seemed best reserved for the written word. To two fellow accounting professors at other universities he wrote:

> . . . I have decided to decline the offer—and I should probably have my head examined in some detail; any contributions toward this examination will be appreciated. . . .
> The offer was very tempting—including fringe benefits

that would make a college professor's eyes pop wide open (example—a furnished automobile with all expenses paid by the company—a membership in the Arlington Club with all bills footed by the company—etc.). Furthermore I would have wound up with one job rather than three—probably a lot less pressure, and a lot more free time. That's a real twist on most people's image of the college professor's life, isn't it—to consider taking a job in industry to ease off on the pressure and find some free time. I couldn't help but drool a bit as I heard those executives describe how they spent their weekends from Friday afternoon to Monday morning, while I mulled over the vision of the class I teach on Saturday morning, and my Saturday afternoons in my study struggling away on a "reasonably accurate" but basically lousy textbook that at least half the accounting professors in the country believe probably shouldn't be published anyway.

However, despite all this I couldn't quite get rid of the idea that education was somehow a cause that would give me more personal satisfaction than the insurance business in the long run, and that reasonably competent college professors (and even maybe deans) were somehow a scarcer commodity at the present time than vice-presidents. I finally decided that what was really tempting me was the thought of avoiding all the desperate problems the University of Oregon (and all other universities) are going to face in the next decade with a veritable flood of enrollment increases in the face of all kinds of financial difficulties—and I couldn't help the gnawing and bothersome feeling that I would be running away from a worthwhile endeavor at a time when its need was greatest and the going looked pretty rough. I don't know whether this adds up to all the reasons, but that's about the best I can do for a rough summary. . . . I feel better now that the decision is made—and no lingering regrets. It was a nice pipe dream while it lasted, though.

His proclivity for writing considered, it was natural that his most unguarded evaluation of his impending move to the president's office would also come in writing: a two-page, single-spaced letter he typed himself to his parents, then living in San Diego, California.

250 PALOMINO DRIVE
EUGENE, OREGON
JUNE 8, 1968

Dear Mom and Dad,

Since things will get a bit hectic around here shortly I'd better take this opportunity to get a letter off your way. As the enclosed clipping indicates I will not be on sabbatical leave next year, but instead will be taking on a new and bigger assignment. Both Jeanne and I have a hollow feeling in the pit of our stomach which will no doubt persist for some time since this is a pretty big jump, even on an interim basis, and one always wonders whether he is equal to the demands that will be put on him. It's one thing to run a segment of an organization—even a fairly large segment—and quite another I'm sure to be up where the buck stops, running the whole show. You ought to know, Dad, because you've always been pretty much in the position of being your own boss. Of course in a state university one is never that much in control—he has a system chancellor, a state board of regents, and a lot of other public elements looking over his shoulder—but there is at least some similarity between the president's spot and the guy who owns the company or is a senior partner. I'm sure there will be many times when I fervently wish I were back in a professor's office where all I had to worry about was teaching classes and writing books. Fortunately the book writing business is in a natural lull for next year—the newest revision of the Intermediate book is just out—and after that who knows; I may decide to grit my teeth and say goodbye to all those beautiful royalties and jump off the precipice into academic administration for good. I'd hate like all get out to toss away that source of income, but I'm finding that the process of keeping a series of texts going is not nearly as much fun as writing them originally. We've used the royalties to provide for the kids' college education and for some luxury extras, but have never let our standard of living get adjusted to more than our regular salary income, so if I decided there might be some things I'd rather do with the remaining years of my career than revise and update books I think we could manage. Fortunately, Jeanne is a gal who finds many things more important than money and who is willing to make such decisions on non-monetary grounds. Fortunately also she

15

will do beautifully the variety of things that will be required of a president's wife.

I've had a number of opportunities to become a candidate for a college presidency, but all at much smaller and lesser schools—state colleges like San Diego State for the most part—and I've simply said I wasn't interested. One reason I took this on, at the sacrifice of my sabbatical year, is that it is only for a year. (A search committee will spend the year combing the country to find the replacement president). Thus I have an opportunity to give the thing the good old college try with no commitment beyond one year. If I wind up thoroughly hating the job, that will be a valuable piece of information and I can still make a respectable exit back into a professor's chair. If I manage to stay ahead of the mobs and find enough interest and excitement to compensate for the worry, strain, and long hours, I'll probably take a look at the next offer or two that comes along and see where they lead. So it looks as if the country boy from Wyoming sits facing another fork in the career road and some hard choices that have a large effect on what happens to this segment of the Johnson family in the years to come.

The story of Flemming's resignation from the presidency is complex. One does not ordinarily leave a presidency of a major university to head up a good, but small private undergraduate college. I suspect there are about three factors in his decision. First he is 62 and going strong—he is a guy who dreads the idea of retirement—and the Oregon State System has a firm rule that presidents step down at 65. Macalester, on the other hand has no such rule and assures him that he can continue in their job indefinitely—thus he's trading three years for an open-ended job. Secondly, the Wallaces who founded and own the Reader's Digest are interested in Macalester, and have apparently agreed to bankroll a major program of quality improvement and possibly expansion. No one has reported the figure but rumor has it at upward of $10 million or so—and the rumors go as high as $50 million. Not knowing how much the Wallaces have, it's hard to judge, but I gather the Reader's Digest has not been exactly a marginal publishing venture. Thirdly, and related to the second, we are currently in fairly serious financial difficulty. We had a badly restricted budget from the last legislature (for 1966-68) and Oregon's economy is badly hit by the slump in building and by high interest rates . . . so we haven't very high hopes for the next few years. Flemming came here from *big* government, he was essentially an optimistic, let's go ahead and do it and worry about the money later, kind of a guy, and as a result we've done some very good things, but are badly overextended. Guess who is going to have the unenviable job of trying to put the pieces back together and get the institution back into something approaching solvency? And guess how popular that process is going to make him with all concerned? And guess how the comparison is going to look between where we were going under Flemming and that awful year when Johnson was in there? Oh well—it ought to serve to keep the search committee on the ball and working hard during the year anyway! Oh yes and on top of that federal research grants are being badly hit by the $6 billion budget reduction which means that on top of slim state support, Uncle Sam will be pulling back his support from higher education. Then as an incidental matter, two of our deans resigned (for reasons unrelated to the president's leaving) in the last few months, and two more will be retiring during the coming year. There are also a considerable number of optimistic and cheerful people who think we're due to have some student uprisings on our hands come Fall term. This gives one some basis for the conclusion that Flemming may be the smartest guy in the state of Oregon. For Christmas you might consider sending an extra large bottle of aspirin tablets. . . .

[The letter concludes with family news.]

Much love,
Chuck, Jeanne, and kids.

Three:
Get Rid of That Man Flemming

In retrospect, Charles Johnson's analysis of Arthur Flemming's resignation was astute as far as it went. Flemming himself would eventually confirm many of the reasons for leaving: Oregon's mandatory retirement rule, Macalester's open-ended retirement policy, Macalester's greater financial resources for innovation and experimentation. Oregon's finances, by contrast, were in a "downturn." Flemming had even begun to accommodate himself to that fact by tightening up on his own free-spending management style. When he was invited to Macalester, he "struggled with this decision for quite a while," he said, but in the end he was guided by the "feeling that there would be substantial sums of money to try out innovative approaches to education that would have national significance."

Flemming gave another reason for leaving, a reason curiously absent from Johnson's analysis. Flemming told his Advisory Council on one occasion that he had drawn down his "credit at the bank." He meant his "bank account" of public support. It was an eloquent way of saying that he had experienced a gradual erosion of public goodwill, the cumulative effect of making too many unpopular decisions and too many outspoken

19

comments on political and social issues. The problem, he said, was endemic to public administration: "After you have been in an administrative job for five to seven years, you have drawn down enough credit at the bank that you should realize that you're not going to be as effective as you were when you started."

In Flemming's case, it was an understatement.

Flemming had been in office for seven years, and at the time of his resignation in 1968, the University of Oregon had not seen a more controversial president in the sixty-nine years since the resignation under fire of Charles H. Chapman, an Easterner who had alienated the frontier Oregonians with his fancy ways, such as his employment of a Japanese servant at his home.

Oregonians would talk about Flemming long after he was gone, and they would talk in superlatives. He had been the best of presidents; he had been the worst of presidents. His tenure had been a period of "unparalleled growth and national prestige"; it had been an "unmitigated disaster." It depended on which professor you asked.

"The university has experienced the greatness of Arthur Flemming, and the spirit of that greatness will remain in the university's heart forever." . . . "You can't make an opera singer out of a jackass, and you can't make a university president out of a traveling do-gooder, nor can you muzzle a fool." Both comments were about Flemming; it depended on whether you read the words of a representative from student government or those of a housewife from Southern Oregon.

Where was the real Arthur Flemming? Buried, no doubt, somewhere beneath the snowdrifts of rhetoric.

One faction saw him as the super-glib Washington bureaucrat, the outspoken liberal Republican and Methodist layman who preached love and brotherhood but cast political stones from the glassed-in sanctuary of the university campus. He was the big-shot politician trampling free enterprise with heavy-handed governmental meddling. One needed to look no further than the "cranberry incident" of 1959 to document that assertion. That was the time Flemming, as Eisenhower's Secretary of the

Department of Health, Education, and Welfare, ordered the disposal of several tons of Thanksgiving cranberries said to be contaminated with a cancer-producing chemical weed killer. The first contaminated cranberries, as tested by the Food and Drug Administration, had turned up in Oregon, one of four cranberry-producing states. Many Oregonians, farmers in particular, were bitter, and they never forgot.[1]

The other faction saw Flemming as "larger than life," to use the words of a university coed. Student leaders considered him the "greatest university president in the country for understanding student problems and standing up to the politicians." This faction saw him as Oregon's foremost champion of social equality. He was the one man in touch with the times, the one educator in Oregon who wasn't frightened of the politicians and the moneyed-old-grad reactionaries, the one educator who might help Oregon shake its lethargy and guide it, dazed and shaken, into the twentieth century.

That neither view captured the real Arthur Flemming did not matter now that he was leaving. What mattered were the emotional extremes themselves. How might they affect the tenure of the next president? Some professors would, in retrospect, be reminded of the French expression, *Après moi le déluge* (After me the flood), a phrase used to describe the reign of the eighteenth-century monarch, Louis XV, whose alienation of important segments of the population helped to set the stage for the French Revolution, which came during the reign of his successor, Louis XVI.

Whatever his faults and virtues, Flemming remained an astute political observer. He knew his bank account of goodwill was approaching deficit status; he also knew that an anti-Flemming underground was alive with political intrigue that spring of 1968. That, in itself, was no reason for resigning; he had, after all, survived a far more vicious right-wing political attack in 1964.

The 1964 attacks on Flemming—a right-wing group had circulated petitions urging his dismissal as president, but the Board of Higher Education upheld him—were the result of an accumulation of incidents. When he first took office, Flemming held press conferences at which he would respond to reporters' questions on political issues. The board finally asked him to stop his political commentary, which he did willingly enough. Then in 1962 he announced that Gus Hall, the secretary of the U.S. Communist party, would be allowed to speak on campus.[2] This precipitated an almost hysterical right-wing campaign to prevent the speech. The ensuing spectacle prompted some 10,000 students to hear the speech instead of the hundred or so that the student sponsors had originally expected. The site was moved to the football stadium, where the speech proceeded without incident.

A political tempest ensued, then quickly subsided. It blew up again in 1964 after a series of incidents on the university campus: the publishing of "dirty poems" in the student literary magazine, *Northwest Review*, the showing of a "pornographic film" at the Student Union, and finally, the disclosure of the biggest scandal of all, the "Lolita Case."

The latter was a lurid story of sex and perversion that unfolded chapter by chapter like a modern (and very bad) novel. . . . In *Chapter One* a thirteen-year-old girl (call her Lolita), who is a plump, friendless, and very unhappy person, is violently raped. She can't bring herself to tell her parents about it because of a family misunderstanding. She runs away from home and discovers sex on terms other than rape. *Chapter Two* finds Lolita enjoying a primitive pleasure in sex; she even begins experimenting with various perverse techniques. She finds a modicum of social acceptance in promiscuity. She is found out by the police, however, and made a ward of the juvenile court. *Three*, the court finds her incorrigible. By now she has developed nymphomania into a creative art. She likes college boys. She randomly telephones their living quarters to arrange "dates." She answers a classified advertisement for a sports car, posing as a prospective buyer and using sex as collateral. *Four*, she spends one hectic night on a fraternity sleeping porch, hopping from bed to bed. *Five*, she's discovered by police one night in a student's apartment. The whole scandal explodes in public. She tells all. She admits to sexual relationships with some sixty men, mostly college students, thirty of whom she can positively identify. *Six,* the case goes to the Grand Jury. The jury declines to indict any of the thirty men on the ground that to prosecute them would be to require Lolita to repeat in open court the lurid details of thirty encounters, a task the jurors felt would cause the young woman undue emotional hardship. In an unprecedented public report, the Grand Jury urges the university to take disciplinary action against the students. . . .

A presidential nightmare. The university's response was to "investigate" and to wonder privately how the Grand Jury could expect a nonlegal body like a university to set up the quasilegal machinery to prosecute thirty cases of rape without such legal sanctions as sworn testimony, privilege, subpoenas, and perjury and contempt provisions. If off-campus justice required the accused to face their accusers, might not campus justice require a similar procedure? Or did campus justice presume guilt until innocence is proven?

The first wave of right-wing attacks came shortly afterward. LID OFF U OF O GARBAGE ran the headline in a right-wing paper, the *National Eagle,* published in Portland by a fundamentalist preacher named Walter Huss. Dirty poetry was the subject of the first attack.

THEY'RE PRINTING WHAT ISN'T FIT TO PRINT!!! AT YOUR EXPENSE—with Arthur Flemming, President of the University of Oregon, AS A MAJOR SPONSOR and with ultimate responsibility belonging to MARK O. HAT-FIELD, Governor, State of Oregon and National Convention "Keynoter" for the Republican Party! ! . . . . . .
FIRST LET US ASK YOU A QUESTION:
Do you consider the following fit to print at public expense by the University of Oregon? WE QUOTE:

> "Who knows better
> 2 thousand years of work yourself to death
> building God's house
> tending God's ducks & pigs
> killing God's enemies
> KISSING GOD'S ASS"[3]

SURELY, YOUR ANSWER IS A SHOCKED "NO" ! !
BUT THAT IS ONLY A MILD SAMPLE OF WHAT IS
BEING PRINTED AT THE UNIVERSITY OF OREGON
AT PUBLIC EXPENSE AND IN THE NAME OF ACA-
DEMIC FREEDOM, FREEDOM OF THE PRESS AND IN
THE NAME OF "EDITORIAL INTEGRITY"!!

Two weeks later readers were treated to another chapter of the
story, as viewed by the *National Eagle*, under the headline
PART II: U of O GARBAGE.

SCANDAL in major proportions exists at the University of
Oregon.

Pornographic motion pictures have been shown to students there.

Thirty students who had improper relations with a
13-year-old girl have gone unpunished.

Material has been printed extensively at the university
which is obscene, sacrilegious, pornographic and Marxist.

These and other abuses have been pointed out from
time to time, with absolutely nothing done about it by Dr.
Arthur S. Flemming, the "moderate liberal" president of
the university.

Acting to prevent or correct scandals is what elected
officials should do—but they're not doing it.

Nothing has been done about it by Governor Mark Hat-
field, also a "moderate liberal" who appointed Flemming.

Nothing has been done about it by Wayne Morse or
Edith Green, who supposedly represent the people of
Oregon in Congress. . . .

Everything that has been done has been done by private
citizens—and thousands throughout the state are indignant
about conditions at the University of Oregon.

Probably more than any other single person in Oregon,
Walter Huss, director of Freedom Center, has done much
to bring these matters to public attention.

"The people are still in power in Oregon," Huss said,
"and if anything is done about these conditions the people
themselves will have to take action. The only way Governor Hatfield will act, is to know that if he doesn't he will
no longer remain Governor. As for Flemming, he has
demonstrated over and over again that there is no point in
trying to get him to change his ways. This leaves only one
alternative—and that is to bring about his dismissal."

Though Huss continued to attack Flemming and the university through the summer of 1964, the storm subsided. The scandal did no apparent damage to the university's enrollment, which took a sharp upward spurt the following fall, surpassing for the first time in three decades the enrollment of a sister institution, Oregon State University.

The anti-Flemming talk did not stop; it merely retreated underground. Oregonians talked about him behind closed doors and in hushed tones. They warned any journalist who might be present, "If you quote me I'll be forced to deny I said it." In the four years following the right-wing attacks, very little of the anti-Flemming invective reached public print.

And with the shades pulled, what did they say about Flemming? They certainly did not talk about the growth in quantity and quality of the faculty or about the U.O.'s newly won national prestige. They did not talk about increases in research grants or about new programs in research and teaching. Or if they did they gave credit to someone other than Flemming.

They preferred to talk about how Flemming was allowing the university to go to hell. He had allowed the students to get away with murder; he had eliminated curfew hours in the girls' dorms; he was permitting the boys and girls to visit each other in their rooms. They said the tragic results of the Flemming "permissiveness" were illustrated in grim statistics (the statistics, if indeed they existed, were alleged to show a sharp increase in the number of unwed pregnancies among university coeds since Flemming's arrival in Oregon).

They said that Flemming was forcing peculiar eastern seaboard ideas on unsuspecting Oregonians; that he had hauled in a lot of colored people to make trouble in Oregon where there had not been trouble before; that he had emasculated the important administrators on the campus, preferring to run the university by himself. They said that while he had given lip service to worthy traditions—fraternities and athletics, for example—he deliberately tried to tear them down: the former by insisting that fraternities live up to the spirit as well as the letter of the no-racial-bias rule in selection procedures, the latter by such devious means as refusing to fire a losing basketball coach and by not building a football stadium fast enough.

They said that he was too outspoken on social and political issues; that he'd hired dangerous and seditious faculty members committed to revolution and black power; that he was allowing the hippie element to run the university; that he'd allowed the university to degenerate, in the words of one alumnus, into a "gold-plated whorehouse."

Even within the university Flemming was controversial. Only Flemming, his faculty detractors noted, would have the temerity to change the founding date of the University of Oregon. To the dismay of faculty historians, he changed it from MDCCCLXXVI to 1872. The discrepancy went largely unnoticed outside the university campus where people seldom bothered to decipher Roman numerals. Yet there it was, on the Great Seal of the university, for instance: one date on the seal adorning the cloth backdrop for commencement, another on the seal affixed to the presidential letterhead. Was the university born in 1872, the date it was granted a charter from the state legislature? or 1876, the year the first classes opened? For nine decades the date had been 1876. It was a fact, irrefutable, literally chiseled in stone, as unchangeable as the rugged face of the mountain depicted on the seal (Mount Hood) or the simple verity contained in the university's motto: *Mens Agitat Molem: Mind Moves Matter.* Flemming changed the date to 1872. He hadn't done this arbitrarily; he merely persisted until he had worn the opposition to shreds. When he ordered the seal redesigned with the new date in bold Arabic numerals, the faculty opposition retreated underground to await Flemming's retirement, which they hoped would not be long in coming.[4]

Citizens outside the university continued to assemble documents—letters, depositions, affidavits, and reprints—to support the case against Flemming. Incidents were said to have been "hushed up" by the authorities. One document was a coed's letter home. "I was standing by my sink in my bra and pants getting ready to wash out a blouse," she wrote, "and the

26

door opened and shut." The visitor was a "huge, dirty, drunk Negro man" who grabbed her ("I stood there shaking and sort of crying"), but he finally left, apparently fearing the consequences of being caught in a girls' dorm. The files bulged with semisalacious material, such as one coed's graphic description of an encounter with a teacher. It was forwarded to an anti-Flemming group by her father. "You have my permission," he said, "to use this information in any way you see fit."

. . . There were three of us in the room after all the other students had brought their projects to be graded, this professor, one other girl, and myself. . . . I let the other girl go first for grading. She pulled something out of a sack and I could see that it was a sardine can with the upper half rolled back and an object in the can partially over the edge. They both laughed. He said, "You get an A."

I asked what it was and why it was so funny. They both looked at me in disbelief. After he graded my project, I was almost out of the door and he stopped me and asked if I really didn't know what her project was. I said that I didn't, and he kept really, really laughing. Then he said, "You're in college now, you should."

I was terribly embarrassed when he asked me, "Do you want to know?" I said I didn't think so. And then I didn't know what to tell him, and he said something like, "You have to grow up sometime; it's about time, and I'm going to tell you." My cheeks were blazing. "It's what a man puts on his penis before he screws." I said, "I don't think it's your place to tell me." He said, "You don't have to be so goddamn pious." I was mad. Nobody talks about it like that. He said, "That's the trouble with you, Laura; I'll bet you even go to church on Sundays."

"Well, as a matter of fact I do."

He said, "Man, if you are in college and haven't learned that yet I feel sorry for you. That's one of life's biggest pleasures."

I said, "What is?"

He said, "To screw, sweet, to screw. I live each day just to screw. It's great."

I turned around without a word and walked out the door. . . .

By 1968 the files of the anti-Flemming underground were fat with new kinds of material: accounts of drug use among students, the yearbook's portrayal of a "pot party," the militant rhetoric of a black-power advocate named Clyde E. DeBerry, a member of the university's faculty. News accounts of a speech DeBerry had given in the spring of 1968 at Riverside, California, were freely copied and distributed. *The San Bernardino Sun-Telegram* reported:

> Dr. Clyde E. DeBerry, professor of sociology at the University of Oregon, is prepared to kill people—white people.
> This is because DeBerry is black . . . and he sees black power as the only way to improve the lot of his black brothers. And he is willing to kill white people to gain black power and to keep it.

The speech had been given to some twenty white school teachers. It left them, according to another newspaper account, "in a state of mild shock." DeBerry was quoted as saying a lot of people would like to fire him from his job at the university but they didn't dare. "I've got a power base of over 500 blacks in Eugene that are ready to burn the place down if they try. . . . If they decide to burn down the university, I'll be out there burning with them."

The racial situation on campus was tense, Flemming's opponents said, and his response was to do nothing. He had done nothing about DeBerry, nothing about the black student who slugged a dean in the mouth, nothing about the increasing harassment of white clerical workers by black students.

With such documents collected in the spring of 1968, the anti-Flemming underground was ready to move topside. One such group began a letter-writing campaign urging the State Board to fire Flemming. "For God's sake," wrote a lawyer from Roseburg, "get rid of that man while the university is still worthy of the name."

Within weeks, Flemming resigned. The anti-Flemming group took no credit for that; they could scarcely believe their good fortune. Now, operating on the momentum of their campaign, they wanted to influence the selection of Flemming's successor. They sought a meeting with a group of influential deans and professors at the university. The meeting was held June 28 with two lawyers, Dudley Walton of Roseburg and Eugene Brown of Grants Pass, as the major spokesmen. Both men were alumni of the university's School of Law. Charles Johnson, the acting president-designate, had been invited but was unable to attend.

"All over the state," explained Dudley Walton, "we kept running into the same point of view. We found it in the blue-collar worker pulling the green-chain at the lumber mill, and we found it in the salaried executive shuffling papers in Portland. They wanted to lay it on the line: get rid of that man Flemming before he leaves the place in shambles."

Now with Flemming's resignation in the bag, they had come to make clear what they expected from the *new* president: "a man with the guts to straighten out the mess ... a man to restore the proper academic climate ... a man to stop the university's getting involved in social issues. . . ."

They quoted at length from the thick file of anti-Flemming documents. They dropped ominous hints that they were prepared to take their cases to the people, hold public hearings around the state if necessary.

"We simply cannot have another Flemming as president," said one man. "In fact, we can't have anybody even remotely associated with the Flemming administration."

"What we need as president of the university," said Walton, "is a General Westmoreland."

A General Westmoreland? That was a startling contrast to the views of student leaders at the University of Oregon. Only three months earlier, a group of students staged a sit-in at the administration building to back up demands that they be allowed equal representation on the faculty committee being formed to search for Flemming's successor. There could be no doubt about the kind of man the students were seeking as the new president.

WE WANT ANOTHER FLEMMING

That message emblazoned on a placard outside the scene of the sit-in, made very clear, and a little frightening, the dimensions of the gap between some citizens of Oregon and some student leaders at the university. Graced by the admiring eyes of student leaders, Arthur Flemming had assumed the dimensions of a Greek god. In their eyes the Flemming façade was marred by only one flaw. He tended to be a lightning rod for angry citizen strikes more properly directed elsewhere. He unwittingly allowed Oregon's citizens to take refuge in the belief that their only problem was Arthur Flemming. It kept the citizens from facing unpleasant truths. Citizens, the student leaders said, blamed Flemming for coddling militant blacks on the campus, instead of facing the problems of racism in Oregon.[5] They blamed Flemming for student unrest rather than seek the real causes of youthful frustration, which ranged from small-town hypocrisy to corporate and military exploitation. They blamed Flemming for "permissiveness" rather than ask themselves why a young person should be forced to give up his civil rights and become a second-class citizen just because he is a college student. Such was the student view.

And now, with the gulf never wider between town and gown, with the gap never more awesome between youth and age, Flemming was leaving. He was stepping down from an educational-administrative platform scorched with the inflammatory rhetoric of both extremes, the citizens who wanted his successor to be a General Westmoreland and the students who wanted another Flemming.

An apprehensive mood prevailed. The spring had seen the destruction and violence of the riots at Columbia University. Would Oregon succumb to the epidemic of violence? The spring also had seen, among citizens of Oregon, a demand for blood at the University of Oregon's quiet little sit-in. The police should have been called, heads should have been bashed in, obstreperous students should have been brought into line.

And now onto the precarious, volatile presidential platform

stepped the tall, gangly, bespectacled Charles E. Johnson, the man with the deep voice and the toothy grin.

Johnson lacked Flemming's political clairvoyance. By his own admission, Johnson was a political innocent. He once startled a faculty colleague, Vernon Barkhurst, with an example of political naïveté. At a luncheon of fraternity alumni, Johnson overheard a conversation that bristled with angry denunciations of Flemming. He asked Barkhurst confidentially, "Is Flemming not well liked out around the state?"

Barkhurst was stopped short by the question. Was Johnson kidding? Barkhurst, then the director of admissions and alumni, was encountering almost constant anti-Flemming tirades in his travels through Oregon.

"You mean you haven't heard?" asked Barkhurst.

"Heard what?"

Johnson appeared to be both serious and ingenuous. As dean of the College of Liberal Arts, he lived in the hothouse atmosphere of academia. There the rampant weeds of politics had no place amid the delicately flowering cultures of science and the humanities. Johnson apparently saw no political significance in Oregon's anti-Flemming hysteria.

Four:
The First Day

The first of August dawned warm and a little hazy showing promise of another hot day. It was Charles Johnson's first day in his new role of filling the "mighty large pair of shoes" left by Arthur Flemming.

Johnson admired Flemming. He saw him as the personification of Onward and Upward. Every problem, by Flemming's view, was an "opportunity" for service, every storm a means of enjoying the sunshine, every unhappy today a challenge to look forward to a better tomorrow.

And the Flemming fiscal style. That, too, was onward and upward—do it and worry about the money later. Johnson winced occasionally as he watched Flemming commit the university to programs for which the money was literally nowhere in sight. Some older, more conservative, old-line administrators were appalled. Flemming used money he didn't have (but hoped to get) as "seed" funds to start new programs that might qualify for federal and foundation grants.

Once, when it looked as if the university might lose its chance for a federal grant for construction of a center for training and research in mental retardation because the state was $50,000 short in matching funds, Flemming announced dramatically to the Board of Higher Education: "I will personally guarantee that the university will have the $50,000 when needed." He didn't actually have the money; he only hoped to get it. Perhaps it would come from enrolling more students—their wallets bulging with tuition money—than predicted in the budget. Perhaps it would come from some new foundation grant from which the university could skim off as "administrative overhead" 34 percent of the grant's wage and salary allocation. Perhaps it would not come at all. What then? Flemming appeared unconcerned about that possibility. As it turned out, the money was there when needed. It was always there through the Flemming tenure, an era of unparalleled growth on the nation's campuses through ever-increasing enrollment and through increasing federal and foundation support.

It was a little like buying stock on margin in the 1920s.

Such actions, Flemming explained to Johnson, were "calculated risks." It was a technique he said he had learned from Robert Clark, who was Johnson's predecessor as dean of the College of Liberal Arts and who later became the university's dean of faculties before accepting the presidency of San Jose State College.

"It was clear to me," Flemming explained, "that Bob had taken a calculated risk when he brought in Terrill Hill. Here was a professor of chemistry, nationally known, a man of tremendous prestige. Bob didn't really have the money to bring Terrill here. He had to break through his salary ceiling, and I'm sure he engendered some hostility from others on the faculty. But Bob said, okay, we'll use this man as a starting point for developing a distinguished program in the sciences. By the time I came here as president, he'd already attracted Virgil Boekelheide, another distinguished scientist. We were getting a very strong nucleus. It was these fellows who came to me and said, 'Look, the National Science Foundation is going to make some institutional grants for improvement in science. How about our getting in on the ground floor?' Well, to get that considered I had to say, 'Yes, we'll commit some of the income that we think we're going to get from increased enrollment in order to get this grant.' "

It was a gamble, but it paid off in 1965 with a four million-dollar NSF grant for general improvement of the sciences. The five-year grant allowed the university to develop computer facilities and to hire still more outstanding scientists. Of course, it also carried a commitment to pick up those salaries on the expiration of the grant in 1970, but that was five years away.

"Bob's theory," Flemming said, "was that you develop some steeples of excellence and you get support for them. Then you develop other steeples of excellence on the foundation of the first. I've very definitely followed that philosophy."

Flemming also believed that any money coming to the university—whether from football gate receipts, dormitory income, or tax funds—was transferable throughout the institution. One result was a decline in administrative fiefdoms on campus and an increase in administrative hostility. Administrators in many departments—dormitories, student personnel, athletics, the business office—grew hostile toward Flemming. The Flemming fiscal policy, nonetheless, freed the university to take advantage of fleeting opportunities. The calculated risk formula helped bring the university a 710 percent increase in "gifts, grants, and contracts": from $2 million to $16.2 million during the Flemming tenure.

Flemming's numerous detractors insisted, of course, that the credit belonged elsewhere, but Charles Johnson credited Flemming. It was Flemming who created the proper "atmosphere" of administrative encouragement to allow the academic flowers to bloom. And it was this that Johnson hoped to emulate when he spoke of keeping the university "moving ahead." But now, in 1968, even Flemming's optimism was "guarded." Flemming said in his last meeting with the faculty in July that the fate of higher education's finances depended largely on what happened at the negotiating table in Paris. "If the Vietnam situation is cleared up, I see no end to the expanding economy of higher education, both at the federal and state levels." What might happen if the Vietnam situation were *not* cleared up Flemming didn't say.

That was now Charles Johnson's problem.

The new acting president was up at 6:30 that first morning,

his usual rising time. As was his custom, he spent a few minutes with the previous day's *Register-Guard* (ninety-seven degree weather and the passage of a school budget were the top news items). He tuned to TV's "Today" show at seven, glancing at it intermittently while reading the paper.

After breakfast he finished dressing: a white shirt, a narrow, horizontally striped tie, and a gray suit. Into his reddish-brown attaché case, initialed "CEJ," he placed an assortment of candy bars and bags of peanuts. They would serve him for lunch on most of the days to come. He seldom bothered with lunch. He never took a break for coffee. The murderous pace was Chuck Johnson's style. It had been no different during the eleven years he taught accounting at the School of Business Administration or the subsequent five years as dean of the College of Liberal Arts, a segment of the university that included 61 percent of the student enrollment.

He certainly did not expect his new position to change his style. He was still "Chuck" Johnson. To a close friend who had written that he planned henceforth to address him as "President Johnson" and not presume too much on the "Chuck" title, Johnson retorted, "Well, I won't mind if you forget."

He updated his biographical resume to include his new title, but otherwise it remained the same: Charles Ellicott Johnson, born September 7, 1920, Worland, Wyoming; married to Jeanne Seal in 1942; three children, Craig 21, Karen 20, and Kylene 13. The "Ellicott" was his mother's family name. Rose Ellicott was a tall, dark-haired, attractive woman who died of complications of childbirth at the age of twenty-nine when Charles was five. She was a quiet woman, reserved, almost stoic, the kind who would never say anything bad about anybody and who would never let on if something was wrong.

Those traits had been inherited by her son, Charles, who at forty-seven now wore his black hair, graying at the temples, in a crew cut. Perhaps it was from his father, Palmer Johnson, that he inherited his stubbornness. Crew cuts were outrageously out of style in 1968, and not even Craig, his fashion-conscious son (then in the Army in Korea) had been able to persuade him to change.

"Come on, Dad, let your hair grow out a little," pleaded Craig.

"No, then I'd have to comb it all the time."

"You could drop your sideburns down a little."

"Oh?"

"Well, at least stop buying those baggy pants. The way they flop around they're gonna bruise your ankles."

He eyed Craig's fashionably tapered, tight-fitting slacks. "I'd rather have bruised ankles," he said, "than to have to screw on the kind of tight britches you're wearing."

His suits remained uniformly conservative, mostly gray or light blue, usually purchased through a mail order shop in Chicago. He bought two pairs of pants with each suit in deference to his wife's complaint about his habit of cleaning the ashes from his pipe by tapping it on his knee, often ruining still another pair with live ashes.

He had smoked the pipe since his college days. The tobacco he smoked invariably was mildly aromatic, though the brand mattered less to him than the size of the container. He bought tobacco by the pound. He insisted on buying everything in whole units, pounds, quarts, gallons. It was a crusade. Nothing infuriated him more than to see an item offered for sale at, say, fourteen and three-quarter ounces for a dollar seventy-nine. Was that a better buy than a competing item at fifteen and one-half ounces for a dollar ninety-five?

To combat these nefarious malpractices, he founded an organization called the Buy-by-the-Pound Society (B.B.T.P.S.) whose membership totaled four, including his wife and the Hardies, who lived in the neighborhood. He installed himself as president. No one could be more amiably fiendish than Johnson, presiding over the monthly meetings, plotting the boycotts and other fearful economic pressures the B.B.T.P.S. might bring to bear on uncooperative merchants.

The B.B.T.P.S. was, of course, a paper tiger. Its president remained an unpretentious man. And a precise, highly disciplined man.

It was now eight o'clock. He kissed his wife good-bye.

Jeanne Seal Johnson, a vivacious, dark-haired woman, bore a

faint resemblance to his long-dead mother. The resemblance was purely physical. Where Rose Ellicott was quiet and reserved, Jeanne Seal was gay and ebullient—and a little mischievous. She was a small-town girl from Verndale, Minnesota, the daughter of a storekeeper, the energetic high school cheerleader who played in the school band and dated the captain of the baseball team and served as salutatorian of her eighteen-member graduating class. After graduation she moved to Minneapolis to attend secretarial school. There she met Chuck Johnson, a freshman at the University of Minnesota.

Jeanne liked to tease him, a show of attention that delighted the serious-minded Chuck Johnson and also triggered his own wit and charm. He told her funny anecdotes about all the foolish things he'd done as a child, and her responding laughter was one of appreciation and acceptance. He liked that. Years later, when people asked how she came to marry him, she'd say, "I won him in a Ping-Pong game." She explained that Chuck and his friend would offer to play the losers in table tennis matches at the Methodist youth foundation. "So I and my girl friend would always arrange to lose our matches so we could play these guys."

One evening Chuck Johnson took Jeanne Seal to dinner. The evening went well until dessert. He said casually, "Oh, say, I've got something here for you." He fished a small box from his coat pocket. Inside was an engagement ring. She was flustered, completely taken by surprise. He had never talked seriously of marriage before. In fact, he'd never even mentioned it.

Clutching the attaché case with its cargo of peanuts and candy bars, the new president walked through the back door to the big double garage. Two cars sat there, the Oldsmobile and the Volkswagen. As usual, he chose the Volkswagen.

It seemed the more manageable of the two cars. Certainly it was vastly simpler mechanically. He developed a distaste for big cars with their automatic drives and fancy trappings ("Just more things to go wrong"). He fared very poorly with all things mechanical; even the new electric can opener wouldn't work for him. But cars were the worst. He hated shopping for them. Once, when he encountered an overenthusiastic car salesman ("I'm sure we can fix you up, Mr. Johnson; just let me talk with the manager....") he left and never returned. When his daughter, Karen, offered to shop for the second family car, he gladly consented and approved her recommended choice, a cream-colored Volkswagen, sight unseen. He gave it a name: Karen's Folly.

He always looked uncomfortable curled inside the tiny Volkswagen, his height forcing him to hunch down over the wheel. He seemed not to mind. He pulled away from the wide cement driveway and headed north on Palomino Drive.

His house melted into the distance. In a few hours he would return to that house. He would always return to that house. He loved the *feel* of it with its long, ranch-style sprawl, its flagstone facade, its wood-paneled living room, its big master bedroom with the super-king-sized bed that allowed him to stretch out to his full dimension. It was the right kind of house for a country boy forced to live in town.

The house stood at Number 250 Palomino Drive. It sat on a flat, double-sized lot, behind a well-manicured lawn watered by a semiautomatic underground sprinkling system. A rose garden, his special pride, bloomed to the south of the house, and a fountain dominated the backyard.

The fountain was a mound of rocks carefully cemented into place with water bubbling out of the top and spilling down the sides into a pool at the base. An ugly stump had been there originally, he explained to visitors. It was the remnant of a tree blown down in a ferocious windstorm in 1962. One weekend he tried to chop out the stump, but the deeply entrenched roots defied the ax.

When he paused to rest, wiping perspiration from his fore-head, he saw them—a scattering of tiny green people scampering from beneath the stump, shouting excitedly.

"Stop!" they cried. "This is our home."

Johnson was aghast. He had no idea that little people lived

there. It was then that he decided on a solution vastly simpler, and easier, than chopping out the stump. He would hide the stump beneath a rock fountain. It seemed an equitable solution to a perplexing problem in social relations.

As he sped down Palomino Drive, the neighbors' houses glistened in the morning sun. The subdivision, formally known as "Westward Ho," was informally called "Horsey Acres." It was a cross-section of Middle America. It contained a high proportion of working wives, and the houses represented the material results of the combined incomes. Each house uniformly dominated a lush, green lawn. A cement driveway spliced each lawn and led to a double garage. Each garage contained some of the trappings of middle-class affluence: cars, boats, trailers, kids' bikes, charcoal grills. Middle America. Most University of Oregon faculty preferred to live on the other side of town in the elegant old houses on University and Potter and Harris streets just south of the campus or in the modern houses that clung to the tree-clad hills farther out. The occupants of Westward Ho's flatlands seemed like expatriates of rural America. No doubt many of them had, like the Johnsons, grown up in small towns or rural areas in the twenties and thirties and were recapturing a small piece of their childhood by living in Horsey Acres.

The drive to the campus took less than fifteen minutes. Though traffic on the Ferry Street Bridge, spanning the Willamette River, was intense by small-town standards, the distance was short. Eugene was a pleasant lumbering, agricultural, and university community of 79,000 persons, a growing community, and by all appearances a prosperous community. The tiny Volkswagen sped down the ramp on the south side of the bridge and onto Franklin Boulevard. Johnson parked the car in one of the faculty parking lots two blocks from his new office in the university's administration building (his presidential reserved parking space had not been designated yet). He walked briskly. Already the temperature was a balmy sixty-three degrees, and lawn sprinklers were at work to preserve the cool, green look for which the campus was widely known.

The new president burst through the door of the outer office of the presidential suite at precisely 8:15. Clutching his attaché case, he strode briskly past the desks of two secretaries.

"Good morning," he said with a toothy smile.

He disappeared into the private office beyond—the President's Office. The office presented an aura of quiet opulence, with its green carpeting, its cherry-wood paneling, its built-in bookshelves lining one wall. He wondered how he would ever fill those shelves. The office was spacious and airy, with a high ceiling, a lot bigger than his living room at home.

He plopped into the big red-leather chair behind the desk.

Charles E. Johnson, acting president. President Johnson.

Janice Medrano, a dark-haired, thirtyish woman who was to be his "administrative assistant," stood by his desk, speaking, looking very flustered.

"I'm embarrassed to ask this but—" she was saying. It turned out that Flemming had not yet vacated the office. Johnson cheerfully allowed himself to be shunted to a tiny side office for the day.

The transfer of presidential power from Arthur S. Flemming to Charles E. Johnson occurred unceremoniously around four that afternoon at the Eugene airport. Flemming waved good-bye to Johnson and boarded a plane for the first leg of a flight to Minnesota.

Johnson returned to find a stack of papers on his desk. A hand-written note on orange paper caught his eye. It was from the chancellor of the Oregon State System of Higher Education. Perhaps it was important.

"With this as our first official transaction during your tenure," the note read, "the prospects appear to be good!" The note, attached to a letter from a university graduate, was signed informally, "Lew." Chancellor Roy E. Lieuallen occupied an office just above Johnson's office and presided over all ten units in the State System.[1] He was Johnson's "boss," though Lieuallen saw himself as working "with" rather than "above" the institutional presidents. Like Johnson, Lieuallen was a country boy, having grown up in the hot, dusty, wheat-farming country in eastern Oregon.

The letter accompanying Lieuallen's orange paper note came

41

from a woman who had graduated from the university thirty years earlier. The letter and a check to the alumni fund had somehow been misaddressed to the Chancellor's Office.

"If you are not careful," she wrote, "the University of Oregon will become one of the major centers of real learning in the United States. . . . Please don't turn the university over to the people who are obsessed by fears, either of students or whatever it is the people get afraid of. The result is sure to be heightened disorder. My New English Bible says, 'You fathers, again, must not goad your children to resentment, but give them instruction, and the correction, which belong to a Christian upbringing.' "

Johnson reached for a pen and, in his first official transaction of record as acting president, wrote a note to Ray Hawk, the university's director of public relations: "What is our procedure on writing thank-you letters? I'd be glad to sign one to this lady—this is a very heartwarming reaction!" He put it in the "out" box—whereupon the machinery of the President's Office moved into action. . . . The memo typed for easier reading. . . . The material forwarded to Hawk's office located just across the lobby of the presidential suite. . . .

In a few days a letter came back, ready for the president's signature. ("It is all too rare in this day of blaring headlines about student unrest and disorders on some of our campuses to find someone like yourself who has a feeling for the students. . . .") Johnson signed the letter, and it was soon in the mail. The remaining documents—the woman's letter, the note from Lieuallen, the carbon copy of the presidential reply—were placed into a new manila folder labeled THANKS, LETTERS OF, which was then inserted under "T" in the presidential filing cabinet.

Five:
The First
Confrontation

In the succeeding days Charles Johnson established for the presidential suite an atmosphere of good humor and Western informality. Gone was the air of aloof dignity—the "tomblike atmosphere," as one secretary called it—that had characterized the Flemming years. Replacing it was a comfortable, pipe-smoking, rather tweedy affability.

Once, as he strolled down the outer lobby of the administration building, Johnson encountered a tall, lanky student wearing cowboy boots and a bright western shirt. The unmistakable odor of horses emanated from the young man.

"Oh, boy," said Johnson. "There's something in the air that reminds me of home."

The young man's discomfort disappeared as he saw Johnson's grin. "I tried to scrape it off. Where's home?"

"Wyoming," said Johnson, pausing to light his pipe.

"No kidding. I'm from there, too."

The early days of his presidential tenure swept Johnson into the mainstream of institutional management like a tiny canoe being picked up out of slack water by the swift currents of a powerful river. The ominous roar that some people claimed to

43

hear downstream—turbulence of unknown dimensions accompanying the return of the students in September—was a comfortable six weeks away. The presidential canoe, meanwhile, began probing into some of the swift currents, including the swiftest and trickiest of all: the financial operation. First, he had to learn something about it. The university, he discovered, was a $180,410.95-a-day business. The figure represented the university's average daily impact on the community's economy as calculated by the business manager.

Despite the trouble the university seemed to cause the otherwise tranquil community of Eugene, despite the "commie-pinko-pervert-revolutionary" students and the "radical professors who preach revolution"—despite these basic flaws—the university possessed one redeeming asset. It was the community's largest single purchaser of goods and services.

The facts were in the business manager's report. Dormitory residents annually consumed 504,000 fresh eggs, 250,000 pounds of meat (not including poultry and fish), 61,000 gallons of whole milk, and 15,500 gallons of skim milk. At the Erb Memorial Union, students annually consumed, among other things, 13,000 gallons of soup and 104,000 hamburgers. The Erb Union also harbored an undetermined amount of drug traffic (marijuana sold at about ten dollars a lid, a statistic not mentioned in the business manager's report), but, in truth, even the most radical of students bought the produce if not the politics of Oregon's farmers.

On-campus consumption was only part of the picture. Although the university's dormitories were usually full, they housed only 21.4% of the university's 14,000 students. Most students (62.6%) lived and ate off campus, primarily in apartments or in the homes of parents or relatives. Many students were married (29.9% of the men and 19.2% of the women). All of them brought money to the community.

The university's payroll, for 5,300 full- and part-time employees, was the largest in the county: $28.5 million. The university "is a stable and substantial business," said the business manager. Its population (students, faculty, and staff) of

19,000 made it equivalent to Oregon's seventh-largest city—"it makes a strong economic impact in the state." To insure that no one missed the message, the business manager prepared a statistical summary.

Table I: University of Oregon Expenditures 1968-69

General education purposes	$18,269,000
Special research and extension service	13,686,000
Auxiliary activities and related enterprises	6,130,000
New building construction	3,110,000
Bond interest and principal	1,008,000
Student aid	3,472,000
Agency and affiliated independent bodies	3,412,000
Student loan fund	763,000
Total University of Oregon expenditures	$49,850,000
Estimated expenditures by students	10,000,000
Estimated expenditures by visitors	6,000,000
TOTAL ECONOMIC IMPACT ON COMMUNITY	$65,850,000

The facts, the columns of figures, were President Johnson's stock in trade. He understood them well, the hopelessly dull and gray documents, the language of the accountant: the blacks of balances and surpluses, the reds of deficits, the double lines underscoring the totals. His CPA-trained eyes glided over the trackless wastes of tables and charts and balance sheets like a hungry kingfisher coasting over the water in search of food.

At a superficial first glance, the university seemed to be in excellent fiscal health. On Johnson's desk lay the State System's financial summary, *Operating Budget for the Fiscal Year Ending June 30, 1969,* an eighty-five-page document. The University of Oregon, as one of ten agencies represented, occupied a mere six pages into which were compressed $38.5 million worth of activities, the items considered essential to educational endeavor, including the annual water bill ($47,000), the cost of diplomas ($6,525), the Department of Mathematics ($462,816).

As an accountant, Johnson knew, however, that budgets are fluid and changeable. The document before him, like a photograph, depicted reality for only 1/100 of a second.

Already the picture had changed. Before he left, Arthur Flemming had approved extra-budgetary commitments totaling $190,200, including an additional $66,000 for the Computer Center, an extra $23,000 for teacher education, another $30,000 for the School of Law. And though Johnson had declared publicly that "all commitments by President Flemming will be honored by my administration," privately he could only hope. The money was nowhere in sight.

Except on paper. True, Flemming had left a balanced budget. But he had balanced it merely by inflating income estimates to what his advisers considered an unrealistic figure. Of course, he'd *always* done that through the years of his tenure. And he'd always been right.

His optimistic prediction suggested that the university would receive $1,165,000 in "indirect cost credits" from federal and foundation grants and contracts. These represented reimbursement for the university's overhead costs in administering the work covered by the grant. Under the State System's "A-21" formula, the university charged 34 percent of the wage and salary allocation of the grant as overhead, or what accountants called "indirect cost credits."

At first glance, it looked like the kind of statistical legerdemain that only a man of Johnson's CPA background could comprehend. Actually, it was rather simple. A million-dollar foundation grant might have $200,000 of the total allocated for wages and salaries. The university skimmed off 34 percent of that—$68,000—as administrative overhead. It budgeted the money as income, just as it budgeted state tax funds. And to some degree the money was transferable within the institution, at least by Flemming's administrative philosophy.

But the university would not know until the year was half over precisely how many grants and contracts it could expect to receive. The trend was downward. Perhaps the university would get only $16 million worth this year instead of the $17 million or more it hoped to get. Perhaps only $3 million of the $16 million would be allocated to wages and salaries. Then only $1,020,000 would come in as indirect cost credits.

And that, by the best guess of the business office, was as high as it was likely to go—or perhaps $1,040,000 at the most, still short of the budget by $125,000.

Balancing the optimistic Flemming budget depended on reaching two additional goals:

1. The university's fall enrollment would have to reach its predicted level of 14,665 students. If it *passed* that mark it would get more money out of tuition excesses, as much as $400 to $600 for each extra student. If as many as 300 extra showed up, as usually happened during the Flemming era, the university could enjoy a financial bonanza of as much as $180,000. It could also lose money if enrollment failed to meet the prediction. So whatever the learned professors said about "pursuit of excellence," the administration was intensely interested in numbers—"warm bodies," as the business office cynically called them.

2. Enough professors and secretaries would have to leave their jobs during the year to permit the university to reach a 2.37 percent "vacancy experience adjustment factor," another arcane accounting term, but again rather simple. It referred to dollars not spent while a position was temporarily vacant through death, resignation, or retirement. In a fiscal emergency a vacant position could be "frozen" (not filled) or it could be "underfilled" (such as a $12,000-a-year professor replaced by two $3,500 graduate teaching fellows).

It was all pretty shaky. It would be late October before the enrollment tally was known, and January before the picture on indirect cost credits became clear.

The president could, of course, take immediate action to control the "vacancy experience adjustment factor."

He called Clyde Patton, head of the Department of Geography. As dean of the College of Liberal Arts, Johnson had approved and sent to the president the appointment of a new professor of geography at $18,000 a year. By the time the document had run the bureaucratic channels and reached the president's desk, Johnson *was* the president.

"I understand the dean has approved this appointment," Johnson told Patton. "I'm afraid I'm going to have to overrule the dean. To be perfectly frank, Clyde, the president knows a lot more about the university's financial problems than the dean ever knew. In fact, the dean was pretty naïve."

Both men sensed the irony. Neither laughed.

Johnson desperately needed to find funds to support some twenty tenured professors whose salaries came from "soft money": foundation grants. The grants would expire next year, and no extra salary money was in sight.

But Johnson's accounting eye was quick to find food in the desert of statistical reports. When the budget office pointed out a discrepancy in the State System's proposed budget allocations for 1969-71, he pounced. The discrepancy existed in the university's graduate level student-teacher ratio (10.6 to 1) as compared to a sister institution, Oregon State University (8.0 to 1). Again, it seemed arcane, but Johnson immediately perceived its significance: at the graduate level, Oregon State had more professors in proportion to students than did the university.

Was it possible, he asked Chancellor Lieuallen, that the university might secure additional faculty positions next year in order to equalize this imbalance? If so, Johnson calculated, the university might gain as many as twenty-two positions.

It was possible, the chancellor conceded. He promised to review the situation.

Johnson pressed harder. "On the basis of our conversation," he wrote Lieuallen, "I understand that there may be factors influencing these ratios that explain the difference in such a way that we would not be justified in asking for a larger new position allocation. If such factors exist, I need to know them in order to explain them to my staff. If your review indicates that our case has merit, I would urge that you give this matter serious consideration in your 1969-70 budgetary allocation decisions."

Such was the work of the university president. Most of it was hopelessly dull and burdensome, dragged down by grinding paper work and by countless conferences about money or the lack of it. For all its tweedy talk of houses of intellect and the pursuit of truth, the university ran on money. When Johnson compiled a list of the five "problem areas" he foresaw in the year ahead, finances were dominant:

1. Maintain academic excellence—and improve it if possible—in the face of a severely restricted budget.
2. Convince the Board of Higher Education and the legislature of the need for financial support.
3. Find ways for students to make an "active and orderly" contribution to the educational process.
4. Strike the proper balance between undergraduate and graduate education in committing financial and personnel resources.
5. Establish priorities among the competing demands being made of universities across the country: "If we do not have the means to be all things to all men, we must decide what are the most essential elements of our mission and then make the hard choices to put excellence above ubiquity."

The list was noteworthy for the absence of a reference to student turbulence. Point 3 only hinted at that question. Did he expect trouble on the campus in the fall? How did he plan to handle the rampant problems of disruption, violence, radicalism, black power, and drug addiction? Would he strive to "clean up the mess?" They were key questions. Johnson tended to sidestep such questions. Privately he shared Flemming's belief that "to brag about how you plan to handle trouble is to invite the very trouble you hope to avoid." Johnson also shared Flemming's optimism about students. Instead of drawing battle lines and rattling sabers, Johnson said, the university might benefit by involving students, in partnership with faculty and administration, in a pattern of "controlled change." This, he said, would help the university to respond in a flexible manner

49

to pressure for change. It would also help to avoid confrontations between "highly polarized groups which see each other as adversaries to be defeated rather than as responsible partners engaged in a search for better ways of attaining mutually desired objectives."

Johnson favored a strategy of "controlled confrontation," bringing all parties to an issue together for public debate in an atmosphere of relative calm. It was naïve, he recognized, to assume that calm could prevail at all confrontations. If a problem deteriorated into a "crisis situation"—one in which coercion and force are involved—the university must seek to find the line between "legitimate protest" and "intolerable actions" that infringe on the rights of others. But the line was likely to be a "gray area," rather than a sharply delineated one. He must have maximum administrative flexibility in meeting the crisis.

Johnson appointed a three-person "crisis committee" (one student and two professors) that would be called together quickly in the event of trouble to advise the president on possible courses of action.

Open communication with students, Johnson knew, required a lot of the president himself. Flemming had dealt directly with student leaders. They were unlikely to settle for lesser administrators. So it was that on the second day of his presidency, Johnson was visited by a ferocious-looking young man who resembled a clean-shaven Che Guevara. His name was Roy Bennett. He wore a dark-blue beret, cross bandoliers of leather, and high boots. He spent twenty minutes with the president.

"What was *that?*" asked a professor, entering Johnson's office as the young man was leaving.

"I think that was my first confrontation," said Johnson. It had been a mild one. Bennett claimed to represent an organization called the Sons of Liberty and had presented ten "requests for quick action by the faculty," upon such items as: allowing students on faculty committees, opening faculty meetings to the public, and eliminating academic credit for military science courses.

"A couple of these make pretty good sense," said Johnson. "Listen to this: 'To eliminate any fatal accidents and to encourage peaceful settlement of all disputes, *no* person should be permitted to carry firearms, ammunition, or any other items manufactured with the intent of killing, maiming, or otherwise disabling.' That's one I'd go along with."

"I didn't notice," said the professor, "did he have any bullets in those bandoliers?"

"I don't think so."

"What do you plan to do with these demands?"

"I notice they're addressed to the faculty and not to the president," he said. "I'm thinking of presenting them to the faculty at the first meeting this fall."

Johnson, meanwhile, began to enjoy the renewed contact with students. "I never realized how isolated from students the dean's office was." He had always felt comfortable with students. In mid-August, addressing a group of graduating seniors, he indulged in lighthearted banter. ("Imagine my surprise to learn they'd *already* named a building after me."[1]) Among the "benefits" of their forthcoming role as alumni, he told them, was an alumni magazine that spoke with candor about the "absolutely awful things the administration is letting the faculty and students get away with now." Another was the security of never suffering for lack of mail. The university planned to send them a steady stream of alumni fund-solicitation letters. "When we wish you happiness and material success, we really mean it from the bottom of our hearts."

His contact with the outside public grew less pleasant. When a delegation of the town's citizens presented him a petition requesting the dismissal of the militant and controversial black professor, Clyde DeBerry, Johnson listened courteously. He promised to discuss it further. But he perceived that they were talking about off-campus "life-styles," not classroom performance, and he doubted that the president had much control over such matters. The stridency of the wording on the petition surprised him, however: "The citizens of our committee are determined that this man be called to account for his actions and that he be discharged and not allowed to conduct classes. . . ."

An equally bitter trickle of letters focused on another problem. Copies of a new student-produced magazine, *Onset*, had been mailed to incoming freshmen. One of the letters asked Johnson whether, after reading *Onset*'s discussion of drugs, liquor, hippies, and assorted campus problems, he'd want his daughter to attend the University of Oregon. That amused Johnson. Karen *was* attending the university. But the letter disturbed him by its rancor. It said, "I've heard and seen pictures of the 'student lie-in' protest in which the university administration 'knuckled under' and gave in to the demands of a handful of so-called 'students' and hippies. It's a disgrace to allow this type of coercion to get by, and I believe the sooner the state rids the education system of such short-sighted administrators the better it will be. I hope my daughter will never be involved in such criminal acts! . . ."

The alumnus said he no longer intended to send his daughter to the University of Oregon. He planned to send her to Oregon State instead.

In flipping through copies of *Onset*, a sixteen-page offset production which he had not seen before, Johnson noted that most of the information about "campus life" came through a *Playboy*-type interview with three prospective freshmen discussing what they thought campus life would be like.

He wondered how his daughter, Karen, might react to the letter. A few days later he found out. In the living room after dinner, he showed it to her.

Karen exploded. "It's stupid! I can't believe that an educated man could write such a letter. I wish I could answer it myself. Boy, I'd tell him off!"

"What would you say?" asked Johnson.

"I'd tell him how *stupid* his letter is!"

"Now that wouldn't do any good." Johnson lit his pipe and puffed thoughtfully. "Calm down. Use a little logic. Why do you think his letter is stupid?"

Because, she snapped, the writer had taken the word of three students out of more than fourteen thousand. Three students! Indeed, they weren't even students; they only intended to be.

"So here's this *idiot*," she said, "who takes as gospel the word of three kids who haven't even attended the university yet. Now that's what I'd call pretty stupid."

"Yes," said Johnson thoughtfully, "I think some of that could go into a letter of reply. I kind of go along with some of that. But you wouldn't get very far using a lot of emotional name-calling, though, would you? That would mean you're no better than he is. All right, what's your next point?"

"The part about not sending his daughter to the university," she said. "It shows they don't really trust her. They don't have any faith in the way they brought her up. If they can't trust her at the University of Oregon, can they trust her *anywhere* outside their own house?"

"That's not bad for point two. Now how about point three?"

"You sound as if you want me to write the letter."

"That's not a bad idea, providing you can avoid being emotional and argumentative."

Karen did write the letter—twice—on ruled notebook paper.

"I read with much interest and admiration your letter of Aug. 27," she began. ". . . The admiration was for your concern as parents. . . . You asked my father if he would allow his daughter to attend 'such a school' as the U. of O. He not only would, but he did. I was free to choose any school I wanted after high school graduation, and Oregon was easily my choice. . . . If (your daughter) starts drinking the minute she leaves your sight, what does that say for the strength of her parental-taught standards? Mine stuck with me, whether my parents are around or not. . . ."

Karen, attractive, dark-haired, vivacious, occasionally explosive, took pride in her father, and the feeling was mutual. She looked upon him with a mixture of affection and awe. Though she considered him naïve in many ways, the naïveté often seemed to contain a certain craftiness.

He believed in the basic integrity of people. He never locked the doors to the house except when on extended trips.

"Dad, someday somebody's gonna come in here and steal us blind," she once said.

"Has anybody robbed us yet?"

"No, but—"

"Well, there you are. Ninety percent of the people are basically honest."

"I know a lot of girls in the dorm who are a lot less than 90 percent honest," she said. "They cheat on tests."

She seemed to get nowhere in educating her father to the realities of life. But the craftiness she thought she saw in him suggested that perhaps he wasn't really as naïve as he let on. Perhaps he was merely taking the approach that if you let people know you believe in them, 90 percent of the time they'll try to measure up to your expectations.

Well, it had worked with her. Like the time she stole the candy bar. She was ten or eleven then, and she and a friend had been caught by the store manager and sent home. The manager had called their parents. When Karen arrived home, frightened, her father greeted her as though nothing had happened.

Later that evening, he asked her a couple of questions. Did she really think it was all right to take something that didn't belong to her?

"No," she sobbed.

How would she feel if someone had taken something from her, something she'd worked hard to earn?

He didn't even raise his voice. Yet in retrospect those questions seemed more painful to her than if she'd gotten a spanking.

A certain craftiness. She sensed it again in the way he dealt with her reaction to the letter from the alumnus. Crafty, and very subtle.

A trickle of students began to arrive on the campus by mid-September. By late September it became a torrent. With the 2,600 freshmen on the campus came the daughter of the alumnus Karen had written to. ("She's here after all! That's really cool," Karen said.)

At 1:52 a.m. Sunday, September 29, the first of three explosions ripped the U.S. Naval and Marine Corps Reserve Training Center, located across town from the campus. A twelve-ton crane, two bulldozers, four dump trucks, a personnel carrier, and a trailer, all property of "B" Company, Tenth Engineer Battalion, U.S. Marine Corps Reserve, were destroyed or heavily damaged. There were no injuries. The loss was estimated at $106,000. The work was clearly that of saboteurs: "It was a well-organized effort, not the ordinary arson job," said an officer. And it fit the pattern of bombings of military buildings on or near campuses of several colleges and universities on the West Coast.

It was more than coincidental, in the minds of many citizens, that within a week after the U.O. opened to students for fall quarter, a military installation should be blown up. The Age of Violence had descended on the normally quiet university town of Eugene, Oregon.

Six:
Dirty Words

First the explosions at the Naval Armory, then a shooting incident. At a near-campus ice cream parlor one evening, a .32-caliber bullet mysteriously ripped through a window. A ricocheting fragment of the bullet grazed a girl's leg. These incidents and others—such as the attempted dynamiting of the local Democratic party headquarters the previous August—did nothing to allay the "feeling of apprehension" that gripped Wandalyn Rice as she arrived back on the campus that September.

Wandalyn Rice was in her junior year this fall, a tall, slim, blonde young woman who studied journalism, got good grades, and wrote articles for the campus newspaper, *Oregon Daily Emerald.*

The violent incidents and the potential for further violence were reason enough for apprehension. But there was more. Police-demonstrator clashes in Chicago during the Democratic party convention in August had raised the ire of many politically active students. Their own interests, represented by the candidacy of Senator Eugene McCarthy, had been shredded by Machine Politics, they said. The most vocal of students seemed disenchanted by the choice available—Nixon, Humphrey— what's the difference? To the most volatile of left-leaning students, the whole aspect of Chicago, from machine politics to police brutality, spelled out an approaching fascist repression. "From Chicago," declared a member of the new-left group, Students for a Democratic Society, "we learned that the entrenched driving elements of America today will not yield to demands for justice without a brutal fight. The experiences of blacks confirm that the system will resort to murder if necessary." Meanwhile the war in Vietnam ground on. The Selective Service System continued to compel young men to fight a war many of them abhorred. Several university students planned to face jail rather than induction.

Adding to Wandalyn's apprehension was the memory of the three-day sit-in at Johnson Hall the previous spring. "That was a very innocent thing," she told a friend. "If something like that happens again it could really be ugly. We realized this last spring when the riots occurred at Columbia University a week or so after Johnson Hall. There it was, kids getting hit on the head by police. If it can happen at Columbia, it can happen here.

"And the new president, Johnson. Well, nobody knows anything about him except that he's an accountant, which doesn't sound too good. With Flemming gone, maybe the new man won't keep his cool. That's all it would take. Just let some administrator do something stupid enough to rile up a bunch of kids so you have to call in the police. The university could blow up."

Wandalyn also noticed subtle differences in the new freshmen on campus in the fall that made her feel a further degree of unease. It was as if they were of a different generation. For one thing the freshmen seemed to enjoy picking up anecdotes about the university's early days and repeating them as mystical legends of a bygone era. One story told of a group of athletes who corralled some hippies and gave them a haircut.

"Bygone era?" Wandalyn exclaimed. "That happened during my *freshman year.* That was only two years ago!"

The freshmen talked differently, too. Wandalyn remembered attending a class in political science a year earlier where discussion turned to obscenity as a political issue. "A boy in the class got terribly embarrassed," she recalled. "He kept referring to *that word.* That's how he put it. He said, 'You know—*that word*—you'd be shocked if I said it.' I thought that was pretty funny."

Now the new freshman girls used *that word* as casually as they wore hip-hugger pants and high-laced boots. It was the freshman girl's way of proving she was "with it," Wandalyn concluded.

There were other changes.

"Do you realize," a classmate remarked to her, "that our class was the last class in the university to use *beer* as its symbol of rebellion?"

"I hadn't really thought about it," she said.

"Well, it's true. The other classes drink, but that's not their symbol of rebellion. I met a freshman girl the other day who has gone through marijuana, LSD, mescaline, and speed. Now she's decided that she's through with drugs. She doesn't need them anymore. And she's only a *freshman.*"

A new student culture had arrived. Perhaps that was why the story on page three of the *Daily Emerald* that Friday morning created only a minor stir on campus. Though she worked for the *Emerald,* Wandalyn was among the last to see it. She overheard a youth at the Student Union coffee shop. "Wow!" he said. "Look what the *Emerald* has done."

"What?" she asked anxiously.

In Johnson Hall, Acting President Johnson was also reading the story on page three. His assistant, William Blevins, a young man new to the President's Office, had brought it to his attention. "This is something you might want to be aware of," said Blevins calmly.

"Oh, boy," said President Johnson softly. "I suppose this will get us a bad press."

ORGANIZATION PROPOSES "DEMOCRATIC" UNIVERSITY

A group of University students and faculty called the Mothers Fuckers recently sent a list of 10 proposals for change in the University to Acting President Charles Johnson.

These proposals, "the first month's goals" of the organization, were all directed towards the group's aim of "obtaining participatory democracy in the University community," said Roy Bennett, chairman, in an Emerald interview Thursday.

Johnson proceeded to turn the proposal over to the Faculty Senate, according to Bennett. The items were then referred to the Student-Faculty Council by the faculty at its general meeting Wednesday. The proposals ask that the faculty and the Faculty-Senate meetings be open to the public . . . and that there be no faculty members on the Student Conduct Committee.

The group also advocates student participation on committees choosing new faculty members, complete student control over student finances, and participation of graduate students on the committees determining requirements for degrees. . . .

Johnson recognized the proposals. Roy Bennett was the young man who had come to Johnson's office wearing boots, beret, and cross bandoliers. But the list of proposals had changed. Johnson did not recognize the one for "complete student control over student finances," for example. And the organization's name was the biggest change of all. What became of the "Sons of Liberty"?

"I'd suggest we try to find out what happened," said Johnson.

It was a bothersome thing—no doubt he'd get a question or two about it at the next meeting of the Mothers Club—but he did not give it a very high priority. A university president, he had decided by now, must ration his time. He had to decide what's important. Probably the *Emerald* problem would be handled somewhere short of the presidential level. And right now the enrollment figures loomed important: 11,454 on the seventh day of registration, short of the 14,665 target but 600 ahead of the same period last year. He was optimistic.

A few days later the *Emerald* printed a correction. It had been "regrettably misinformed" about the name of the organization, the paper said. "The alleged chairman of the group, commonly known as the Sons of Liberty, maintained the name

60

of the group had been changed to that which was printed. However, there is no recognized student group by that name."

So that was that. Just one of those unfortunate things. An "inexperienced sub-editor," Johnson learned from a journalism professor, had been badgered by the group's chairman into using the name in print.

It surprised Johnson a little, however, to note the rancor in some people. A member of the university's own staff had written to the Board of Higher Education, with a carbon copy to Johnson: "I just wonder how much longer we will be compelled to endure such *filth.*"

"That's this guy's sense of loyalty to the university," said Blevins bitterly. "Sending a letter like that to the board."

"I'll have a chat with him," said Johnson.

It was good to have the obscenity issue out of the way. New problems arrived daily.

Students complained that the class registration process was slow and inefficient. Many classes filled up within the first hour, and hundreds of students had to be denied places.

The Department of Chemistry reported that students had started forming waiting lines at 4:00 a.m., standing in line until registration opened at eight, to be assured of places in certain classes required for graduation.

Departments asked Johnson for more money to add class sections. Mathematics and English said lack of funds forced them to use inexperienced graduate students to teach many classes. In English, graduate students were teaching all but two freshman-level literature classes.

The grounds maintenance men were equally strapped for funds. "We asked for a budget of ninety-nine cents per square foot of grounds space," complained the superintendent. "All we got was sixty-nine cents."

There was no extra money.

New kinds of problems arose.

The weekly report of the Office of Student Services cited a "rather high-spirited week" in the dormitories: "Problems with men entering the women's rooms and sleeping areas . . . three

61

panty raids . . . an unidentified male running around a dorm complex in the nude . . . a female dorm resident hospitalized from use of drugs. . . ."

Rumors arose that one student, suspected of being emotionally unstable, had purloined a map of the campus underground utility tunnel system and was threatening to plant dynamite under key buildings, each explosive charge to be detonated by remote control unless certain demands were met. Campus security patrols were alerted.

Now a point of alarm: a flyer was circulating around the campus that described how to make Molotov cocktails and booby traps. A detailed diagram showed how to place explosives in hollowed-out books, the books to be placed on library shelves. When an unsuspecting student or librarian removed a booby-trapped book, the explosion would shatter the shelves and possibly kill or maim the person. One such explosion might spread terror throughout the campus, might even shut it down.

Now a new question about an old problem. A professor asked how Johnson planned to respond to the *"Emerald* problem."

"Silence," the professor added, "would appear to be tacit approval."

Such inquiries puzzled Johnson. The editor had printed a correction and had taken steps to prevent a recurrence of the incident. In short, the person responsible had exercised the proper authority. What exactly did people want the president to do? Exact vengeance?

But Oregonians, for whatever the reasons, seemed unwilling to let the issue drop. An organization called the Taxpayers Protective Association flayed the university in its October newsletter.

FILTH—AT TAXPAYERS EXPENSE

The Taxpayers Protective Association Inc. does not desire to print filth in its lowest form in our newsletter. If you can face filthy language, the type you would expect from the gutter instead of from educated people, phone the U of O (342-1411) and ask for the Oregon Daily Emerald office. Ask the girl that answers their phone to fill in the missing word in the following article. Some of our officers have already done so, and she spoke it as nonchalantly as if it were common usage.

The article referred to above is in the OREGON DAILY EMERALD of October 4, 1968 and reads as follows:

A group of University students and faculty members called the M------F------ [see note above] recently sent a list of 10 proposals for change. . . .

[The article was reprinted in its entirety]

Whether or not you call the Oregon Daily Emerald, we can assure you that the language is not the type you would use in the presence of your children or their friends.

Are the Taxpayers of Oregon willing to pay for—or accept for free—policies at the U of O that will give its cloak of respectability by permitting the publishing of filth? . . .

The association printed an extra 1,000 newsletters and circulated them to important people across the country, including legislative candidates in the forthcoming November 5 election.

"Free speech should be controlled," declared the association's president, Charles Potterf, a gruff-talking manager of a radiator repair shop in Eugene. "If I was head of the university, some heads would roll. There has to be a boss with the power to stop trouble. Johnson knows he's got trouble, so why doesn't he do something? When the school administration is intimidated by misfits, chaos results. To allow a mad dog to run at large is inviting nothing but chaos."

The newsletter succeeded in raising the ire of some politicians. One legislative candidate was so "shocked" by the *Emerald* obscenity that he asked the district attorney to initiate criminal prosecution. "I, too, was shocked by the profanity," replied the DA, "but, unfortunately, under recent United States Supreme Court rulings, this is not a prosecutable offense."

A couple of dirty words. Just what was it, Johnson wondered, that caused citizens to react so strongly?

Profanity was suddenly big news, and journalists began interviewing the new president on the subject. An obscene phrase, Johnson said in one interview, is singularly unpersuasive. "It's a fact of university life that ideas expressed intelligently and in acceptable language receive the most careful consideration. Of all the techniques of persuasion, the use of obscenity is the least effective."

But the journalists seemed to have a fixation on obscenity.

"How did the dirty words get in the *Emerald?*" a reporter asked.

"Because of an outright lie on the part of one of the revolutionist students," Johnson replied candidly. "The student alleged that the student group had changed its name to the obscene name printed in the *Emerald*. That was a deliberate lie."

Did he encourage revolutionary students to come to Oregon?

"No, we'd like to see them stay completely away. We prefer to have nothing to do with him."

Did he approve of the flyers on making Molotov cocktails and bombs?

"Flyers and brochures of every description are handed out regularly on campus," he said. "They're disturbing, but they are not illegal. We're disturbed as much by the fact that they're printed on university equipment as anything else. We could pull the duplicating machine out, but what would that do? It would deprive the other students of a valuable and often necessary service."

How many "revolutionary" students did the university have?

"It's hard to say. Maybe thirty. Maybe fifty. But I want to distinguish between the 'revolutionary' and the 'activist' student. We welcome the activist. He may be the direct cause of more than a few gray hairs and wrinkled brows in the administrative offices. We know he will create problems. But we also know that his interest in the university is constructive."

When the reporters returned to their city rooms, Johnson reflected on the nature of the public interest in higher education. Was it limited to obscenity, troublesome students, and football? He, like other university presidents, often repeated Clark Kerr's famous remark as president of the University of California: the major requirement of a president is to provide football for the alumni, parking for the faculty, and sex for the students.

He also heard the derisive laughter that greeted an Oregon professor's comment to an alumni meeting that "the University of Oregon seems to be doing a good job of providing two of those three."

Considering Oregon's shaky gridiron record of recent years, the alumni obviously felt that football could not be one of those two.

Even so, a football weekend was a pleasant diversion, and Johnson looked forward to the game with the University of Southern California coming up on November 2. As a campus tradition, the football weekend had changed drastically in the sixteen years Johnson had been on the faculty. Gone were the pregame pep assemblies, the pom-pom girls, the fraternity skits, the speeches by the coaches and the president. A lot of alumni complained that the "Oregon Spirit" was gone. There hadn't been an Oskey-wow-wow yell for nearly forty years. And it did not escape alumni attention that some of the student body did not even rise when the band played the *Star Spangled Banner.*

But one persevering tradition was the President's Box. It remained a matter of prestige to be invited to join the university president and his wife in the presidential section of the stadium: fifty seats on the fifty-yard line. The president earned some goodwill points by passing the invitations around to Important People. And Acting President Johnson perceived that he needed some goodwill points.

That Saturday afternoon, in the game against "Goliath" (i.e., U.S.C., the nation's Number One football team), the seats of honor next to President and Mrs. Johnson, went to the governor of Oregon and his wife, Mr. and Mrs. Tom McCall (Oregon '35).

The afternoon at the stadium was rainy and blowy. Charles Johnson wondered aloud how U.S.C.'s legendary halfback, O. J. Simpson, might fare on the slippery turf. Simpson was considered unstoppable: he had gained no fewer than 196 yards per game this season. Even Johnson, who privately could take football or leave it alone, was excited by the prospect of watching Simpson in action. He also went into the game cheered by news of the final enrollment figures: 14,858—almost 200 *above* the budget. At $400 for each "overrealized" student,

65

the university stood to gain $80,000 in extra revenue. Great news. Win or lose, this was going to be a fine day.

Unlike the deluxe, upholstered seats in the covered and electrically heated section of the stadium on the opposite side of the field, the President's Box was in an open location, exposed to the elements. Proposals arose occasionally to build a roof or move the box to the covered section. Each time the proposal was rejected on the ground that the university had to be careful about putting on fancy airs that would suggest class snobbery or an ostentatious show of opulence. This was in keeping with Western informality. The president of the university drove a motor-pool Plymouth instead of riding a chauffeured limousine. And, in a perverse way, the president's guests considered it high camp to suffer with him on the hard wooden benches exposed to the elements—as though intellectualism had won over creature comfort.

Nobody expected the Oregon "Ducks," as they were known, to slay Goliath. The team did astonish the governor and 35,000 others in attendance, however, by pushing U.S.C. all over the field. Oregon ran up 359 yards offense against U.S.C.'s 196. And every time the legendary O. J. Simpson carried the ball he ran into a brick wall. In twenty-five carries, he managed to accumulate only sixty-seven yards. With just moments to go before the game's end, the score was a 13-13 tie.

And in those moments, Goliath slayed the Ducks by scoring the winning touchdown.

Even so it was a "moral victory" for Oregon. That was the feeling at the postgame cocktail party sponsored by the Alumni Association that evening at a motel not far from the stadium. The party was well under way when Johnson bid the governor and his other distinguished guests good-bye (including two U.S. congressmen) and hurried on to the motel. The talk was light and amiable. "Do you realize that Simpson made only two-point-four-eight yards per carry? . . . Great defense. . . . Keep it up and we'll be in the Rose Bowl in a couple of years. . . ."

Sometime during the evening the tone of the conversation changed. The old grads had downed a few drinks. They drifted toward the new president, a man easily spotted because he towered above everybody else. Standing beside his wife, Jeanne, he clutched a glass of Scotch and soda, nursing it along all evening, as he listened to what the alumni called their "serious concerns." Sometimes he had to bend down so that, in the din of the cocktail chatter, he might not miss a word of the Voice of the Alumni.

I've been concerned for some time about the direction the university seems to be taking. . . .

Frankly, Dr. Johnson, it's reached the point where I'm ashamed to say that I'm an Oregon graduate. . . .

Someone has got to stop this foolishness and get down to business. . . .

Dr. Flemming certainly didn't help to stop this trend . . . all we hear around Salem is "thank God he's gone." . . .

Now this business about boys in the girls' bedrooms . . . my daughter certainly doesn't entertain her gentlemen friends in the bedroom of our home. . . .

Isn't it time we stop mollycoddling those hippies and filthy bastards? . . .

Our joy truly overflowed when Flemming left. . . . I don't envy you, cleaning up the mess after seven years of over-permissiveness. . . . In Hood River the image of the university is the lowest ever . . . that bastard Flemming all but destroyed the fraternity system. . . . It'll take years to repair the damage . . . the administration has goddamned well knuckled under to the students and you know it . . . excuse my French, but you should have kicked the sons of bitches in the ass. . . . It's all Flemming's fault. . . .

He listened attentively, he asked questions, he delivered calm explanations. When he was momentarily alone with his wife, he remarked to her, "These people will never know the great things Arthur Flemming has done for Oregon. I don't know how to begin to tell them. I'm not even sure they *want* to know."

When the last inebriated alumnus had left, Johnson spotted a colleague across the room who looked equally beleaguered.

"Whew!" Robert Bowlin, the dean of men, chuckled

67

amiably. He said he'd never seen so many unhappy alumni. "With Flemming gone, I suppose people see this as a chance to influence change to bring the university around to what they think it ought to be. And heaven knows how many different views that entails."

"I think they've blown our warts and blemishes out of all proportion," said Johnson. "People are losing perspective. Our own alumni are losing their sense of humor. Whatever became of humor?"

"I don't know. Gone with the times, I suppose."

"Whatever became of the Max Shulmans of our time?" Johnson said. "Do you remember him? Remember *Barefoot Boy with Cheek?* We need an up-to-date Max Shulman, someone who can take a serious situation and make light of it without being sarcastic or in bad taste. We don't have anybody like that around the campus."

"The students are so grim and serious."

"There are plenty of funny things to write about. Tonight, for example, I've never heard so many dirty words used to complain about obscenity on the campus."

"Say, I *do* know one guy," Bowlin said, "a real funny guy with the typewriter. I'll give him a call and ask him to write something."

"I wish you would," said Johnson. "Seriously."

Bowlin did make the call. But for whatever the reasons, the words calculated to put matters into "proper perspective" were not written.

A few nights later a bomb exploded in the university's ROTC building, causing several thousands of dollars damage. No one was hurt. The incident was, indeed, quickly forgotten in the wake of the *new* obscenity issue. Obscenity suddenly was big news, and the press wallowed in it. Said one report:

A handbill that seemed certain to arouse another controversy at the University of Oregon was being distributed on the campus Wednesday and Thursday.
The printed 8½ x 11 sheet on yellow paper advertises a U.S. Memorial Week at the U.O. next week. . . . Possible

objections to the handbill would probably center on the use of an obscenity that created a public controversy last month when it appeared in an edition of the Oregon Daily Emerald. . . . And on a drawing appearing on the upper one half of the sheet that—if not "obscene"—could at least be described as offensive.

Erb Memorial Union Director Richard Reynolds said Thursday 4,000 copies of the handbill had been printed on a machine in the EMU and paid for by SDS. . . .

The flyer was not quoted or reproduced; no doubt it was considered too obscene. It advertised a series of antiwar, anti-draft meetings, stating in part: "Students for a Democratic Society presents a U.S. Memorial Week," or "Feeling Caught up in the System." Radical Film Festival Nov. 12 & 14. Columbia revolt, the Motherfuckers, Boston Draft Resistance, Pentagon demonstration, Black Panther Huey Newton, and more. . . ." The drawing depicted a fat man, squatting, nude except for his military cap, "eating" young men and "defecating" them as soldiers.

"It's god-awful," one university administrator told his secretary. He handed her the leaflet face-down. "Don't even look at it; just put it in the file," and that's what she did.

"Oh, boy," said Johnson as he saw the leaflet.

The experience at the alumni party apparently convinced him that he ought to take some action; he wasn't sure what. The pamphlet certainly wasn't illegal. It could have been handed out on the steps of the Capitol Building in Salem. He wondered, however, whether the university equipment ought to be used to print such materials. But when he posed that question to the Student Administrative Board, a committee comprised mostly of students, and charged with the operation of the Erb Memorial Union (and its printing equipment), he got a chilly reception. He got outright hostility on the part of several radical students who had infiltrated the audience.

"I know," Johnson began, "that to you it may appear to be a strange world that gets upset over a childish thing like printing the words on this leaflet. . . . I'm asking you to advise me on how I should answer these people who will be calling up in the next three or four days asking what sort of university I'm running."

He leaned back in his chair, lit his pipe, and awaited the answer. One girl among the spectators exhibited a curious, dreamy demeanor, floating around the room officiously, playing a transistor radio, tossing paper airplanes, holding up a sign behind the president: NIXON IS OBSCENE. She lifted her finger in an obscene gesture.

The committee, after considerable discussion, concluded that Johnson should go out and fight fearlessly for free speech. Johnson left the meeting feeling that little had been accomplished. "I'm not sure I should have bothered," he confided to a colleague, Robert Bowlin.

"They seemed totally unwilling to look at the overall problems the university is faced with in terms of its statewide constituency," said Bowlin.

"I'd hoped to get an open and informal discussion of the problem," Johnson said. "What I got instead seemed to be a hardening of points of view into something approaching a confrontation."

Somewhere along the line, he said, there had been a serious breakdown in communication with students.

The expected new wave of protests over the flyer was slow in coming. Perhaps that was because the letters were going to the governor's office instead. One was from a custodial employee of the university. "The filthy things that go on here is terrible," she said. "Printing such material that I have enclosed in this letter is just a small part of it. Can't something be done about this?"

The governor was quick to reply.

"The dodger you sent me was absolutely disgusting," he said. "I am horrified. . . . I am even more concerned to realize that it is coming from our state university. I am notifying university officials of my concern, and I am requesting that they take appropriate action to prohibit this sort of trash in the future."

Governor Tom McCall wrote a letter to Charles Johnson. Shortly thereafter he left for a trade mission in the Orient.

The first Johnson knew of the letter was when a newspaper reporter called him for comment.

"Letter? What letter?"

The news was on the air. The governor had written a letter to Johnson warning that the "depraved nonsense" represented by the SDS flyer must be stopped. Then the presses rolled.

The headlines seemed gigantic.

OFFENSIVE HANDOUT CRITICIZED BY McCALL

The *Register-Guard* reported:

> Gov. Tom McCall has served notice to the University of Oregon that it had better put an end to obscene publications by student groups.
>
> Failure to do so, he warned, is likely to result in restrictive action by the next State Legislature.
>
> The warning came in a strongly worded letter to acting university President Charles Johnson, dated Wednesday and made public in Salem Thursday. . . .

Johnson knew only what he read in the papers. Publicly he said nothing. Privately he was incensed.

"Why on earth would McCall want to put that in the papers?" he said at home that evening. His teeth clenched tightly on his pipe.

"Politics, maybe?" Mrs. Johnson suggested. "Being against obscenity is like being against sin and in favor of motherhood."

"But he's going about it in the wrong way," said Johnson. "Doesn't he realize he's making the problem more difficult? It forces everybody to become more deeply entrenched in their positions." It was one thing, Johnson said, to discuss the issue privately, quite another to make a public scandal out of it. Johnson felt he had made a start on the problem. He had consulted the appropriate faculty and student groups. He planned to appoint a student-faculty committee to draft a new policy on the use of university printing equipment.

It would take time, of course. That was always the way with a university. Universities were ungainly monsters to administer,

71

simply because they *were* universities with rich heritages of academic and intellectual freedom. Any university that allowed its president to crack down with an iron fist on people with whom he happened to disagree would no longer be a university worthy of the name. It would lose the precious and fragile commodity known as freedom. Either that or the kids would blow it up.

The governor's letter arrived in Johnson's office the following day, Friday, about two hours before he was due to leave for a football trip to Berkeley, California. A secretary rushed it to his desk. "I think this is what we've been waiting for," she said.

NOVEMBER 13, 1968

Dear Chuck:

I want to thank you and Mrs. Johnson for having us as your guests at the USC-Oregon game—certainly a thrilling and enjoyable occasion.

Not so enjoyable, however, is the trickle of protest letters I received today from a number of citizens in your area who enclosed a most offensive dodger issued by Students for a Democratic Society. This is the second mailing piece in this disgusting vein which has been brought to my attention recently.

I understand that these dodgers are processed on an ASUO machine. The events advertised on this one were to be held, I see, at Erb Memorial and tickets were available at the SDS table there.

This seems to imply acceptance by the whole student body. I know this is not the case and must insist that this kind of depraved mischief be stopped.

There's no one more fair on free speech than I, but after seeing its abuse in these and other recent instances, I'm afraid your way-out people are inviting restrictive sanctions by the Oregon legislature such as those adopted by the Ohio State Assembly.

I plead with you to exert a measure of control so that a generally excellent campus climate is not drastically altered through an ever-gathering backlash reaction.

Sincerely,
Tom

Johnson scanned the letter quickly. He gripped his pipe tightly in his teeth and swung around to the portable typewriter on the table behind him. In the minutes before departure time he wrote:

DRAFT
11/15/68

Honorable Tom McCall
Governor
State of Oregon
Salem, Oregon 97310

Dear Governor McCall:

Thank you for your recent letter which I learned about in a number of radio and television broadcasts, as well as in the press, before having received it in the mail. . . .

That was only the first draft. He would change the letter at least five times in the next ten days. After the weekend at Berkeley, he returned to it, struggling a little with his emotions as displayed in the opening paragraph. He tried version after version, each a little less petulant than the preceding one.

Version #2 (added to the original paragraph): "The letter did not reach my office until Friday morning, Nov. 15."

Version #3: "I regret that the circumstances of your trip to the Orient, plus my own trip to Berkeley, resulted in your recent letter being released to the news media before I had received it and had an opportunity to respond."

Version #4: "This is in response to your recent letter."

Version #5: "This is in response to your recent letter in which you express what I hope was a friendly warning of growing public irritation over the actions of a student organization on this campus. . . ."

He finally settled on version #5. He told inquiring journalists that he would not release his letter to the press "unless Governor McCall wants to release it." The letter never did reach the public eye, and it appears in print here for the first time.

. . . I appreciate your concern about a problem currently facing this as well as every other major university in the United States today. I can also sympathize with your initial reaction to the handbills distributed by the local chapter of the Students for a Democratic Society because,

73

frankly, my personal off-the-cuff reaction was quite similar. After studying the problem and after having discussed it with my administrative staff, faculty advisory groups, student leaders, and a fair number of alumni, parents, and citizens of the community, however, I have concluded that there are serious disadvantages to various actions which might be taken in an attempt to suppress this kind of material that seem to outweigh by a fair margin what advantages I can discover.

To give you some idea of the nature of our situation: The University of Oregon currently operates on the premise that students who come to a university should have reached a stage of adulthood that makes it desirable for them to begin to assume responsibility for their personal actions, tastes, and moral behavior. If they violate the law, students are subject to prosecution and punishment by the general law enforcement machinery of the community. The University cooperates fully with law enforcement agencies and makes no attempt to shield students from the consequences of illegal acts. The University applies sanctions only when student conduct directly interferes with the University's primary educational mission or its subsidiary responsibility to provide an environment in which the business of education can proceed effectively and without interference. In addition, the University gives students an opportunity to participate fully in the formulation of policies and rules pertaining to student conduct, student organizations, and on-campus extracurricular activities.

The Students for a Democratic Society is a recognized student organization, subject to the policies, rules, and regulations of the Student Administrative Board. If the preparation and distribution of the miserable, vulgar handbill in question is illegal, we regard that a matter for the law enforcement authorities to decide. I am advised that it probably would not be possible to frame a constitutional law that would prevent the distribution on, for example, the steps of the State Capitol. If this advice is correct, then it is at least a serious question whether the University (whose very existence depends on freedom of inquiry and expression of ideas) should adopt policies that would attempt to prevent the distribution on the campus of written material that could be legally distributed on any street corner in the State of Oregon. . . .

Johnson quoted an Oregon Supreme Court justice's comment that democracy depends on a free exchange of ideas which in turn depends on freedom to read and listen. The burden of having to sort through "dangerous and offensive" materials is a price "that we should be willing to pay," the justice said. Johnson went on:

> It is never very pleasant for a college president or a governor to face the prospect of being "fair on free speech" or expression in relation to the kind of vulgarity represented by this pamphlet. Unfortunately, most issues of free expression have to be fought on just such slippery, muddy turf because unless the expression in question offends a considerable segment of the public the demand for suppression is never raised. It is ironic that many of our most cherished principles must be jealously guarded by protecting the freedom of persons or groups with whom we are neither in sympathy or agreement. It is perhaps even more ironic that in this letter I find myself defending the freedom of a few student radicals who by careful and calculated design aim to discredit the university and its administration by means whose only test is whether they serve this end. For however outrageous the specific acts of the members of the SDS, we can be sure they know exactly what they are doing. The University of Oregon cannot afford to lose the goodwill and support of the citizens of the state; but neither can it afford to solicit such support at the price of adopting policies that compromise the basic principle of freedom of expression on our campus. The question is whether, with the help of our friends, we can avoid being crunched in the jaws of this kind of pincer movement.
> There is also a simple pragmatic argument for allowing a group such as the SDS, to have the same freedom to speak and act—laudably or reprehensibly—as members of society at large. If they choose to abuse this freedom by offending public sensibilities they are likely to be held accountable by the vast majority of the student body they want to influence. Vulgarity as such has seldom been a very successful medium of persuasion, as any professional molder of public opinion or seeker of support for a cause will testify. In a sense the resort to this kind of communi-

cation is a tacit admission that shock treatment is necessary to attract attention because the argument on an intellectual level has somehow failed to win support. Thus I am not sure it is even a good tactic to adopt policies that protect such groups from their own excesses. I would prefer that they stand and be counted on the merits of their own actions, forms of communication, and medium of expression. If we do violence to our principles of free expression just to deny them a forum on their own terms, we in effect provide them with a legitimate issue, wrapped in the United States Constitution, by which they might rightfully rally the support of responsible persons whom they could not attract on the dubious merits of their cause. . . .

The letter concluded with an invitation to discuss the issue further. Johnson then appointed the student-faculty committee to formulate policy on university printing equipment. In the agonizingly deliberate manner typical of a faculty ad hoc committee, the group would spend almost nine months discussing the problem.

Seven:
Hair

Somebody called from the university's budget office. "You remember that extra $20,000 we thought we had in the budget yesterday—we couldn't figure out where it came from?"

"Yeah?" Johnson said warily.

"Well, we just figured out where it came from. An error in arithmetic. We really don't have it."

Johnson laughed uproariously.

"You think it's *funny?* We're another $20,000 short."

"I'm laughing through my tears," said Johnson.

Laughter was a hallmark of the Johnson administration. Recent events had caused a temporary decline in the quality and quantity of laughter. Then, that Wednesday morning, hearty guffaws suddenly reverberated through the presidential suite.

"Bill, come, take a look at this!"

Bill Blevins, his assistant, found Johnson leaning back in his chair, a big grin on his face, waving a copy of the morning's *Emerald*.

"Boy," said Johnson, "ol' Charlie really got himself in trouble this time." He pointed to a front-page interview with

Charles Potterf, the radiator repair shop manager who was president of the Taxpayers Protective Association. It was Potterf who had published the anti-university diatribe, "Filth at Taxpayers Expense," in the association's newsletter. The *Emerald*'s photo showed a scowl on Potterf's face that seemed to match the headline: TAXPAYERS ASSOCIATION HEAD SAYS 'UNIVERSITY GOING OUT OF CONTROL.' The story began:

> "I don't like the socialistic trend going on up there. The University is going out of control and I think it's about time somebody does something about it. You people holler for free speech, but when you start using obscenity and that sort of c—, I think you're abusing it."
> The above ideas were expressed by Charles Potterf....

At first glance the story appeared to be a straight interview. But whenever it quoted Potterf's own coarse language, it used euphemistic dashes for the four-letter words. The result was subtle satire.

> ... Potterf said the articles in the Taxpayers Association newsletter were "retaliation for what some of those sh—heads up there are saying and doing."
> He said the association, which was organized in March 1967, first became concerned with the situation at the University when then university President Arthur S. Flemming allowed controversial speakers like Gus Hall and Stokely Carmichael on campus.
> "The University lost its sense of values when Flemming was appointed," Potterf said....
> "From then on it was all downhill for this place," Potterf said. "There'd be those rabble-rousing speakers up there at the student union and all those c—head kids eating it up.
> "Why, just a month ago there were a couple of communist recruiters on the terrace for a couple of days. I think that's a g—d— poor state of affairs," Potterf said....

"But you know," said President Johnson, "in a way I kind of admire old Charlie, in spite of all the trouble he's causing us."
"You do?"

"Well, yeah. Here's this poor guy, not much education, tilting at the university, putting his foot in his mouth. But, by golly, he says what he really believes. That takes real courage. You've got to admire the guy for that."

Johnson's pleasure was brief. In Oregon, obscenity was no laughing matter. Governor McCall's well-publicized letter brought much anti-university mail. McCall soon had 250 letters and thirty-two petitions, most of them calling for a swift crackdown. Conditions were so bad at the university, confided one woman, that she had it on good authority that a freshman girl had closeted herself in her dormitory room for weeks, too petrified by fear to venture out even to the cafeteria. And campus morals were at such low ebb, she added, that "the men openly boast that the girls make good mattresses."

A tiny minority of letters, most of them from the campus itself, took exception to McCall's comments. A coed wrote that "a vast majority of the students had no knowledge of the handbill before the press raised the issue. Had people over-looked it, the whole incident would have faded away within twenty-four hours. The actual SDS movement on this campus is non-existent, primarily because they really can't find an issue." Another student identified himself as a member of SDS at the U.O. "I feel I can answer the obscenity question quite succinctly," he wrote. "The SDS cartoon which we printed *was* obscene because it portrayed an obscene situation: the military machine devouring young American youths and defecating mold-fitting, trained killers. The New York SDS organization is called 'Up Against the Wall, Motherfucker,' not as a threat to the establishment but simply because that phrase is what a policeman says to you when he sees you walking around at night with long hair or a black skin. This infamous obscenity is a product of the defenders of the law."

And Bill Bowerman, the university's nationally famous track coach, said the campus problems resulted from seven years of "running around in so many different directions that no one, least of all the man at the head of the ship, took the time to get rid of the accumulation of manure." He said Johnson faced a task not unlike that of Hercules who in Greek mythology was able to rid the Aegean stables of manure in a single day by diverting a river. Johnson's job would be easier, Bowerman said, if "so-called friends of the university" would rid themselves of the habit of "taking pot-shots and throwing rocks at the university."

For the moment there seemed little prospect of that. The rocks and potshots, in the form of letters and phone calls, began to assume a wearisome appearance of sameness. Alumni presented gloomy reports of the decline of the university's reputation in various communities, much as a meteorologist might cite readings of barometric pressures. Conditions were stormy everywhere.

Portland. Falling trend. "The university is on a downhill slide," said one alumnus. "We desperately need to turn the tide and start making friends, not losing them. The casualties of the past seven years are frightening."

Lakeview. Uncertain. "I am sick of what has been going on at the university generally, and I have yet to run into anybody in the general public who does not agree with me."

The Dalles. Dangerously low. "I must sadly report that the reputation of the university has been at low ebb in this area."

Corvallis. Falling. "More and more I am encountering classmates who are sending their children to other schools and who have abandoned all idea of loyalty to the university."

The logic of some of the letters defied Johnson.

You are going to be in the same position as England was with Hitler after Chamberlain's policy of appeasement. (The analogy escaped him. Why was defending the principle of freedom of speech, as guaranteed in the First Amendment of the Constitution of the United States, and as interpreted by the Supreme Court, to be considered "appeasement?" On the contrary, to have compromised the constitutional principle and applied censorship because of outside political pressures—that would be appeasement.)

Are you afraid of the leftists and the pornographic peddlers? Perhaps you are afraid of the much-used and much-abused "legal rights." (Well, he certainly felt himself on the side of law and order. A legal right was something to be respected. Was he expected now to take the law into his own hands? To act as judge, jury, and executioner? That was only a step away from vigilante action.)

I am sure that you do not use such words in conversation with your wife and daughter. (Indeed not. But wasn't that a little beside the point? He could defend others' rights to use them, if that is the law of the land, without using them himself.)

When in heaven's name will they restore some sanity to the university's image? (Sanity is not something you apply to an image, though he supposed that the combination of meta-phorical expression and literary license made the point clear enough. In any event, it was a wife-beating kind of question, and he had no answer.)

Frankly we would like to see the colleges returned to the old system when the administration was in control and the decent young people were protected from the minority. (He certainly was sympathetic with that point. To have been a college president thirty, twenty, even ten years ago was a much more agreeable prospect. Universities used to be less complicated to administer when people generally agreed on their purpose and direction and when the campus was, in a sense, immune from the law. In those days a president might arbitrarily expel a student or fire a professor and get away with it. Today if he acted without due process he could be taken to court.)

I used your picture in the paper for plain toilet paper, and it wasn't even good for that—too slippery like you are. (The writer was complaining about obscenity. What irony.)

I am appalled at how much publicity such a disruptive element in our society receives in the news media. (He certainly agreed with that.)

Johnson insisted that the letters be answered. Ray Hawk answered most of them in his position as director of public relations. Hawk passed a few of them to Johnson when he felt the writer's status, as a prominent alumnus or a legislator, deserved a presidential reply. But occasionally Johnson dipped into the piles of letters and pulled out missives from "average citizens." To some he wrote personal replies, typing the rough drafts on his typewriter at home. No one could explain why he took time from a busy schedule to write such responses; perhaps he merely wanted to put his thoughts in writing, a form of communication at which he excelled. To a Portland man who said he'd lost sleep worrying about the university, Johnson replied:

> . . . Ideas are the main business of a university, and we have a conviction that if all ideas, good or bad, offensive or inoffensive, well or badly expressed, are available for examination at a university, those of worth will endure, and the foolish or invalid ideas will find their rightful place in the trash basket. Members of a university community are not willing to have anyone, even a president, act as a censor and tell them in advance which ideas they need not consider and which they should. . . .

To a housewife in Portland he wrote:

> . . . I must admit to a personal belief that the real obscenity lies not so much in mere words (which can be spewed forth at random by a mindless computer) but in all schemes that thwart the realization of full humanity in our society. On the other hand, I do not approve of the use of words that violate current standards of good taste. . . .

Johnson was to reiterate these views countless times in the weeks ahead. Ray Hawk, seeking to defuse the public hostility, had arranged for Johnson to speak to the state's "opinion leaders": blue ribbon groups of civic leaders, alumni, legislators, newspaper editors. Johnson seemed to make headway with such groups. His conversation, as he sat in meetings sprawled over a chair, his hands fumbling with his pipe, seemed to soothe people. After hearing Johnson speak in Portland a wealthy alumnus asked a professor, "Is Johnson under consideration for the permanent presidency? I hope so. He'd make a good one." The professor was startled. The alumnus had seemed devastatingly hostile during the meeting.

Another group, comprised of mothers of U.O. students, voted to endorse Johnson for president after hearing him speak. Indeed, whenever they confronted Johnson in person, Oregonians found him less the evildoer, more the open and sincere administrator facing problems not of his making, skillfully and cautiously picking his way through the minefields of protest and reaction. Often it mattered less what he said—though audiences usually agreed that his words were persuasive—than the way he said it. He exuded a pleasant mixture of quiet, rural charm and just enough tweedy intellectualism to be interesting without being threatening. He definitely was not a "smooth operator," a term often applied to his predecessor. He remained the country boy from Wyoming who used terms like "oh, boy," "gee whiz," and "doggone." Oregonians felt comfortable with him.

"If we could just get the president out around the state to meet the people in person," said Ray Hawk, "I think we could begin to turn the tide of public reaction in our favor."

That, of course, was impossible. The president's time was spread too thin already with meetings, luncheons, speeches, appointments. Members of his secretarial staff agreed that they had never seen an appointment calendar quite as solid as his. But on Thanksgiving, he did allow himself a full holiday.

It was a pleasant day. Karen had brought several college friends home for Thanksgiving dinner, among them her long-time friend, Julie Keith, a pleasant, dark-haired girl with an easy smile. Charles Johnson invariably liked all of Karen's friends, even the erstwhile boyfriend that his wife couldn't stand. But Julie had long been a favorite. He had immortalized her by using her name in one of his books in a hypothetical accounting problem.[1] He also felt free to tease her. The teasing began two years earlier when she had been included in a family weekend at the ocean beach. At the beach cabin that evening, he and Karen taught Julie to play a game called Risk. She listened patiently to his instructions ("Don't expect to win the first time; it takes experience."), and to his razzing as the game got under way. ("Watch out, Julie, we're really gonna pull the rug out from under you!")

Julie won handily. He emerged with a new respect for Julie's "voodoo powers." He "blamed" her for everything that went wrong the rest of the weekend, from the beach fire he couldn't start ("Julie makes me nervous") to the Volkswagen that got stuck in the sand and was almost swallowed by the incoming tide ("It's all Julie's fault; doggone it, Julie, why did you let this happen?").

Julie was amused and flattered by the attention, especially when he kept at it after becoming acting president. When he hit a sour note playing the organ that Thanksgiving Day, it clearly was her fault ("Julie's up to her old tricks again"). For an hour and a half he played the organ while the students sang *Old Mill Stream* kinds of favorites. Occasionally the three girls, Julie, Karen, and another girl, Sally Meisenhelder (a future daughter-in-law)—the "Lemon Sisters," they called themselves—sang close harmony.

Julie found evenings and weekends with the Johnsons to be lively circuses, particularly when Karen and her dad got to cracking jokes. Yet she felt that Johnson, for all his amiability, remained aloof. She wished she could know him better. She wished that she could just talk quietly with him about a serious issue. That, she believed, is how you get to know a person. Johnson's wisecracks, she concluded, tended to tell her, "Don't get too close."

"By the way, Dad," Karen was saying, "it's nice to see you again." Karen was a sorority girl now, living away from home. "Do you realize that I tried for weeks to get an appointment with you just to say 'hello?' I finally got it, but then—guess what?—it was canceled. How do you suppose that makes you feel when your own father cancels out on you?"

"I could probably spare you a few minutes late in March."

"That's really cool."

"Just don't ask for money."

"By the way, Dad, what are we having for dinner today—grapes?"

"No, we're *not* having grapes. I told those kids we don't eat grapes at our house." He turned to his wife. "Jeanne, I trust you'll go along with that."

"Well, I'm not all that fond of grapes anyway," she said. "But what's *this* all about?"

"Dad got his picture in the *Emerald* again," Karen said. "Honestly, Dad, you looked so *grim* in that picture, sitting there with your chin in your hand. I thought maybe you'd just eaten a typical dormitory meal."

Johnson said he'd met earlier that week with a group of students seeking to have the dormitories stop purchasing table grapes from California growers involved in a labor dispute with farm workers led by Cesar Chavez. The question had come up earlier in the fall, and he'd referred the students to the Housing Office. Now a conflict had developed. The Housing Office said, "If the students want to boycott grapes, why don't they just stop eating them?" The students said they tried that, but the grapes merely came back later in salads or gelatin desserts. Now they planned to compromise by conducting a poll of dormitory residents and reducing the purchases of grapes according to the percentage of students who said they didn't want them. Johnson told the students that the university would cooperate to whatever extent possible, perhaps by providing an alternate on the days grapes are served.

"But according to the *Emerald*," said Karen, "Dad says the university itself will not take a stand on grapes. Right?"

"That's about it. I think we have a pretty good precedent in the Friday menus that provide alternatives to Catholic students. In providing these alternatives, the university is not taking a stand on religion. It's merely accommodating students who want to exercise their individual convictions."

The dinner conversation weaved in and out of campus affairs and personal experiences: classes, midterm exams, sorority life, boyfriends. Karen said she had dated a boy who discovered midway through the evening that she was the president's daughter—"that was the politest date you ever saw." The talk also touched briefly on current events: Jackie's marriage to Aristotle in October, the violence at San Francisco State College where the president was twice forced to close the campus, the Hong Kong flu epidemic now beginning to sweep the country, the Apollo moon shots. Apollo Seven, the earth-circling mission, had been completed in October; Apollo Eight, the moon orbit, was scheduled for December. "If everything goes all right," said Johnson, "we should have a man on the moon by 1970 or '71."

The governor's letter was only briefly mentioned. The release of the letter to the press was now reported by the governor's aide to have been an "unintended mistake." The governor himself was still out of the country, apparently unaware of the furor.

"It might have been a mistake, all right," said Johnson. "I'll admit I was a little surprised when it came out in the papers before I'd received a copy. The more I thought about it later, the more I concluded, 'This just isn't the kind of a letter a governor writes for public consumption.' "

He asked how many of the students had seen the controversial SDS flyer. None had.

"That just proves what I've been saying all along. Here's a flyer that's created all kinds of havoc outside the campus, but scarcely a ripple inside the campus. Why? Because bad taste is the wrong way to get your point across."

Karen said she'd been handed an "anti-administration" flyer at the Student Union that so angered her that she ripped it to shreds.

"The trouble is, that makes you as weak as they are," he said. "You can look at it, you can read it, you can hand it back, you can throw it in the garbage, but you don't have to rip it up. That drags you down to their level."

The holiday was soon over. Johnson was back to work on Friday with a full calendar of appointments. Among them was an interview with two reporters from the *Oregon Journal*, a Portland newspaper. They were on the campus, they said, to explore the university's problems and write a series of articles.

Johnson shared with them the views he'd been expressing in recent weeks, with occasional added flourishes: "When the issue at stake is freedom, the university ought to fight with every means at its disposal—go down in flames if need be—to resist public pressure or strict censorship." He also talked of the power of ideas, of student disruption, of the "gray area" that shrouds the "line of tolerability" between acceptable and unacceptable student behavior. Yes, he said, there *was* a point at which he'd call in the police. But last spring's Johnson Hall sit-in wasn't it; there was, after all, no destruction or actual interruption of university processes on that occasion. Calling the police, he said, was a very serious step. The experiences on other campuses indicated that the result was usually more trouble, not less. And SDS was vastly overrated, he said; its membership probably consisted of no more than thirty students.

"But these students can attract large rallies, can't they?" suggested a reporter.

"Oh, five hundred if they get the right cause," he said. "At one time I think they could get five hundred to discuss an anti-Vietnam issue. But the anti-Vietnam sentiment extends over a broad range of students. It's not a monopoly of SDS by a long shot. Now the grape issue—I suppose you can get a hundred students who are very sympathetic with the migrant grape problem."

"Since SDS seems to be at the root of some of your problems, have you made any effort to censure them?"

"We've obviously indicated displeasure. Let me tackle this in a different way. In looking at the problems created by groups that are doing things with which we don't agree, or that members of the community find offensive, we look at our Student Conduct Code. It is basically the policies, rather than the incidents, that we are involved administratively in examining—continuously, as a matter of fact—and strengthening or improving."

"Is there a rule that covers obscenity?"

"Okay, let's take that as a case study. Here is an organization that goes to the student print shop and prints a flyer that many people find offensive. What do you do? All right, what about this organization? How did it get recognized? You turn to the *Student Handbook,* and you find that—I'm reading now—*'The university as a public institution will not allow its facilities to be used for clandestine purposes. Therefore to insure against the formation of secret societies, every organization seeking recognition must submit information concerning the following.* [A list of requirements followed.] *Recognition of a group or organization grants to that group the right to the use of university facilities and to identify themselves with the university—."*

Reporter: "It doesn't matter what the organization does or what kind of group, just that they be recognized?"

"That's right. *The group agrees to accept such regulations and administrative procedures as may be necessary to protect the essential functions of the university, to allow an equitable sharing of time and space, and to assure the reasonable health and safety of the community.'"*

Reporter: "In other words, a Communist group could open on campus, declare itself, ask for membership, and be recognized."

"That's right, as long as it's not against federal, state, or local laws."

"What about an adviser? Does SDS have a faculty adviser?"

"Yes."

"Do you know who?"

"Mr. Froines. F-r-o-i-n-e-s. John. Professor of chemistry."

Johnson said the responsibility for student conduct had been delegated to student-faculty committees. The president himself was unlikely to act beyond censure—"censure in the sense that we tell them we think they're acting very childishly."

"Have you done that?"

"Oh, yes."

"You have—in an official statement to them?"

"Not in an official written statement. I met with the Student Administrative Board and let it be known that I didn't think much of the SDS pamphlet, but I did not officially write a letter to them."

Having delegated responsibility, the president was unlikely to withdraw it arbitrarily. "I don't put a string on responsibility and draw it back on whim." The risk of possible bad judgment or irresponsible behavior was a desirable one: "Otherwise what would this university be teaching the next generation about responsibility? We would merely be giving them busywork. This nation is a democracy, remember, with a court system that allows a judge to make a mistake and sometimes allows the guilty to go free. That's the price you pay for a democracy."

He said the university's policy was to treat students as adults. "When they come to us they're eighteen years old. There has been a lot of talk about setting eighteen as the voting age. We start with the premise that (a) generally speaking, students will be held responsible for any acts that violate the laws, and (b) we will cooperate with law-enforcement agencies and make no attempt to shield our students from actions taken against them when they have violated the law."

Reporter: "Do you have great faith that groups like SDS, or a Communist group if one opened here, would not garner much attention or membership?"

"Well, yeah, I have a personal faith that communism is not a very attractive idea in the United States, and I think students are a cross-section of the United States. Look at the Communist party. Look at the number of people that it's been able to attract. Look at the political polls that suggest college students tend to reflect the political views of their parents. I think students represent a pretty good cross-section of the country. If the country is not particularly enamored of communism, then I don't think students are particularly enamored of communism. We've had two incidents on campus that would give you some evidence of this. One of them occurred some time ago when Gus Hall—"

"Oh, yes—"

"Remember him? Well, Gus Hall attracted a tremendous audience because the outsiders guaranteed him an audience. If he'd just been brought to the campus they'd have had no more than a hundred students there. But because of all the uproar, well, I guess we finally had to hold it at Hayward Field. I was a faculty member then and, walking away from Gus Hall's speech, I was completely unimpressed. He's not a very effective speaker. His ideas were pretty vacuous. That's exactly what all the students were saying. I overheard a couple of students commenting, 'What's all the fuss about? Here is a guy who impresses me as hardly worth the time; I wish I hadn't bothered to come out.' The students were just utterly amazed that the State of Oregon and Washington, and I don't know how far up and down the coast, could be so upset about this man coming here and making a rather stupid speech. Well, the other thing is that we've had a gal who came down here and recruited for the Communist party on the porch of the Student Union."

"Came down from where?"

"I guess from Washington someplace. I don't keep track of such things, but I've never had a report that there were more than five or six people around that table at any one time."

The *Journal* articles were scheduled to appear in mid-December. Even as they were being written by reporters Rolla Crick and Walli Schneider, a new campus issue had formed, exploding with the fury of a sudden mountain thunderstorm, accompanied by the customary shock wave of adverse reaction. This time the issue centered on an aspect of intercollegiate athletics.

At first glance it did not seem a very important problem. It seemed to be one of those countless little "brush fires," as Charles Johnson called them, that left him with a "feeling of frustration that I don't find time to deal with the question of how we can move ahead to improve the quality of education."

The "hair issue," as it came to be called, exploded early in December, on the day of the season's first basketball game for the freshman squad, to be played at Clark College in Vancouver, Washington. The previous evening the freshman basketball coach, a vigorous, enthusiastic man named Frank Arnold, asked members of his team to appear neat and well-groomed, with shaves and haircuts, based on the rules applicable to basketball players: ". . . We sincerely believe these rules are based upon common sense and a logic which will not be oppressive to any individual. . . . You are recognized by all as a basketball player, and you will be asked to conform to standards set by coaches in areas we feel are important to team success and campus and community acceptance. . . . When appearing as a group in public, we will be neatly dressed, shaved, and without excessively long hair. . . ."

Arnold was in his second year of coaching for Oregon. Sports fans saw in him the solution to Oregon's lagging basketball fortunes of recent years. Few coaches worked more enthusiastically or conscientiously to recruit outstanding athletes who would play, first for the freshman team, and then go on to perform for varsity coach Steve Belko.

Coach Arnold, according to subsequent news reports, took aside two black players, Bill Drake and Bob Moore, who wore their hair in "natural" or "Afro" style. He specifically asked them to get haircuts.

The two players were incensed. So were many of their black friends. The players had just come off the freshman football squad where nothing had been said about the length or style of their hair, they said. Black players on the varsity basketball team had longer hair, apparently with the coach's acquiescence. Lew Alcindor, UCLA's legendary basketball great, had longer hair. And white players, many of them, had longer hair, the only difference being that they combed their hair flat instead of letting it grow out for the stylish African "natural."

The blacks appealed to Arnold to change his edict. He refused. They then appealed to the Faculty Committee on Intercollegiate Athletics, the agency that handled grievances in athletics. But faculty committees moved with the efficiency and finesse of a well-rusted Rube Goldberg contraption. With the bus leaving at 3:30—it was now close to noon—the chairman said it would be impossible to convene in time. The problem was referred to Johnson, marked "urgent."

Johnson asked the litigants to assemble in the conference room at 2:15. Coach Arnold was there. So were representatives of the Black Students Union. Fifteen other blacks came, uninvited.

To Arnold's dismay, Johnson allowed them to stay, although they were noisy and abusive. They hurled angry epithets at Arnold, among them innuendos about what they called the "racist policies" of the Mormon Church, of which Arnold was a member. Arnold, apparently, was given little chance to defend himself or to present his arguments. He was appalled that Johnson would allow the blacks to be so abusive.[2]

Johnson hewed to a different philosophy on such meetings. He considered them "controlled confrontations." They were a calculated policy of getting all the litigants in a room and allowing them—amid the heat of dispute—to work out a solution. The policy derived largely from an awkward experience he'd had earlier in the fall. At issue then was a dispute as to whether students should have to pay for bus rides to football games at the stadium, located three miles away. Student leaders said Arthur Flemming, before he left, had promised them free rides. The Department of Athletics countered that maybe he did, but the money was not to come out of athletic funds. Each side, meeting privately with the president, gave a different version. Each version had to be checked with the other side in a subsequent meeting. Meeting after meeting brought little progress. Johnson finally settled the matter by allowing free rides financed by funds from the president's meager reserve. But he complained that the "sloppy administrative procedures" must not be allowed in the future. "We're not going through *this* kind of nonsense again. On the next dispute, we're going to get everybody together in the conference room and hassle the whole thing out then and there."

"That could be a little like going into the lion's den," said his assistant, Bill Blevins.

"Sure it could. But in the long run we'll be further ahead by working in the open, cards on the table, and we'll get out decisions much more quickly."

The meeting with Coach Arnold on the hair issue was just such a lion's-den confrontation. For almost an hour Johnson calmly listened to the impatient rhetoric, occasionally asking a question or making a comment.

"It's pretty obvious," said one of the blacks petulantly, "that nothing's gonna happen at this meeting. The blacks are getting fucked over by this university."

Said another, angrily, "All you're gonna do is sit on your white racist ass, defending your coach, and not do a goddamned thing."

Johnson remained calm. "That's not the case at all. I merely want to get all of the information out in front of me so that I can make a decision. I'm not going to make a hasty decision. Clearly we have a time factor here—it's past three already and the bus leaves at three-thirty—but I don't want to rush into things."

Each side was adamant. Johnson finally moved the meeting to his office, excluding the uninvited blacks, where the arguments might jell with fewer people and in a calmer atmosphere.

Coach Arnold said that if the players went on the bus without haircuts, he would stay at home. The blacks said the coach insisted on applying white standards to black hairstyles which the black culture did *not* consider sloppy. Indeed, the remaining black students, in this calmer atmosphere, appeared to agree with most of what the coach said. Yes, they agreed, players should be well-groomed when appearing in public. Yes, the coach had the right of strict disciplinary control over matters relating to team performance. If there were rules governing the length of hair, however, they must have been made before black players came to the teams.

Arnold was adamant. His decision had been made he said.

"Frank," said Johnson, "I wish you'd reconsider." To Johnson the issue seemed trivial, yet he knew how strongly the black people felt about it. It symbolized a part of the continuing fight of the blacks to gain, in reality, the kind of civil rights promised all citizens by the U.S. Constitution. Black people were attempting to throw off the feeling that blackness was a handicap to be overcome. They were attempting to generate a feeling of genuine pride in blackness and in African ancestry. Hence the Afro haircut.

"Frank," said Johnson to Arnold, "I wonder if you aren't making a hasty decision. Here's what I'd like to suggest. Let's buy ourselves a little time. Let's talk again next week when we can discuss the issue without time pressure. Right now the bus is ready to leave. Without committing yourself to any particular view, why don't you go along this time, and then we'll talk some more on Monday?"

Arnold declined.

Johnson glanced at his watch. "You really leave me no alternative," he said. He turned to the director of athletics, Leonard Casanova. "Cas, do you have another coach you can send?"

Casanova nodded. "I suppose we could send Nick Jones."

Within minutes the two players were on the bus, en route to Vancouver. Coach Arnold stayed home.

Johnson issued a statement: ". . . hairstyle should not be a condition of participation on athletic teams at the University of Oregon." He then asked the Faculty Committee on Intercollegiate Athletics to review fully the personnel policies of the Department of Athletics, a task that would require almost six months.

Eight:
The Funny Side

In October, Ray Hawk, the director of public relations, asked
his secretary to keep a tally of the "letters of complaint" now
flooding his office. The secretary, a trim young woman named
Marlene Stroh, began the tally when the issue was *Emerald*
obscenity, and stopped it in mid-December in the middle of the
haircuts-for-athletes issue. At that point, flooded by too many
letters requiring replies, the beleaguered Mrs. Stroh gave up.

Her tally represented only a fraction of the letters pouring
into the university. Other departments, particularly alumni,
Development Fund, and athletics, were equally inundated. But
the tally, covering a period of ten weeks, seemed to portray
graphically a cross-section of public attitudes.

95

Table II: Letters of Complaint

TOPIC OF COMPLAINT	NUMBER	PERCENT
Haircuts for athletes	41	29.3
Emerald obscenity	31	22.2
SDS flyer	24	17.2
Harassment, disruptions, etc.	8	5.7
In support of Gov. McCall	6	4.3
Opposing Gov. McCall	6	4.3
Yarowsky destruction seminar	4	2.8
Educational issues	2	1.4
Miscellaneous	18	12.8
Totals	140	100.0

The "Yarowsky destruction seminar," another new controversy, appeared trivial—but so had "hair" and "obscenity." An Associated Press dispatch described a university class in "Visual Semantics," taught by a professor of art named Morris Yarowsky. For one session of the class Professor Yarowsky had asked students to bring "something of value" to the class and then destroy it. One student smashed a ringing alarm clock with a sledgehammer. Another smashed a television set. A girl lathered her face with red soap and shaved off an eyebrow. The story got national attention, even a paragraph in the *New York Times.* "I know there are a lot of idiots in the world," said one of the complaint letters, "but it beats me why they have to be hired by universities." Yarowsky was a new faculty member, a "visiting professor," who in three years had attracted a large following of students by his charm and by his funky, avant-garde ideas.

The "hair" issue continued to dominate the mail, and, inexplicably, it had the state in still another uproar. If Johnson saw "hair" as symbolic of social attainment among the black population, most athletic fans saw it as symbolic of further erosion of administrative control. A content analysis of the forty-one "hair" letters in Mrs. Stroh's tally showed an average of three points of complaint per letter: that the president had undermined the coach's authority, that he'd knuckled under to a bunch of "uncouth colored folks," that he'd better start getting some backbone. Eight alumni said they'd not contribute another cent to the alumni fund (a check of names showed that five of them had not given the first cent); seven high-school coaches said they could no longer encourage their best athletes to attend the University of Oregon. Two writers said the president "obviously" would rather coach the teams himself; another said the team members "play like bums, they might as well look like bums." Finally, there was the inevitable comparison with a former president: "Pardon the expression, but this sounds like a trick Arthur Flemming would pull."

Despite many letters of support, Coach Arnold backed down after four days. He had "spent many hours examining every facet of the problem," he said, and he concluded that his request for personal grooming had been based on personal tastes which were "unintentionally oppressive to some individuals. . . . President Charles Johnson has so directed that hairstyles should not be a condition of athletic participation. I will support him in this decision. . . ."

Many fans saw it as a "gun-to-the-head confession." Had Arnold been less popular with Oregon fans—had he not been the great hope for the future of Oregon basketball—the controversy might have been less strident. But, alienated by years of mediocre teams, and alienated further by what many fans took to be anti-athletic machinations of the Flemming administration, the fans struck back.

President Johnson was surprised by the intense hostility. Indeed, in a coldly logical context, the world of the athletic fan seemed strangely disquieting. It appeared to be part emotion, part fantasy, part political power.

Student leaders had compared the Department of Athletics to the Department of Defense. They said athletics were guided by an "athletic-business-political" complex, a power base largely independent of the university's administration. Most

97

state university presidents tended to sidestep the issue. They were content to support intercollegiate athletics on blind faith alone. They were prudently wary of tampering with it or bucking the community power structure. They preferred to justify athletics in terms of campus solidarity, character building, and rapport with alumni and the general public.

Now some of the student leaders had begun to question these concepts, and Acting President Charles Johnson did not discourage them. When, for example, the student leaders wondered why football players were transported to spend the night before a home game in a posh motel near Eugene, Johnson wondered, too. Furthermore, when programs dedicated to providing education for minority race groups were starved for funds, why was the athletic program allowed to wallow in luxury? Johnson promised to look into the question.

It was not the only puzzle. He wondered, too, what perverse logic caused a newspaper sports writer to conclude that the "hair" decision might be blamed for the varsity team's subsequent defeat in a basketball game against Nebraska. It was "loss of morale," the writer had said. "A Friday dispute over hairstyles had obviously left the Ducks rattled. They were tense and mistake prone. . . . Arnold's future now has to be clouded. The acting university president in effect cut his legs out from under him as a coach."

An alumnus had clipped that report and sent it to Johnson with a strident letter.

"I really don't understand this," said Johnson, fishing the clipping and the letter from a pile of documents on his desk and passing it across to his colleague Ray Hawk. He said it was but one example of the kind of letters he'd been receiving lately.

"These people don't know me," Johnson continued. "I don't know them. Yet they feel perfectly free to attribute all kinds of motives to a decision about which they do not have all the facts. Now here's a man with a college education. On the basis of a somewhat emotional and warped newspaper account, he takes it upon himself to send me a letter like this."

Hawk scanned the letter and noted the name at the bottom.

The writer was a prominent professional man in southern Oregon. The letter bristled with crude, often contradictory, innuendoes: the president had knuckled under to the two-bit demands of a couple of novice athletes; this will mean the complete demise of any hope for competitive athletics at Oregon; clearly the president had decided to coach the teams himself, relegating the coaches to mere figureheads; the general public is mighty fed up with the U.O.'s appeasement of minority groups; it makes the writer sick to see the university destroyed with increasing acceleration by weak administrators; if the minority groups don't like such great all-American virtues as discipline and standards, why don't they leave?

Hawk perceived that Johnson found this letter more repugnant than other, far-more-strident missives such as the one asserting that the university had become a "haven for creepy, sloppy, foul-mouth slobs. . . . When this black trash becomes the tail that wags the dog, it's gone too damned far."

That letter was unsigned, thus beneath contempt in Johnson's view. But the effect of the other letter lingered, perhaps because it caused Johnson to realize that reversing an entrenched and largely emotion-based perception of the university's "tarnished image" was a task more awesome than he'd imagined. Perhaps his accounting background even complicated the problem, since according to cold logic, facts and figures ought to add up and balance out, assets against liabilities, with neat double lines under the totals. Still, Johnson was not entirely a cold logician. Beneath his precise, unflappable exterior lay the heart of a humanitarian and idealist.

Ray Hawk had ideals and humanity, too, but he was ever the pragmatist administrator. A stocky, athletic-looking man of fifty, a colonel in the Air Force Reserve, and a former dean of men, Hawk possessed an uncanny perception of the political and social crosscurrents. Yet he retained an element of flexibility that permitted him to move with these currents rather than be ground down by them.

Hawk seemed inexorably drawn into the administrative vacuum that plagued Johnson in the early months. Administratively, it was a "building" year. The university's management team consisted of a combination of older men, many of them largely bypassed by the Flemming administration, and new men, inexperienced in the jobs they held.

The chief administrator for the academic side of the university was Charles T. Duncan, a lithe, graying man of fifty-four, a former dean of the School of Journalism, who was a conscientious but inexperienced temporary replacement for Harry Alpert, the dean of faculties who was now on leave in Europe.

Leonard Casanova, a personable former football coach, was also new—and a little uncomfortable—in his position as director of athletics, a sensitive "target" area for activists and militants seeking to force social change. By December, the pressure proved to be too great for Casanova; he asked for a sabbatical leave, and a young man named Norval Ritchey became the acting director of athletics.

Donald Schade, an eager young accountant and a little in awe of Johnson, the CPA president, was also new in the crucial position of head of the university's budget office.

Johnson's chief secretaries, Christine Leonard and Janice Medrano, though both experienced workers, were new to the presidential office routine. At some point during the changeover from the Flemming to the Johnson staff, the correspondence files for the entire month of June 1968 disappeared and were never found again.

The president's chief staff assistant, William Blevins, a devoted young man, came from a background of student personnel work and was without prior experience on the presidential level.

Elsewhere were the older men, notably William C. Jones, nominally the dean of administration in charge of the nonacademic side of the institution. At sixty-nine Jones was within a year of retirement. Ideologically opposed to what he considered the cavalier fiscal and administrative policies of the Flemming administration, he had been gently nudged aside by Flemming—allowed to keep his title, but largely stripped of responsibility. Johnson hoped to reengage Jones, an experienced administrator who had been president of Whittier College from 1944 to 1951 and acting president of the U. of O. in 1960-61. But Jones seemed, for whatever reasons, unable to reestablish himself as a figure of authority.

So it was a building year, at a time when the problems and the relentless pressures for change were never greater. Ray Hawk found himself increasingly undertaking, by request or more often on his own volition, responsibilities for which he technically lacked the authority. Hawk actually held two titles: assistant to the president for federal relations (i.e., helping to secure federal grants), and acting director of university ("public") relations. Hawk had no prior experience in the latter role, though as dean of men he'd worked extensively with public groups as well as with students. Now, in his new role, he frequently quelled irate alumni by reminding them of their own undergraduate misdemeanors ten or fifteen years in the past.

"I just don't understand the logic of some of these people attacking the university," President Johnson often said, but Hawk believed he detected in this stance certain subtle signs of executive insecurity. These included Johnson's seeming unwillingness to ask for help when he clearly needed it, his tendency to be a loner, his proclivity for keeping problems and uncertainties to himself, and his inclination to cut short discussions when caught with a weak argument. That a new president should harbor uncertainties seemed to Hawk perfectly normal; but that Johnson refused to admit these uncertainties and seek help with them bothered Hawk a little. It was often Hawk's aggressiveness, rather than Johnson's request, that caused Hawk to move uneasily into the awesome administrative vacuum.

Hawk did not always agree with Johnson. He was wary, for example, of the presidential stance of cooperating with the students who urged a boycott of the California grapes. Hawk agreed fully, on the other hand, with Johnson's "hair" decision. True, it had been made in haste and had left hard feelings on the part of Coach Arnold. But it was not Johnson's fault that the problem landed on his desk scarcely more than an hour before deadline. In truth, it should not have landed there at all;

it should have been handled by the athletic department. But Johnson had handled the problem coolly and logically, Hawk believed. Johnson allowed emotions to dissipate in the smoke-puffs of hyperbole, and then penetrated the emotional haze to the logical arguments, finally arriving at a decision based not on expediency or compromise, but on principles that would last as long as the university itself endured.

"Well, Chuck," said Hawk, responding to Johnson's puzzled query about the emotional attacks on the university, "when you're a public figure, it's just a fact of life." Hawk felt slightly uneasy, a little like a father commiserating with a small boy who had lost a pocketful of pennies by being too trusting in people. "It doesn't matter whether you're a politician or the head of a corporation or the president of a university. People will come at you from all sides with emotional arguments. Even educated people. A college president isn't going to win any popularity polls, especially in these times. I think the university's best course of action is to continue to work with the opinion leaders around the state—the key people. We're having the newspaper editors down next week, and I think we'll get some real mileage out of that. If we can get *them* to understand the complexities of today's university, then they'll carry the word to the rest of the people. Now about the letters—"

Hawk again felt uneasily aware that his words sounded naïve.

"—There are a couple of procedures we can use. Some presidents are pretty thick-skinned. They want to see everything that comes in. Other presidents don't want to be bothered. They want their people to screen out all this junk and take care of it. I, personally, would be happy to have these kinds of letters routed to my office so you won't be bothered."

"No," said Johnson. "No. I want to see it. I want to see all of it."

There was further evidence to suggest that Johnson was unduly bothered by the criticism, which he claimed not to understand. In a speech to a parents group in Portland he complained about newspaper stories that portrayed only the bizarre events on the campus. He talked also about the "dozens of letters of complaint."

102

I don't remember receiving a single letter when our alumni magazine was rated one of the ten best in the country, when a film on sex education for children received a national award, when a TV program by one of our English professors, *Poet's Eye,* was awarded national recognition by educational television, or when our debate team walked off with regional and national honors in competition.

We have over 100 prominent speakers on our campus every year on almost every learned field imaginable . . . but let a speaker appear to advocate resistance to the draft, or opposition to the war in Vietnam, or the wonders of communism and we make headlines immediately.

It may sound as if I'm complaining—I'm really not. I realize that news is made by the spectacular, the unusual, and the controversial. That's simply a fact of life.

The University of Oregon, along with other major universities, is in a paradoxical situation in 1968. Never have so many well-qualified applicants demanded admission, never has the national and international prestige of our faculty and scholarship been higher. And yet we are under increasing attack from the right and the left and the center.

Johnson went on to cite three "fundamental principles" that guided university life. First was the "rule of law . . . that is the servant and superior of us all, the kids as well as the cops, the accused criminal as well as the prosecuting attorney." Second was "love of learning" as the "pilot of life . . . that learning is good in and of itself," and not merely because a degree holder earns more or that college graduates add more to the gross national product. Third was freedom of expression and inquiry as essential to the learning process—freedom to pursue truth wherever it may lead, freedom of students to learn, to make mistakes, to express ideas.

Perhaps there was a time when a university president could stand comfortably aloof in his idealism and abstract intellectualism, quoting Jefferson and Milton and Alfred North Whitehead, satisfying audiences with dazzling displays of erudition they didn't really understand but were too embarrassed to question. But that time was gone.

The question-answer period following the speech touched on

more pragmatic problems. Did he *really* believe a professor has the right to say anything he pleases in the classroom? What about the professor who allegedly told his students, "Go out and shoot your parents because they are racist"? Was it true that the boys and girls were visiting each other in the dormitory rooms? That the health center was dispensing birth control devices? That the drug problem had gotten out of hand?

When he explained that students coming to the university were considered adults, that the university at nearly 15,000 enrollment could no longer act as sheriff and substitute mother even if it were so inclined, that the concept of *in loco parentis* (the university acting in place of the parents) was dead—killed off by two decades of parental permissiveness in the homes, as a matter of fact—the discussion lasted far into the night.

The experience was a revelation. Clearly, abstract principles were no longer what citizens wanted to hear from university presidents. Yet if they didn't understand the principles, how could they understand the practice? He toyed with analogies. He typed this note to himself, for example, and placed it in a loose-leaf notebook he called his "speech book."

Speech idea:

In modern manufacturing plants is an instrument of modern electronics which probes crucial forged parts with "silent sound" to make sure they are free from flaws that would weaken them and cause them to fail in service. This instrument, about the size of a television set, is called a Sonoray flaw detector. It enables industry to perform nondestructive testing—inspection without harming the object. With destructive testing the object must be sawed apart or broken before it can be examined.

Analogy—University is in a sense a nondestructive testing device. University as an educational forging operation is a place where you can hammer and mold your innate capacity into a sharp and shimmering intellectual tool. It also provides some nondestructive testing devices to help you discover both strengths and flaws and then do something about them.

In another "speech idea" he suggested that the antics of the younger generation were like hiccups: "good for nothing, unlike coughing and sneezing which clear air passages. Hiccups simply annoy. The problem is to distinguish hiccups from reflex actions which, though equally annoying, serve a useful purpose."

There was no record that he ever used those ideas in a speech. He did, however, deliver countless speeches, often limiting them to a "few comments about the university" to be followed by question-answer periods. His answers to the questions were open and candid. To Embert Fossum, a crusty retired Army colonel who served as alumni director, Johnson seemed to exhibit an old-shoe affability in front of the most hostile alumni audiences imaginable. And after Johnson had charmed a hostile group with his straightforward, country-boy sincerity and candor, Fossum began hearing private remarks from alumni in the audience: how about removing the "acting" from President Johnson's title? Fossum wrote the Presidential Search Committee suggesting consideration of Johnson's name. "Johnson was the coolest head in the room," said Fossum of the many hostile alumni meetings. "He is unfailingly straightforward, honest, and charming, even when his listeners are not. He commands their respect and gains their goodwill."

What amazed people was Johnson's capacity for patience and his ability to absorb without flinching the barbed arrows of groups pushed to the point of irrational hostility. A remarkable phenomenon.

But no one stopped at this point to ask a pertinent question. Where did he get his release from emotional tension? How much can a man absorb?

Did he smash things? Never.

Yell obscenities? Once, when the power mower wouldn't start, he yelled, "Doggone machinery!" But that was the limit.

Shout at the kids? Never.

Yell at colleagues or subordinates? Never. Once, when Bill Blevins, another sensitive man beneath a cool exterior, apologized to Johnson for having blown his top at some "obnoxious guy who came to my office," Johnson said, "No need to be sorry. That's exactly what a guy ought to do when things get to him. I admire your capacity to do that. I think *I* ought to do that more often." But he never did, so far as any of his colleagues could recall.

Did he fight with his wife? Seldom. They seemed to have a tacit understanding of their respective roles: he the man of the house, a virtual law unto himself; she the lady, the helpmate who would support him in what he wished to do. Their only major point of disagreement was on child care. If a rule were violated by the children, punishment ought to be fairly automatic by Johnson's philosophy. If Craig came home with the car two minutes beyond the agreed-upon curfew, then he must suffer the consequences, usually a loss of car privileges the following weekend. Mrs. Johnson tended to be more lenient. "Shouldn't we ask Craig *why* he was two minutes late?"

So where did Johnson get his emotional release? Or was he, indeed, that rare man of sensitivity who had no emotions—or at least no need to display them?

Where indeed?

Humor.

In his speeches he usually opened with a humorous story. There was the one about the legislator who had been corresponding with a student. When the student voiced concern about certain actions damaging the university's reputation among Oregonians, the legislator reassured him.

"You have absolutely nothing to worry about," he said. "No one, absolutely *no one,* could blacken the university's image any blacker than it already is."

It got a respectable chuckle from the audience.

It was also a true story. The letter documenting it was in Johnson's file. Perhaps his attempt to use it as humor belied his unease about it. Humor covers up a lot of insecurity, in the manner of paratroopers cracking jokes to ease the tension just before their jumps.

Not that there was anything remarkable about the Johnson humor. It was a homespun, rural kind of humor. Nor was he an accomplished storyteller. He frequently muffed the punch line, but he kept trying. He clipped anecdotes from magazines and pasted them in a loose-leaf notebook labeled "Humor." He meticulously recorded stories he'd picked up at conferences, and just as meticulously recorded where he'd told a certain story so that he might not be caught telling it twice to the same group. They were scrupulously clean jokes, the most daring of them being the one about the two lost mountain climbers who had just been discovered by a St. Bernard with a brandy flask around its neck. "Look, Jim, yonder comes man's best friend," said one. Replied the other, "Yeah, and look at the size of the dog that's carrying it!"

Sometimes he enjoyed poking fun at his own accounting profession with esoteric humor: A janitor carrying three adding machines, dropped one down a flight of stairs. A young accountant took one look at the smashed remains and exclaimed, "Thank heavens—this one is fully depreciated!"

Some of his stories suggested that professors were equally naïve—compared to a real man of the world. Three professors had gone on an Alaskan hunting expedition. Alone at the guide's cabin one evening, they speculated on why the guide had set the wood-burning stove at chest height off the floor.

The physicist hypothesized that the stove was high to allow a more even heat radiation and save fuel in the bitterly cold Alaskan winters.

The education professor said it was more elementary: the stove is high to allow the wood beneath it to dry out.

The rhetorician said it was a channel of communication, the stove set high so that the light from the fire might shine through the window to illuminate symbolically the dreary Alaskan night and act as a beacon during stormy weather.

When the guide returned he denied all three hypotheses. "Nope," he said. "What happened was we lost half the stove-pipe coming up the river, so we had to raise the stove up high so the other half would reach the roof."

Nobody proposed to write a book about the Johnson humor, but it seemed to serve his purpose—to relieve tension. It placed matters in proper perspective, showing the world that here was a man who didn't take himself too seriously—just a humble country boy from Wyomin', hopelessly incompetent, but willing to learn.

When his humor assumed the form of true anecdotes, he cheerfully served as the fall guy. He enjoyed quoting the chiding remarks of his soft-spoken but subtly witty son, Craig. When Johnson backed the family car over the brink of an embankment, causing the rear wheels to hang suspended in air, Craig said calmly, "Why don't you grease the car, Dad? You'll never have a better chance." And after Johnson gave Craig fatherly advice on the traits necessary for success, Craig replied, "The trouble with being successful, Dad, is that the receipt for it is a nervous breakdown."

Sometimes Johnson fired back. Speaking on the occasion of Craig's high school graduation, he said, "I'm not losing a son; I'm regaining the use of the family car."

Johnson's best humor, his friends agreed, was a spontaneous, ragging, clownish type of tongue-in-cheek repartee, adapted to the occasion. His oral versions of it appear to be lost for all time, since witnesses could never reconstruct examples later; but sometimes Johnson put them in writing. The classic example was his exchange of correspondence with Lloyd Staples, a slim, wiry, amiable man who served as head of the Department of Geology. In 1962, a dozen letters slipped out of a mail basket in Johnson's office and fell out of sight behind a file cabinet, where they remained undiscovered for five years. Somehow the university survived the communications break. The missing documents included a check from Staples to Johnson for $9.18 in payment for lunches consumed at the Faculty Club during meetings of a committee on which they both served. To Johnson, the meticulous accountant, had been delegated the task of paying the bills and then collecting individually from the committee members. When he saw this ancient check, Johnson sent it back to Staples with the following note:

I hold the enclosed commercial document, signed by you, dated January 9, 1962. I have presented this to the bank for collection and they inform me that it has only historical interest to them. Because I have witnesses in high places who can testify that you consumed certain edibles and thus incurred this everlasting obligation, I am presenting it to you for satisfaction. I have waited 5½ long years for restitution and I believe you cannot say I have not been patient. If I do not hear from you within the next five years I shall be forced to turn this case over to my attorneys, Catchem, Convictum, and Fryim. With interest at the normal commercial rate of 1% per month, the debt currently amounts to $17.60, and is growing rapidly.

Staples promptly sent a check for $9.18 with a note, "Please cash this check immediately so I can balance my books!" To his surprise Staples found the new check returned to him a few days later, crumpled, with a hole in the center. The date had been changed from 1967 to 1867. With it was a note from Johnson.

Dear Mr. Lloyd Staples
 The enclosed check was found in the sole of an old boot belonging to a Civil War veteran, Charles Emancipation Johnson, who I believe was a great-uncle on my mother's side. It was obviously written shortly after the War, no doubt in payment of some debt incurred during the conflict. . . . The check was no doubt placed by my uncle in his boot for safekeeping and then forgotten. There was a slight hole in the boot, and it may be that the check also served the purpose of keeping out the elements.
 Assuming the standard 6% interest on personal debts the accumulated balance of this obligation as of 1967 is now $2,352.64.
 Since I assume from the name that the writer of this check is a relative of yours, and since I am sure that you would not want the name of Staples to be besmirched by the blot of an unsatisfied obligation, I trust you will investigate this matter and remit to me $2,352.64 at your earliest convenience.

Charles E. Johnson
Only known living relative of
Charles Emancipation Johnson.

Professor Staples patiently wrote another check, this one for $9.19, and sent it with a psuedo-legal document, tongue in cheek, insisting that he owed only $9.18, but was willing, as an act of charity, to include the extra penny. Back came the check with another note from Johnson.

Dear Lloyd,
   Your recent letter and the enclosed attempted remu-neration were received with interest (although 1c is hardly the kind of interest one can get interested in). . . . After reviewing carefully the document you submit, including all the whereases . . . I am shocked at the contumeliousness of your reply to my carefully reasoned and calmly stated case.
   It pains me that though I spoke only of "just desserts" you chose to describe your ungracious attempt to right this wrong of 5½ years standing as "charity" and yourself as a charitable person.
   I find myself unable to accept this check under the terms offered, namely that acceptance is evidence "that the plaintiff testifies to this lack of guilt" on your part. This is particularly true in view of the fact that I believe I called to your attention some 5 years ago the failure to receive reimbursement and you at that time made pay-ment.
   Thus as I see it, my careful and highly accurate records have saved your hide (and your $9.19), while your guilty conscience (and obviously weak system of accounting) caused you to offer me (under the guise of charity) what I take to be a bribe to keep me from exposing your true character to your other creditors who, if they knew you could be talked into paying all your debts twice, might consider you a poor risk indeed. I myself am led to wonder what skulduggery and double payment of invoices may be going on in the budget of the Geology Department. . . .
                                                  Charles E. Johnson

Enclosure: one negotiable instrument of dubious worth, dated July 1, 1967.

Staples got Johnson on the phone. "You mean I've *already* paid that bill?"
   "Yeah, five years ago."

"And you've been kidding me all this time?"

"Let's just call it a lesson in elementary accounting."

"Well I'll be damned." They both laughed.

Those were the good days when friends like Lloyd Staples could enjoy a laugh, even at their own expense.

How different it seemed now. Whatever happened to humor?

Charles Johnson responded with boyish delight when he did encounter a sample of humor. He found it in one of the least likely spots imaginable: the sports page of the daily newspaper.

Jerry Uhrhammer, sports editor of the *Register-Guard*, had written what he called a "parable." In a faraway country most of the population was black. At a big university the athletes were black with the exception of a few talented whites. All the blacks had long, bushy "natural" hair, which was the style of the day. So did the black coach. The few white players, seeking a white identity of their own—"White is Wonderful"—wore their hair in crew cuts. The coach asked two white players to let their hair grow longer or be off the team. The two players protested, "But our hair is neat, like the rule says it should be, and we don't think it's excessively short." The black coach was adamant. "I think it's too short; let it grow or else you don't play." Throughout the country black citizens supported the coach. They'd frankly been uneasy about this new trend for crew cuts among the uppity whites. A big fuss ensued, and it was all so silly. A black person described as a "cooler head" said, "Neatness is fine; I'm all for it. But it's ridiculous to become so upset about hairstyles. They're always changing. I wish they'd get back to playing basketball."

Johnson laughed and reread the column. He retreated immediately to his den to write the author a letter lavish in its praise.

Dear Jerry:

Just a note to congratulate you on one of the finest and most imaginative sports columns I have seen in any publication during the current season. I refer, of course, to your piece satirizing the "haircut" incident in the Athletic Department at this university.

The sports world may take justifiable pride in its record

of progress in granting the black athlete an opportunity to achieve whatever success his talent and capacity will allow, on the basis of individual merit alone. I hope the University of Oregon can claim some small credit in this endeavor. . . . Your satirical column, in my opinion, was a rather stunning way of helping your readers to see things in their proper perspective. As such it was in the highest tradition of journalism and reflects credit on you as sports editor of a fine newspaper.

Uhrhammer was delighted with the letter. All the other letters he'd received—and he'd gotten quite a few—condemned his column. The Johnson letter provided just the lift he needed.

"There's a good deal of latent racism in this state," concluded Uhrhammer as he thumbed through the letters of condemnation. "Johnson's decision was a good one. It was the only decision he could have made under the circumstances. It was based on the simple and sound principle that a public university has no damned business setting hairstyles for students."

Johnson sent Xerox copies of Uhrhammer's column to the letter writers who continued to complain about the "hair" decision. The column, he said, tended to put things in proper perspective.

Humor had done that. Humor was important.

Nine:
Grapes

As the fall quarter ended in December, Johnson had suffered, in his five months in office, almost constant criticism and abuse. He had defended a Constitutional principle that the people of Oregon seemed anxious to compromise in favor of peace and tranquillity—what they called "law and order."

Well, it *was* law and order he was defending, Constitutional law as interpreted by the U.S. Supreme Court. Most citizens recognized these civil rights, of course; they merely seemed unwilling to apply them to university students. Johnson recalled the psychiatrist who had visited the campus some years before and remarked, "I can think of only two institutions in our society where the leaders are expected to be as repressive as the president of a state university. One is the state mental hospital. The other is the state penitentiary."

Not that Johnson was against tranquillity. The Christmas card he sent his parents depicted the snowbound tranquillity of a tiny nineteenth-century New England village, with a horse-drawn sleigh, laden with Christmas trees, crossing a wooden bridge. Johnson's accompanying message seemed to yearn for a return to academic tranquillity: the peace of the classroom.

Johnson, as the teacher, was described as a "benevolent patron" by some of his former students. He was a learned man, anxious to share his wealth of knowledge with the young. He set high standards, but he worked hard to help students meet them. Nothing was more important to him than a student; research, writing, even supper could wait until the last wayward student had left his office armed with Johnsonian counsel. "I will always teach," he said once, prior to the presidential appointment. "The greatest man in the university is the professor. There is no rank higher than that." Perhaps it pleased him that students fought for places in his classes.

Yet Johnson was an ambitious man. He set high goals for himself and he believed, as had his father before him, that a man's debt to the God-given privilege of life could be paid only by striving to reach one's highest potential. A man must push forward to the limits of his ability. His father, Palmer Johnson, was among the last of the Horatio Alger heroes—a perfectionist and a self-made man, whose formal education ended with the seventh grade. But Palmer Johnson was an avid reader. He had educated himself with such persevering dedication that he easily passed an examination certifying that he had attained a level equivalent to two years of college. Then, by correspondence course, he studied law and passed the Montana Bar Association examination. He even studied for and passed an examination to become a certified public accountant.

Palmer Johnson's hard work, sacrifice, and self-discipline—coupled with his double-pronged expertise in law and accounting—won him his goal of a position of status and affluence despite the Depression. Clearly, he was a remarkable father for a son to live up to.

Charles Johnson's Christmas message home contained a subtle recognition of his father's respect for achievement. His father might even be impressed by the fact that he had reached such a high station in academic life that he did not have to put up his own house lights at Christmas. He was less sure, apparently, of his father's approval of the teaching profession.

Dear Mom and Dad,

... Some men from the Univ. physical plant put up our outside lights for us this year so we've been in full holiday glory for some time, and Jeanne has been holding up splendidly through the round of teas and dinners and coffee hours that the president's wife falls heir to during this time of year. She had one town-gown coffee hour at which 80 women showed up. Since I wasn't here I don't know where she put them all, but I gather it was a successful venture.

I don't know whether we could manage to keep up this pace for more than a year or not, but it's been interesting thus far and doesn't leave much time for worrying about what the future will hold. At least we got through the fall term without any incidents of the kind that seem to be plaguing some of the California schools. We had a couple of close calls in an incident with some of our black athletes and with one of the leftist student organizations, but managed to keep them both under control by working with responsible faculty and student government leaders.

I find that I enjoy the excitement of never knowing what new problem is going to be dumped on your desk each day—but find the process of working one's way through the mass of paper work that pours through the president's office rather frustrating and burdensome. On many days the life of a professor teaching classes and writing books looks pretty attractive. . . .

> Much love,
> Chuck

He wrote again in January. It was a personal, chatty letter filled with family minutiae: holiday activities, the trip to the Rose Bowl, the weather (unseasonably balmy), his good fortune in escaping the current epidemic of Hong Kong flu. The *real* news, quite possibly the purpose of the letter, was buried at the end of the two-page, single-spaced letter, added in almost too casual a manner. It dealt with the possibility of his becoming the permanent president of the University of Oregon.

... This is a legislative year for us—and we will have a committee from the legislature on campus in the next week or so. That should keep things humming. In addition there will be four or five presidential candidates showing up for visitations during January—the committee has narrowed the list to a small number and are now ready to do the final interviewing. The search-committee chairman called on me the other day and told me that my name was on their "short" list—I don't know whether I should be pleased or sad at that news—but at least I guess it means that they think I haven't let the place fall apart so far. But the year isn't over yet, either.

Much love,
Chuck

All very casual. Yet it was curious that, with the exception of the Christmas letter, the communications he'd sent home—together with the two additional letters he would write later in the year—came within days after he'd passed some significant milepost on the road to administrative achievement. The first announced his appointment as interim president. And now this, the first tentative step in the long, involved courtship ritual known as the "presidential search," a spectacle at least as colorful as the whooping crane's mating dance, and evidently just as necessary in its logic-defying gyrations. The process of selecting college presidents was awesomely similar to that of courting a girl, or of being courted, and just as gripping emotionally. The Search Committee's chairman had mentioned Johnson's status on the "short list." It was like being sent a dozen roses.

Johnson told the chairman that his future plans were not yet certain; but, yes, he might be willing to consider the presidency as a possibility if, in the opinion of the committee, the university's best interests would be served by his leadership.

Considering the infamous Johnson naïveté, it was hard to accept that comment as the standard ploy of the presidential hopeful. Yet it was precisely the right thing to say. In accordance with the arcane etiquette of the presidential search process, some coyness was essential; one must never appear too anxious.

The committee's professed interest added a further burden.

Like the girl made self-conscious by the sudden attentions of an attractive suitor, the acting president now knew that his every action would be perceived on the Search Committee members' sensitive antennae, and each decision would be scrutinized as to its implications for the future of the university.

Not all the presidential activities possessed a high degree of visibility, of course. The publicized activities were but the top of the iceberg. Beneath the surface was the real work, the long, lonely hours of paper work, the reports, the letters, the budget summaries, the statements of position.

Daily now, Johnson's desk was literally strewn with dozens of documents. Perhaps it is significant that his desk contained four "in" baskets representing various degrees of urgency, and only one "out" basket. Just a few samples:

The letter from Debbie B. A schoolgirl from Okmulgee, Oklahoma, asked the president's opinion on lowering the voting age from twenty-one to eighteen. "It should be lower than twenty-one," he answered, "but I am uncertain about precisely what it should be."

Graduate Placement Service's annual report. Great demand for graduates, particularly in accounting and sales; accountants with BS degrees averaging $677 a month. Businessmen aggressively recruiting. Whatever their complaints about the university, he mused, they didn't hesitate to hire its graduates.

Departing professors. A report analyzed the departures of twenty-five senior professors; most left for better jobs and salary increases averaging $4,254 each.

More hair. A prominent and wealthy athletic fan to be reasoned with: "The 'Afro' has many of the advantages of the crew cut," Johnson said, "in that the hair stands away from the head and never falls on the forehead or gets in the eyes of the performer."

Arriving faculty. Another statistical report analyzed the "in-migration" of forty senior professors. Most joined the university for advancement and higher pay (averaging $2,591 each), though three had taken pay cuts to leave industry or government service for the benefits of academia—"to get back in touch with young people," as one said.

Updated budget report. The problems that plagued him in the fall now seemed relieved. In the marginal areas not covered by the ongoing budget, Johnson now had the following information.

Table III: Budget Report, 1/69

Wages and salary savings	$134,864.00
Other sources (primarily overrealized enrollment)	286,580.00
Less: indirect cost credits deficit	(96,000.00)
Total resources	$325,444.00
Less: special disbursements approved by President Flemming and by budget committee	275,058.00
Estimated free balance	$50,386.00

True, it looked good, barring unforeseen catastrophes. The university might get through the year financially intact. Now the big problem was next year. The salaries of twenty-two professors whose grants were to expire would have to be picked up on state funds next year, and at the moment he could see funds for only five new positions.

Twenty-four-hour visiting. The university allowed men and women to visit each other in the dorm rooms up to midnight, if approved by the individual dorm (via two-thirds majority in secret balloting). Now, one men's dorm had voted for twenty-four-hour visiting privileges. Johnson vetoed the action. "Sometimes," he explained, "the university for the sake of very fundamental principles must dig in and take a strong stand in spite of adverse public reaction. We have liberal visiting hours now, and I don't think extending them is one of those fundamental principles I want to risk the university's future for." A strange thing happened: nothing. No confrontations, no violence. Some student leaders even expressed admiration for his candor and his courage in bucking the trend of permissiveness.

Guns on campus. A request to allow night watch personnel to carry guns lay on his desk, along with protests by student personnel deans citing the danger of "injudicious, hasty, or panicky action, by inexperienced personnel." Johnson agreed. "No university employee should carry a gun."

Faculty erosion. Professor Blank had received a "serious inquiry" from an eastern university and felt it his responsibility to pursue this feeler in view of the lack of support from the U.O.—lack of equipment, lack of space, overcrowded classes. Four other young professors were said to be similarly uneasy. "We are in need of an encouraging sign from the university," they said. Johnson put the document aside. At the moment he felt only discouragement.

New directions for social services. A seventy-page proposal for a new program to be run cooperatively with Portland State College. He looked at the price tag. A bargain at $268,854.00.

Overworked administrators. An item in the trade newspaper *Chronicle of Higher Education* caught his eye. A professor had studied administrators' work loads and concluded, "It would be only a slight exaggeration to say that those who hold the ten positions covered in this study are always overworked—the president, like the captain, worst of all." Amen.

Contract for police protection. The university maintained no police force beyond night watchmen, but paid the City of Eugene for the services of three full-time patrolmen and one plainclothes detective at $47,473.61.

Dogs. A report of dogs going wild on campus, roaming in vicious packs. An employee was bitten and required painful anti-rabies shots. Almost worse than the dogs themselves, the report said, was the incredible arrogance of their owners.

Keeping up with the day's news. 420 ARRESTED IN SFS DISORDER. Increasing violence at San Francisco State despite efforts of the new acting president, S. I. Hayakawa. KANGAROO COURT CHARGES ROSEBURG DRAFT BOARD. A student from Roseburg, a small community to the south, had, with several friends, turned a draft board hearing into a "theater of the absurd," a mock trial of board members for "high crimes against humanity." The student, Kip Morgan, and his friends were removed by police. It was the same Kip Morgan who had proposed a campus "bureaucratic harassing committee" that would read aloud exam answers in a sociology class and attempt in other ways to make life miserable for bureaucrats. (Deeper in his #3 "in" basket, Johnson had a report stating Morgan was not registered that term as a student; neither was Roy Bennett, the leader of the now-defunct Sons of Liberty.)

CAMPUS UPHEAVAL AT U.O. Series of five articles by the two *Oregon Journal* reporters who had visited him in the fall. One article alleged that a professor had told his students, "Go out and shoot your racist parents"; he turned out to be Clyde DeBerry, who denied the statement and who, as it turned out, was leaving the university for a job in San Francisco. Another article quoted students complaining of public overreaction and news media oversensationalism about trivial problems on the campus. "Where does all this public self-righteousness come in?" asked the student-body president, Dick Jones. "A university is not the only place questionable films can be shown. In Portland you can see anything you want—just walk downtown." A final article cited the formation in Eugene of a "Committee of Twenty-five," a group that would work in secret to wield influence. The article quoted one prominent citizen: "The university needs a president big enough, broad enough, and with experience enough in administration to build the kind of image for the state university that it should have." Then came the bomb—an editorial asserting that a mood of "confusion and uncertainty" pervaded the university and that it was somehow the president's fault for lack of "clear thinking."

Budget memo. Just a reminder that $201,000 worth of salary commitments for next year were not covered by "any presently discernible means." "That's *news?*" said Johnson.

That was but a tiny sampling of the paper work. It was, in fact, impossible to characterize it, save to note that the vast majority of it was excruciatingly boring. In that respect, it was not unlike the management of a modern industrial corporation. A lot of Oregonians assumed the analogy held in other ways, too. A manufacturing plant, for example. It makes a product at a cost of X for raw materials, Y for labor, Z for overhead. The product rolls off the assembly line with all the polish and glow of a fresh new line of television sets. Why wasn't a university run like *that?*

Of course it was absurd to consider college students as "units of production," or as products on the factory shipping dock. The human equation defied such conformity, though a lot of parents tended to deny that truth, as did some students. "I feel I'm in a Campbell's Soup factory—and I'm the soup," quipped one student leader.

Charles Johnson, the PhD accountant, was quick to deny the implications; there *were* differences in higher education, paramount among which was that you do not produce educated minds the way you produce TV sets. Nor do you have, as an administrator, the management flexibility or authority in the university to make shifts to follow new economic or social trends. The academic world does not fit a rigid system of accounting. But, of course, accounting itself is not a rigid discipline. A lot of people do not understand that, either.

"Accounting," Charles Johnson said, "is an exact science based on wild assumptions," a statement he did not originate, but which he kept above his desk as a reminder of the reality.

Ridding the public mind of its misconceptions about accounting had been a life-long crusade. He once told a group of alumni in Portland:

> The picture Charles Dickens painted—of the timid, mousy character sitting on his high stool grubbing over musty ledgers and trying to screw up enough courage to throw another lump of coal on the fire—is beginning to fade. In its place, in modern business novels, emerges the image of a sharp-eyed, soul-less character, devoid of human kindness, whose main joy in life lies in catching some poor soul in the process of filching company funds, or in paring operating costs to the bone, or in finding some obscure tax loophole. But these stories always end happily—the warmhearted administrator finally wins the struggle for power

121

and gets the girl. And as we fade into the glowing sunset, the villainous accountant is seen muttering curses as he slowly drowns in a sea of adding machine tape.

In reality, accounting calls for a man of creative imagination, Johnson said, a man who might work on the management team to help chart courses to new and better horizons on the basis of statistical compilations. ("Using pretty girls to run the accounting machines—a not insignificant improvement over the old days.") The accountant's function, he said, is comparable to that of the skilled navigator guiding the company through the crosscurrents of economic change and around the shoals of financial disaster.

But it remained an inexact process: "For managerial purposes, all sorts of estimates, opinions, and even vague hopes may be stirred into the accounting brew as an aid to making decisions and analyzing performance."

The university also employed accounting procedures. It moved on the basis of hard data almost as faithfully as it moved on the idealism of such educational philosophers as Alfred North Whitehead. Among the key devices used at the university was the "student credit hour" (SCH), an accounting unit that reduced to manageable dimensions the cost of infusing into the mind of one student one academic credit hour of knowledge. A professor who taught a three-credit course to 100 students, for example, would have a load of 300 SCH's for that class.

During fall term of 1968 the University taught 206,062 student credit hours at a cost of $2,838,571. The cost of pumping a credit hour of knowledge into a student's mind thus became $13.78. The university calculated that those 206,062 SCH's were the equivalent of 13,700 full-time students (on the basis that a full student load was fifteen SCH's). This was different from the fall term "head count"—14,858—because not all enrolled students took a full load.

The SCH loads were separated into departmental levels, where the variances of teaching costs were readily apparent. A simplified tabulation of some (not all) of the university's instructional departments in Fall 1968 looked like this.

122

Table IV: Student Credit Hour Loads by Department, Fall 1968

DEPARTMENT	SCH	ALL ACADEMIC LEVELS COST	C/SCH	GRAD LEVEL ONLY C/SCH
Anthropology	5,779	$ 63,749	$11.03	$38.27
Biology	6,655	141,388	21.25	46.91
Classics and Oriental	1,195	28,471	23.83	36.44
English	23,032	207,649	9.02	21.62
Geography	2,581	41,829	16.20	59.70
Geology	3,343	52,718	15.77	70.69
Mathematics	13,598	178,098	13.10	47.11
Political Science	8,946	74,294	8.30	24.46
Romance Languages	6,906	94,423	13.67	55.90
Business Administration	10,550	188,864	17.90	31.23
Journalism	2,876	41,009	14.26	15.86
Law	3,501	67,699	19.34	79.61
Music	4,959	109,172	22.01	46.81
Education	17,144	251,341	14.66	21.32
Liberal Arts total	130,070	1,712,382	13.16	42.16
Professional Schools total	74,678	1,126,189	15.08	26.02
Misc. Courses*	1,314	–	–	–
University Total	206,062	2,838,571	13.78	34.36

* Primarily Military Science courses, run at no expense to the university.

SCH: Student Credit Hours

C/SCH: Cost per Student Credit Hour

Source: University of Oregon Budget Office (Selected Departments Only)

The SCH cost variances were accounted for in several ways. Large departments, such as English, were able to effect savings by presenting large, economy-sized lecture classes. Some departments reduced the SCH costs by offering large "glamour" classes by popular professors (the record was a 2,000-enrollment class entitled "Seminar on Poverty Solutions," taught by a popular, personable, and somewhat-irascible professor of education named Arthur Pearl). Tiny departments could not be as efficient; some contained senior professors whose high salaries inflated the SCH costs. Science departments were limited by the size of their teaching laboratories. Art and Journalism were anxious to maintain small classes in painting and writing to permit individual attention to creative endeavors. Graduate level instruction clearly came at higher per-unit cost, because of the need for smaller classes, more complicated and expensive equipment, and a more individualized student-teacher relationship.

When he was dean of the College of Liberal Arts, Charles Johnson applied his accounting talents to the cloistered world of academia. Convinced that he was making too many decisions on guess work, or on the basis of eloquent pleas of strong-willed department heads, he began to employ data collection methods to help him proceed on the basis of "hard facts." An example of this was a set of detailed and complex "profiles" of the teaching loads, faculty staff, and class enrollments for each of the twenty departments under his jurisdiction. Some departments predictably complained of bureaucratic red tape or of "adding-machine mentality," but the tabulated results graphically demonstrated what the departments had been trying to show all along: the gloomy trends of burgeoning class enrollments and deteriorating student-teacher ratios. The following table was an example of the Johnsonian quantification methods, a seven-year "profile" of the Department of Anthropology. It gave a clear picture of the perils of trying to maintain an even keel amid the swelling waves of student enrollment.

Table V: Statistical Profile, Department of Anthropology

YEAR	SCH	STUD FTE	FAC FTE	ST-FAC RATIO	AVG CLASS SIZE	MAX SCH AT 15-1 RATIO	SCH EXCESS @15-1	FAC SHORT @15-1	FAC SHORT @17-1
1962-63	3,143	210	11.10	19.1	51	2,498	(645)	2.9	2.6
1963-64	3,720	248	12.50	19.8	41	2,813	(907)	4.0	3.6
1964-65	4,215	281	9.70	29.0	49	2,183	(2032)	9.0	8.0
1965-66	4,287	286	11.95	23.9	45	2,698	(1598)	7.1	6.3
1966-67	5,300	353	15.49	22.8	53	3,485	(1815)	8.1	7.1
1967-68	5,799	386	16.25	23.8	60	3,656	(2143)	9.5	8.4
1968-69	5,779	385	15.85	24.3	58	3,566	(2213)	9.8	8.7

SCH: Student Credit Hours (one student taking one hour of class credit).

STUD FTE: Number of "full-time equivalent" students; 15 student credit hours equals one full-time student.

FAC FTE: Number of full-time faculty (part-time teachers account for fractional designations).

ST-FAC RATIO: Number of students per each full-time faculty member.

AVG CLASS SIZE: Average number of students in classes offered by department.

MAX SCH AT 15-1 RATIO: Maximum allowable student credit hours to be taught if student-faculty ratio were maintained at 15 students to one faculty.

SCH EXCESS @ 15-1: Number of student credit hours taught in excess of allowable maximum at 15-1 student-faculty ratio.

FAC SHORT @ 15-1: Number of additional professors required to maintain a 15-1 student-faculty ratio.

FAC SHORT @ 17-1: Number of additional professors required to maintain a 17-1 student-faculty ratio.

To Johnson they were beautiful figures. Precision figures, like those of the instruments gracing the cockpit of a DC-8 jetliner. They were just as mysterious to the untrained observer. Yet to run a business or a university without such data, was like flying a DC-8 without its instruments.

Anthropology's instruments showed an emergency—fire warning lights for engines one and four. To shut down those engines meant that the craft would remain airborne, but at a perilous loss of efficiency. It ran contrary to Johnson's ambitions—"to keep the university moving ahead." The university was not moving backwards, certainly, but it was losing altitude.

The statistics showed that student enrollments had increased alarmingly in Anthropology—85% vs. 45% faculty increase. It meant larger classes. It meant more reliance on graduate students as teachers. It meant a slow erosion of the student-faculty ratio from 19.1-to-1 to 24.3-to-1—something akin to a slowly overheating engine.

The university had hoped to maintain a 15-1 ratio, but, sensing that as a remote possibility, it fell back to a 17-1 ratio. Even at that level, Anthropology clearly needed 8.7 more professors—and had little chance of getting them. Acting President Johnson, with his eye on the budget and mindful of the grant expiration problem, seemed unlikely to approve even one new position. Much would depend on what the State Legislature, convening in Salem in January, accomplished. But education, according to one news analysis, would have a "low priority," somewhere beneath tax reform, reapportionment, welfare, and law enforcement.

Anthropology was but one of the thirty-one[1] academic departments comprising the university in 1969; all of them had statistical profiles about as dismal as Anthropology's. These figures did not tell the whole story, of course; Johnson had another analysis that showed Anthropology utilizing its resources in the manner typical of most academic departments. It was holding to a comfortable 10-1 student-teacher ratio at the graduate level; there was, in other words, no shortage of teachers or overenrollment at that level. Here was a fact of life in the modern (and ambitious) state university. So far as the faculty was concerned, an institution's status and prestige came at the graduate level. It was here that federal and foundation grants were secured, that distinguished faculties were built, that national reputations were attained. It was what the state university "out in Ore-gawn,"[2] as the Eastern Establishment viewed it, must do to keep itself in the academic mainstream. The alternative was too horrible to contemplate: slipping into the brackish pools of an educational backwater.

It was a curious phenomenon. Within the state—among parents, legislators, taxpayers—a university's status lay in the manner it treated freshmen. Outside of the state—among faculties of great eastern universities, among the federal offices in Washington, and among the leaders of professional societies— the status lay in the way it handled graduate students and research. It was another of the town-gown conflicts that nagged at the administration. It did not help that the faculty (with notable exceptions) took a largely elitist attitude, aloof and unconcerned about the opinions of farmers in Fossil, legislators in Salem, or businessmen in Klamath Falls. Wasn't that the president's job?

Yes, it was just one of the many lessons to be learned about a job that defied description. Johnson saw his interim role almost as in-service training: "I'm just trying to learn my job and keep the university running between presidents," he told a news reporter in January. (He did not mention his status on the Presidential Search Committee's "short list.")

Much remained to be learned. The philosophies of management ranged across a broad spectrum—conservative vs. liberal, authoritarian vs. permissive, "benevolent dictatorship" vs. "authoritarian democracy," to name a few. The inscrutable nature of university management—with its problems of aloof faculty, restless students, and anxious public—seemed to require a description less transpicuous.

Bubble up vs. trickle down. Here were two management styles uniquely adapted to university campuses where the analogies with business management—the proverbial running of a "tight ship"—simply did not fit. The modern state university is not a tight ship; it's a ramshackle collection of watertight academic compartments, barnacle-laden, loosely held together by the utility wiring, with each compartment tending to drift along on its own social or political current.

The *trickle down* president is a gentle persuader and manipulator. He does not issue strong edicts or authoritarian directives, but he's firm in letting his convictions and attitudes be known. He speaks forcefully, often with eloquence. He will court and perhaps capture the faculty power structure, a cadre of about twenty-five professors who man all the important faculty committees. He will appoint countless ad hoc faculty committees under the guise of consultative management, but mostly as a means of disseminating his gentle persuasion (or dispersing the responsibility—and the responding flak—in a controversial decision). Eventually the word from on high will trickle down through the organism, like oil on creaky machinery.

The *bubble up* president shows leadership by creating a warm atmosphere that allows the most fragile of ideas and even the most threatening of new concepts to gain prompt attention and careful analysis. No idea is discarded until it has been tested thoroughly in the crucible of open discussion. The bubbler president encourages subordinates to come forth with their ideas, their theories, their problems. He appoints ad hoc committees to scrutinize every idea, every policy, every problem. His speeches radiate Miltonian and Jeffersonian philosophy; he talks about the grappling of truth and falsehood, about the power of ideas, about freedom, about fighting and arguing merely being learning in the making. And he *listens.* He might even employ data collection methods so that the inputs of information will be even more thorough, the chance for error even less. And then, after the last shred of data is at hand, he will act. Or "interact," as he would say. The bubbler president seldom asserts; he asks. He seldom manipulates; he is manipulated (but knowingly so). He seldom persuades; he is persuaded. He does not direct; he interacts. He does not run at the front of a tandem administrative structure; he runs abreast with his

128

colleagues. And the creative output of his interacting team would be greater than the sum of the team members acting individually.

The terms are, of course, academic. No one executive is "pure" one or the other. Arthur Flemming was complex and controversial. Students considered him a bubbler. Faculty saw him as a tricklish bubbler. Administrators saw him as a super-trickler—a gushing fire hydrant who listened to no one. Roy Lieuallen, the chancellor of the State System of Higher Education, was largely a bubbler. "No one serves under me," he once said, "they serve *with* me, and we're all moving together." Perhaps it was a necessary stance for anyone with the temerity to tackle a job that placed him squarely between two craggy monoliths, the Educational Establishment on one side, the Political Establishment on the other. Lieuallen also believed that a college executive ought to have "a skin thin enough to know what's going on and thick enough not to give a damn." He believed an executive had only limited influence on the course of an institution anyway: "Any man who overrates his own influence on events is the man who, in the dark of night, has to live with his conscience."

Charles Johnson tended to be a bubbler president, though he did have tricklish tendencies not readily apparent at this stage of his presidential career. He was, after all, just learning. It may have been his bubble up relationship with students that led Johnson to take an action that would brush him with a brand of political tar that he could never wash off. It would be a learning experience.

The "grape issue," as it came to be called, had started quite innocently.

"Who's Cesar Chavez?" Johnson asked when the question first came up.

Two students had asked the president to support Chavez and his California grape workers by stopping the university's purchases of grapes. They said Chavez was the leader of a committee formed in 1965 to unionize farm laborers, mostly of minority racial groups.

"Tens of thousands of California grape workers have gone

out on strike," said Roberta Hanna, a dark-haired young woman, one of the two boycott leaders. "But instead of relating to the demands of the strikers, the huge agri-businesses used political pressure tactics on the governor of California and on immigration officials. Governor Reagan supplied prisoners as scab labor."

She talked of grape pickers working in 100-degree heat, without sanitary facilities, without water, for incomes averaging only $1,800 a year. Her partner and co-leader of the boycott committee, a tall, extraordinarily handsome young man named Jean Oliver, had lived amid the poverty of rural Kentucky as a Vista worker. "Steinbeck got me interested in the farm workers," he said. "Then I spent time in the Central California valley labor camps. They're forced to live in shacks just like those I saw in Kentucky. There's no sanitation. They live like animals. The men have strength and pride, but they're being destroyed."

They formed an unusual partnership, Hanna and Oliver. She was a radical and erstwhile member of a loose-knit campus organization known as SDS; he was largely a conservative. Yet they worked effectively together, and their arguments were persuasive.

Johnson's immediate reaction was that the university should take no position on labor-management disputes. He was told, with vigor, that by doing nothing—by maintaining the status quo and continuing to buy grapes—the university *was* taking a position. It clearly put the university on the side of the grower.

Johnson expressed sympathy for the plight of the workers; the students, he said, had made so convincing a case that he planned—privately—to ask his wife to stop buying grapes. But for the university to take a stand, no, that was a different matter. He saw the real issue as nonpolitical. Should the university attempt to accommodate substantial numbers of students who wanted to affect (for whatever the reasons, religious, political, gastronomical) the dormitory menus? His answer was "yes"; there were already too many ways in which the university could, even with the best of intentions, oppress students:

forcing them to stand in long lines, denying them entry into crowded classes, holding them apart from close relationships with teachers.

"Let's look at it this way," said Johnson. "Here's a situation where a student comes into a large institution and holds a contract for room and board at the dormitory. As an individual, he has almost no control over the menus. But supposing, say, 30 percent of the students got together and said, 'Hey, we don't like that liver you're serving.' Well, I think the dormitory office would make some effort to accommodate that large a group. Or what about the provisions for Catholic students who don't eat meat on Fridays? I don't recall a single complaint that the university is taking a stand on religion because of that."

The meetings dragged on through the fall and into the winter quarter. They grew increasingly hostile, the boycotters and the dormitory officials crossing swords in angry confrontations in the President's Office. The boycotters said that the dorms were buying grapes in greater quantities than ever, an allegation denied by the dorm officials. Yet they seemed evasive about precise figures.

And how did the dormitory residents themselves feel about grapes? The idea of an opinion poll appealed to Johnson. It was precisely the kind of quantification one *should* use in making decisions. His mind was set now. "When we get the results of the poll we'll have the dormitories cut back by whatever percentage of students say they don't want grapes served. We'll use last year's purchases as a base, because grapes weren't an issue then."

The boycotters wanted a majority vote to determine policy: if 51 percent didn't want grapes, then purchases ought to stop altogether. "No," Johnson said, "under those circumstances we'd cut back 51 percent. If we bought 1,000 pounds of grapes last year, we'd buy 490 pounds this year."

The first poll (40% against serving grapes, 33% in favor, 27% no opinion) was a fiasco. Its design was nonprofessional, its methodology skewered, its validity doubtful, the boycotters said. A new poll was ordered with these results, reported in late January:

Table VI: Grape Poll

POSITION ON BOYCOTT	NUMBER	PERCENT
I have no opinion on the grape boycott	205	18.0
I am for purchasing grapes according to the percentage of students wanting them	281	24.6
I am against the grape boycott (I am for continuing the purchasing and serving of grapes in the dormitories)	324	28.4
I am for the grape boycott (I am for no further purchasing or serving of grapes in the dormitories)	331	29.0
Totals	1,141	100.0

The arguments on methodology and validity did not cease, but meanwhile the whole question proved moot. The figures on grape purchases for the past two years came in. Johnson read them and said, "Oh, boy." They seemed almost to explode out of a copy of a letter from the housing director to the fiscal affairs director.

Dear Mr. Lindstrom:

From July 1, 1967 through June 30, 1968, the dormitories purchased 4,258 pounds of grapes.
From July 1, 1968 through February 8, 1969, the dormitories purchased 6,234 pounds of grapes.
The pertinent information is contained in the attached.

H. P. Barnhart
Director of University Housing

The implications were as clear as they were ominous. The dormitories had purchased more grapes in the first seven months of this year than *all* of last year. Far from cutting back by 30 percent, the dormitories had increased their purchases by *254 percent.* They had increased their rate of purchase from 355 to 903 pounds a month. Even if they purchased no more grapes for the rest of the year, they would still have increased their purchases by (he scribbled out the figures on scratch paper) 48.5 percent rather than cutting by 30 percent.

The grape boycott leaders were incensed. Obviously they had lost, no matter what happened.

But Johnson had made a commitment. He had agreed to abide by the results of the poll, and now he was in the most awkward of positions. What irony. How many times had he warned his accounting students against the dangers of making decisions based on incomplete data? He didn't know the dormitory purchases were gyrating wildly upward, though the students had not been shy in pressing that allegation.

He took the "grape file" home that evening, knowing full well what he'd have to do, despite the remonstrances of Ray Hawk, his public relations man: "We ought to steer clear of any action that smacks of political involvement or taking a stand on a labor-management issue. . . . We'll offend a lot of people in those fruit-producing areas such as Hood River and Medford. . . . We're skating on mighty thin political ice—don't forget this is a Legislative year and one of our most powerful legislators comes from that fruit-producing country down on the Rogue River. . . . We're treading awfully close to a secondary boycott, and we ought to have some legal advice. . . ."

Johnson turned a deaf ear to those comments—it was a little of the trickle down philosophy showing—he'd had quite enough of Hawk's comments and wanted to hear no more. He knew what he had to do.

Ten:
Taking the
Offensive

When President Johnson discovered the university's grape purchases were running rampant, he did what the prudent economic man does upon discovering that he has overdrawn his bank account—stops writing checks. Johnson stopped buying grapes for the remainder of the academic year. News of this decision touched off yet another statewide conflagration.

This was the height of irony. Grapes were not normally served during the winter and spring anyway, purely for economic reasons: the cost was up and the quality down during the off season. To announce in February that the university would purchase no more grapes for the remainder of the year was simply restating the obvious.

It was ironic, too, that it made headlines at all. Some universities had avoided controversy quite simply; they quietly stopped buying grapes. Such a decision could, after all, be justified on grounds other than political. The management of the University of Oregon's Student Union had decided—long before the boycott became an issue—to discontinue grape purchases for a very simple reason. Too many students picked up the grapes in the cafeteria line and ate them before they reached the checkout cashier, thus avoiding payment.

But with the news media's supersensitive antennae zeroed in on the university, it was impossible to do anything quietly. What the university did *not* plan to do became the major story of the day.

Why the university dormitories had increased their grape purchases remained unclear at the time. The Housing Office at first vacillated in its answer, but finally concluded that the reasons were purely economic. Oregon's apple crop had been damaged by a spring frost, causing the price of apples to double to ten dollars a box, while California grapes continued to be available at attractively low prices.

What did it matter? Johnson was in hot water again. It was the grape issue that caused Thomas Garrison's slow burn to boil over.

Garrison, a soft-spoken but fiercely hard-line lawyer from Roseburg, a lumber-mill town south of Eugene, had viewed with increasing dismay the events of the fall and winter at the university. A former mayor of Roseburg, and an influential man in state politics, Garrison started writing letters. To Johnson he wrote, "This decision along with several others has made me conclude that you simply do not have the judgment needed to do your job. Even temporarily."

To the Board of Higher Education and Governor McCall he wrote, "Mr. Johnson's decision is clearly against the public interest." He urged the board to "reverse the patently erroneous exercise of authority by the acting president."

To Governor McCall the grape decision did, indeed, seem to defy logic. "Jesus, what a bum idea," the governor said. "You count the grapes and if you're eating them faster than you were last year you're supporting the farmers, and if you're eating them slower you're supporting Cesar Chavez, so you try to eat them at the same level that you did the year before. That sounds awfully Mickey Mouse."

McCall wrote a letter to Garrison that found its way into the Roseburg daily, the *News-Review:* "It was a case of poor taste and poor judgment for the University of Oregon to involve itself in this dispute." The governor added that he'd been told by the chairman of the Board of Higher Education that "at least four members of the board are highly incensed."

The letter did not create the statewide furor of the previous fall's gubernatorial missive, but it did precipitate a microcosmic controversy in Roseburg.

The newspaper editorially supported Garrison and the governor: "It is time taxpayers let it be known that they expect Oregon's schools to be firmly directed—and with no funny business."

A taxi driver dissented, apologizing to Johnson for the "arrogance" of the editorial: "This is only a small-town paper with much smaller ideas."

Another lawyer dissented further. Garrison's comments, he said, should be filed under "decreasing dividends in the section for sour grapes."

And a farmer, living outside of Roseburg, concluded, "I can see why our young people get so out of patience with us oldsters. . . . What would happen if a university president refused to negotiate with students on an issue that represents what many of them feel is a gross injustice? The battle lines would be drawn . . . and we'd have police and National Guard troops on our campus to enforce order."

It was a bright spot, Roseburg. Its citizens expressed with élan the most divergent views ranging from the hawkish conservatism of ex-Mayor Garrison to the rampant radicalism of the young man who had disrupted the draft board hearing, Kip Morgan, son of a Roseburg logging family.

In contrast, the critical letters from elsewhere in the state had a dreary sameness about them. The issue was different, but the rhetoric was strikingly familiar. The threat from Grants Pass: *Every effort I can muster will be used to have your tragic mistake corrected;* the advice from Newberg: *Be firm, like the president of San Francisco State, it is the only way;* the ominous portent from Redmond: *It might be apples, pears, potatoes, or any other farm product next time;* the crude disgust from Salem: *If you are such a weakling you're not good as an administrator;* the frost from Portland: *When I see pictures of*

*your campus and the type of students there—my blood runs
cold;* the antipathy from The Dalles; *I'll never allow either of
my last two sons to attend this school; the first two came back
with very changed attitudes that I could not accept as bene-
ficial;* the sage philosophy from Hillsboro: *It does not take a
good education to be smart in some cases, just being practical in
many ways is the smartest way to act;* the fading image report
from Portland: *Such action only further alienates the supporting citizen-taxpayer;* the sarcasm from Eugene: *Once again
we should feel reverent as we observe our top administrators at
the university diligently administering their do-nothing policy
of appeasement.*

Ray Hawk, having noted Johnson's sensitivity to such criticism, was beginning to intercept some of the letters and was
answering them himself. But there was no shielding Johnson
from the public anger of Oregon's farm community. The directors of the Oregon Farm Bureau Federation were quick to issue
a statement fairly dripping with emotion: "President Johnson
has been duped by an emotional minority who have probably
never picked a grape in their lives, but consider themselves
spokesmen for farm workers. . . . Where does student control
begin and end? This is the real issue. . . ."

And it happened that the two key men in the Legislature, the
co-chairmen of the Joint Ways and Means Committee, had
agricultural connections: one a farmer from Eastern Oregon, the
other a fruit grower from the Rogue River Valley. The latter, a
man named Lynn Newbry, wasted no time dashing off a letter
to Johnson with a copy to the editor of *The Oregonian.*

I notice in an article in the Portland *Oregonian* that you
have reached the policy of not purchasing table grapes in
support of the secondary boycott against the grape
growers in California.

I am sure that you are aware that secondary boycotts
are prohibited under the Taft-Hartley Act, and therefore
you are in effect accessory to an illegal act. . . . Your
action . . . has the effect of placing economic sanction
upon a group of people with whom you disagree as to their
activities. Since you have adopted the use of economic

sanctions, I can only presume that you would not criticize the Legislature for using the same principle in dealing with the University of Oregon in regard to policies with which we do not agree.

Ray Hawk sent the letter on to Johnson's office with a hastily penned note: "Chuck should answer personally and *promptly*— Newbry a key legislator and fruit grower from Southern Oreg."

Johnson followed Hawk's advice. "The story in the *Oregonian*," he said, "was not only misleading but also in error in its statement of the facts. The fact is that I have repeatedly announced . . . that the university . . . *will not take a position* on this or any other controversy." Johnson's letter traced the route of the decision, the commitment to students, the lack of validity to the claim of neutrality when the university had in fact *increased* its consumption of grapes.

> I hope you will appreciate the irony of the situation. If we have not in fact been neutral it is the growers we have favored. Thus those supporting the workers have a basis for complaint that we have not acted consistently with a policy of neutrality. At the same time groups generally supporting the grower position are loudly making the same claim. Obviously the *Oregonian* story is to a considerable extent responsible. But I admit that this has turned out to be a far more complex administrative problem than I ever anticipated at the outset, and that it is unlikely that the chain of reasoning can ever be explained to people whose emotions are by now thoroughly aroused.
>
> Someone once told me the best test of a fair decision was that everyone involved in the result was equally unhappy. I laughed at his jest at the time; I'm not sure I would even smile today.

The perceptive observer could, in retrospect, detect in this letter a change in Charles Johnson. The difference was subtle, certainly not discernible at the time. Yet it was undeniably present.

It was present in the more aggressive tone of his comments, as though he had adopted an attitude of "defensive aggression," a version of the tactical theory that the best defense is a good offense. And now, in January and February, the sixth and seventh months of his presidential tenure, it began to show more prominently, permeating his speeches, his letters, and his conversations.

For one thing, Johnson displayed increasing impatience with the press handling of university news, particularly in the two Portland newspapers. He was almost beginning to believe what many professors and administrators had been saying all along: that the Portland papers were seizing any opportunity to discredit the University of Oregon to the greater glorification of their local institution, Portland State College, soon to become, by legislative fiat, a "university."

Furthermore, Charles Johnson had had quite enough of being compared unfavorably with the hard-line acting president of San Francisco State, S. I. Hayakawa, whose campus had been embroiled in violence for months. When a prominent alumnus who was a state senator wrote of the "sad state of affairs" at the university—the demonstrations, the permissiveness, the sit-in—Johnson seized the platform to express some of his most sharply worded views to date.

I appreciate your frankness in stating your concerns. I must admit, however, that I am somewhat at a loss for an answer to your comments. . . .
May I say that not only do we share many of your concerns but that we have spent and are spending untold hours and effort working to keep and enhance the progress I have seen at this university in the 16 years I have been on the faculty. I am by this time absolutely firm on only one thing: the problems facing every major university today, like the problems facing state legislative bodies, are not simple, nor will they give way to easy, glib solutions. Most university administrators are groping for answers and seeking wisdom from every knowledgeable source. One exception, perhaps, is the present head of San Francisco State who is bravely presiding over the ultimate ruin of what was once a pretty fair state college—but this is a lost cause and lost causes are relatively easy to bring to their inevitable conclusion. Like the fireman who smashes the premises with an ax in a last desperate effort to bring a

holocaust under control, what Mr. Hayakawa is doing is necessary, but chopping up the place with an ax is scarcely an intelligent technique of fire prevention. Even as an acting president I have no ambition to officiate at either the beginning or the end of this kind of disaster. . . .

Why the change? Although the reasons were doubtless complex, it is not unlikely that one may have been implied in the Newbry letter: he was laughing less. Perhaps he was adjusting to that fact by greater aggression. Perhaps, too, he had gained self-confidence through six months of experience. This self-confidence can only have been increased by the knowledge that the Presidential Search Committee had its collective eye on him.

But whatever the subtleties, the changes were real. Indeed, sometimes he left subtlety aside and bucked straight into the controversies.

"Why all this criticism of the university?" he demanded of a Lions Club audience in Eugene. "Our product is well accepted, with businessmen lined up at the employment center anxious to hire our graduates. Our national reputation is growing. Our research reputation is growing. Then why the criticism? Is it because we are careless with our money?"

He said the university had one of the lowest administrative overhead rates in the country, 34 percent, as figured in the federal grants. A study showed Oregon and Oregon State had the lowest number of secretaries per staff member of any university in the Pacific Eight Athletic Conference. He said the university was attracting outstanding faculty and research grants.

He added, "We aspire to be a great university. We're still quite a ways from that goal. But in the sixteen years I've been here we've come a long way—and each year sees a bit more progress. Now despite all this, I have a desk full of letters from concerned citizens who say that they wouldn't want to send their son or daughter to this awful university and that someone had better get busy and clean up that awful mess at the U. of O."

It was with policies that the university president must concern himself, not individual incidents, he continued. Policies that allow for free and open exchange of ideas. Policies that allow room for dissent. Policies that allow the almost forgotten voice of the student to be heard amid the creaks and groans of the bureaucratic machinery. Policies that treat students as adults and do not attempt to shield them from their responsibilities as law-abiding citizens. "Now you may argue that a wise, benevolent dean could do a good job with wayward young people who get in trouble with the law. My reply would be, 'So could a wise, benevolent judge.'"

And he'd heard quite enough talk about "gutless wonders" as university administrators. He told a group of Rotarians that it was not lack of guts that kept sensible administrators from slashing student throats, but a sense of fairness ("Due process we call it"), and a perception of impending change. The university of the 1970s will be quite different from that of the 1940s or '50s, he said. It was high time the public woke up to that fact.

Furthermore, the American society had shown such an incredible degree of ambivalence, that it was small wonder that the young people were puzzled and upset:

> Society wants the universities to produce young people with high levels of technical competence mixed with a large dose of humanistic concern, but it's unwilling to suffer the inconvenience of the social change that must inevitably follow these young graduates out into the world.
>
> Society wants first-rate instruction for its young, yet it wants to limit the areas of academic inquiry.
>
> It wants young people to learn new things, yet it is disturbed when these new things tend to change their ideas and their outlook on life.
>
> Society wants its own values questioned by the universities as a means of social progress, but it doesn't want professors to ask impertinent questions.
>
> Well, gentlemen, you can't have it *both* ways. You can't have an active, current, *relevant* university and still have tranquility. It has not yet been proven to me, however, that we can't manage in an orderly fashion the changes that must occur in our university.

He seemed to be everywhere at once, writing, speaking, traveling the state—a tall, slim, statuesque figure, impressive as he gave release to sincere convictions riding forward on his deep-timbred voice of authority. He was a rhetorically nimble-footed quarterback on a team suddenly gone on the offensive, running, passing, rolling out, opting for the keep.

And smiling. Not laughing, but at least smiling.

"These are exciting times for one engaged in university administration," he said. "The spirited give-and-take of controversy and the questioning of basic principles produces an atmosphere that is conducive to change and progress."

He continued to talk of moving the university ahead: "I hope we are sufficiently wise and energetic to focus the current spotlight on higher education on the *real* issues and to keep the university moving toward a position among the first-rate universities in this country."

To a legislative committee, on campus to investigate problems of higher education, he cited the supreme irony of public relations: "At a time when the image of the university, by all appearances, is at a low point *within* the state, its reputation, as viewed from throughout the nation, has never been higher."

And the militant students—even *they* served a purpose, he told another group: "They may be making a genuine contribution to the university by making us uncomfortably aware of our shortcomings and imperfections. Sometimes they have to hit us between the eyes with a two-by-four to get our attention."

He even managed to take a subtle jab at the news media in a speech to a group of newspaper publishers: "I'm sure I don't surprise you with the thought that we sometimes feel quite keenly the paucity of the kind of reportorial competence and editorial insight of which we know you are capable."

In another pin-prick thrust at the press, he quoted from Francis Bacon's essay, "Of Seditions and Troubles," a passage on social unrest: "And as there are certain hollow blasts of wind and secret swellings of seas before a tempest, so are there in states. Libels and licentious discourses against the state when they are frequent and open; and in like sort, false news often running up and down, to the disadvantage of the state and hastily embraced; are amongst the signs of trouble."

Johnson continued, "I thought to myself it was interesting that things hadn't changed much in 350 years—it was 1597 when Bacon's essays were published."

It was all pretty subtle. The press, however, needed more than a pinprick; it needed to be hit between the eyes with a two-by-four.[1]

"I read the rest of the essay," Johnson continued, "to see if he had any advice that might be pertinent today. The rest may be pretty well summed up in a key sentence: 'The surest way to prevent seditions (if the times do bear it) is to take away the matter of them. For if there be fuel prepared, it is hard to tell whence the spark shall come that shall set it on fire.' "

Johnson said, "I can think of no way to describe *more accurately* the general strategy being employed in many universities throughout the country today to cope with turmoil and unrest."

Ironically, the press reports of his speech stood in unwitting testimony of his criticisms. They quoted largely peripheral remarks, primarily his oft-quoted comment, "There is no power greater than the power of a good idea" and the obvious point that tensions between youth and adults had resulted in an "abnormal surge of discontent."

And when the session turned to questions and answers, Johnson found himself fielding the same dreary queries. Why had he stopped buying grapes? Why did he not crack down on the vocal minority of students who were causing all the trouble?

Had they not listened to his speech?

The newsmen also missed—or at least failed to report—Johnson's perceptive views on how a university is governed. Johnson went on:

> ... Though a university is a limited society existing for a special purpose, it sweats over issues of governance just as states and cities and nations sweat over issues of governance.

Among states we've tried kingdoms, we've tried aristoc-
racies and dictatorships, and we've tried democracies. In
the history of universities we could point to adaptations of
each of these. The swing in both states and universities has
been from authoritarianism toward democracy. And one
of the things we should remember while we are trying to
protect order—which is of utmost importance—is that in
the history of the development of governance, the major
changes were those that were *won*, not granted. The establishment does not usually anticipate the need for freedom
and grant it. It has to have this need called to its
attention—and frequently it will only pay attention when
it is hit hard. . . .

There are two general ways of talking about democracy.
One is generally attributed to James Madison who wrote
one of the brilliant defenses of our Constitution in which
he described it as a theory of governance based on "countervailing coalitions." This is a pretty fair analogy to the
system of governance existing in universities today. Not
only do we have countervailing coalitions of students,
faculty, administrators, and outside boards of governance,
but within the university's structure we have professional
schools and academic departments each of which has to
some extent conflicting interests and each of which joggles
for special attention, for money, and for the chance to
become more distinguished.

There is another way of talking about democracy, generally attributed to Jean-Jacques Rousseau, which is called
participatory democracy. The Students for a Democratic
Society have rediscovered this approach. . . .

It has been pointed out to me that this sort of democracy does not require respect for normal freedoms of
speech, press, expression in all mediums which we consider
sacred in our country and in our universities under the
concept of countervailing coalitions. Under this system of
participatory democracy a person gets his freedom, if in
fact he has it, from having been a part of the sovereignty
that made the decision. And having been a part he must be
willing to accede to any decision made, however intrusive
and ungenerous it may be toward the interests of some
particular minority group.

I happen to think that this kind of participatory democracy will not work in a society as complex as ours. But the

fact that I believe this is not going to stop some portion, perhaps the most idealistic of our present college generation, from not only holding an opposing point of view but from continuing their attempts to force our attention to this idea.

The first attempt to *force* a political point of view onto the University of Oregon campus came in late January. Johnson was in conference that afternoon when an urgent call came from Richard Reynolds, director of the Student Union. Outside his office at that very moment, Reynolds said, was a riot.

"It's a little frightening," said Reynolds. "People are running and shouting. There's fighting and scuffling. The tension is growing. This has all the characteristics of mob violence. If it doesn't subside in a few moments, we may have to alert the police."

It all stemmed from a "mock trial" of two Navy officers who had set up a recruiting table in the Student Union, Reynolds said. Radical students had approached the table and staged a "guerrilla theater" type of kangaroo court. Somehow this peaceful brand of protest had exploded into violence. The two Navy officers were beaten and manhandled, and their literature was being confiscated and burned. Emotions were running raw, Reynolds said.

Johnson did not hesitate. Excusing himself from the discussion of a new request for a National Science Foundation development grant, he calmly put on his light tan raincoat. From the coat pocket he fished out and put on a flat-topped rain hat.

The scene etched itself in the memories of his office staff: the president standing straight and tall and trim, looking rather like a British military officer. There was a slight smile on his face. He issued instructions: "Bill, we'll need you by the phone—we may have to get in touch with the police." Then, like General Montgomery en route to the front, he marched purposefully out of Johnson Hall and into the dreary, rainswept afternoon.

"Hey, it's the president," a student was heard to say.

"My God," said another.

"He's got a lot of guts, coming over here in the middle of this."

The faint smile remained on Johnson's face. "What's going on?" he asked a student he recognized as one of the campus radicals.

Students quickly gathered around. The Navy, Johnson was told, had been declared guilty of high crimes against humanity by waging an imperialist war in violation of the Geneva accords. The "jury" of fourteen—said to have split its vote—was five for "guilty," five for "not guilty," because the Navy was a "pawn" under control of the fascist American state, and four for "not guilty" by reason of insanity.

Little by little the story came out: the manhandling, the literal ejection of the Navy personnel by force, the burning of their literature and a tablecloth. Johnson noticed the ashes on a speaker's podium called the "Free Speech Platform" on the Student Union Terrace.

Johnson asked questions aggressively. Last fall, he said, a Communist recruiter had visited the campus and set up a table at the Student Union where she handed out literature. Those who objected did not attempt to forcibly eject this person. Was there some reason, he wondered, that now caused the students to believe that the same courtesy should be denied to other recruiters? Supposing the university were to deny the Navy access to its facilities because it was not in agreement with its policies, he said. Would that mean it would have to agree with the policies of those it *did* permit on campus? Who would make those kinds of decisions?

The answers were a litany of antimilitary radicalism: the university's complicity in the military-corporate-imperialistic war machine; babies being napalmed in Vietnam; the need for active protest as a means of supporting the oppressed peoples of Vietnam, Latin America, and the black ghettos in their great struggle for liberation; the need for the people to fight back with increasing determination to avoid being channeled via a one-way street to Vietnam or to corrupt, hedonistic suburbia; the *people* this, the *people* that, and if the government did not stop the war the *people* would stop the government.

The crowd's emotions quickly peaked out, defused in part by Johnson's presence. Here was the president of the university, and he was listening. His height forced him to lean down, so that amid the noise of the crowd he might not miss a word of the gushing rhetoric—the billions spent for weapons of death while millions of people starved . . . the *struggles,* the desperate, life-or-death struggles against archaic moral and political values, struggles by students in Prague, in Berkeley, in Berlin, in Guatemala, in Mexico City, struggles based on issues of human dignity and survival, struggles against authoritarianism and stagnancy and oppression. The people would no longer put up with this bullshit. It was some of the most strident abuse he'd heard to date: "People are dying in this fucking war. . . . Get off your fat ass and *do* something. . . . How can you spread that bullshit about human rights when the rights of so many millions have been violated for so many years?"

Johnson continued to listen calmly. He listened to the Navy recruiters. He listened to his own staff debate the issue of what action the university should take: one group insisting that the university must take swift, punitive action against the students if for no other reason than to protect its public image; the other insisting that the university had no machinery for prosecuting criminal matters, and that if the students had violated the law, they should be prosecuted in the criminal courts downtown.

The day after the incident, Johnson had made up his mind. The university's long tradition of freedom had been violated, he said. "The university has apologized to the Naval personnel. It will hold the participating students responsible under its conduct code and will cooperate with the Naval representatives if they elect to bring charges against any of the offenders for violation of the law."

He added: "The chagrin of the university community was mutely reflected in the charred ashes of material brought to the campus for distribution by the Naval representatives. It was a lamentable sight to see these ashes strewn across the top of the place chosen for the burning—the Free Speech Platform."

Johnson gained wide campus support. Formal statements of support emanated from both faculty and student groups. A faculty colleague, scientist Aaron Novick, wrote Johnson a commendatory note. Johnson, beleaguered by criticism of the grape decision at the time, replied:

> Thanks for your note. A word of support among the brickbats helps brighten my perspective more than you may know. Now if I had been a bit more level-headed instead of pin-headed on the grape issue, perhaps I wouldn't be in quite such hot water. Incidentally, how are things going on the *education* side of the establishment?

The comment revealed a growing frustration. "I'm getting tired of putting out brush fires," he confided to Bill Blevins. "Gosh, if we just had the time to think through the important issues of education, we could plan ahead. We could *prevent* problems. All we're doing now is running a fire department."

Mindful of the possibility of becoming the permanent president, he began to toy with ideas for administrative reorganization. Clearly the current administration of the university—comprised of the smoldering chaos of the Flemming administration, old men approaching retirement or new men inexperienced in their jobs—was not the answer.

Someone had sent him an account of a reorganization at the University of Alaska. Only four men reported to the president: the vice-presidents for academic affairs, research, public service, and finance. It sounded like a good idea, and he made a mental note of it. At present, Johnson calculated, he must have thirty people reporting directly to him. That's the way Flemming had operated.

Some changes, he vowed, would be in order if he became the permanent president. *If.* He hadn't made up his mind about that. His attitude wavered from day to day. Did he *really* want to be a university president?

On the morning of the day he was to give the committee his

answer, his wife had not the slightest clue to his decision. She did not ask. She suspected he didn't know either. It would be entirely in character for him to make up his mind only moments before giving the committee his answer.

From the aloof, Olympian view of the Presidential Search Committee, Johnson remained an attractive prospect, though it was no secret that perhaps ten or a dozen others were on the "short list." Johnson's smooth handling of the Navy recruiter incident did not escape the attention of the committee. Neither did his defense of free expression during the obscenity crisis and the defense of individual rights in the "hair" issue. The committee was split on the grape decision. Some called it awkward, others considered it the correct decision under the circumstances. In any event, the prospect of permanently seating the tall country boy from Wyoming in the big red-leather presidential chair remained, in the jargon of academia, a "viable alternative."

Eleven:
The Search
for a President

Was there an answer, somewhere among the events on the campus, to this most difficult of all decisions—to run, or not to run, for the presidency? Some events reassured him, including the battle-of-the-sexes exchange in the *Emerald* letters column. The boys indicted the girls for lack of "femininity," and the girls complained of limited choices for dates: uncouth fraternity men, pony-tailed hippies, and opaque intellectuals long on conversation but short on action. Some things would never change.

Yet new and strange forces were in motion—the turmoil and tension following the Navy recruiter incident, for example. Several arrests had been made (among them Kip Morgan, the Roseburg youth who had disrupted the draft board hearing, and Roy Bennett, the Che Guevara type of "Sons of Liberty" fame) on various charges relating to the Navy and draft board incidents.

The arrests brought an escalation of demonstrations, marches, rallies, and bullhorn rhetoric on the terrace of the Student Union. They coincided with the formation of a new Black Panther group in Eugene, a group said to be arming itself with carbines and pistols "for defense."

Tensions grew. Protest rallies occurred almost daily. A group of students marched through the campus. Students presented to President Johnson three ''non-negotiable'' demands: (1) amnesty for all "political prisoners," (2) an end to university "complicity" with the military, and (3) an end to "political repression" and university cooperation with police, FBI, and narcotics agents.

When a crowd of 300 gathered in front of the administration building to protest militarism, police states, American fascism, and assorted ills, Johnson emerged from his office to talk of intellectual values and free expression. But the radicals among the audience were impatient, seeming to be more interested in the politics of confrontation than in truth and falsehood grappling on the open forum. Was the president aware, they asked, that the pigs were on campus? The pigs, the fucking pigs—did he know they were snooping, harassing, making arrests? Did he approve? How could he justify this blatant repression against our black brothers and our white brothers?

Johnson stood at the top of the Johnson Hall steps, cool, tall, and unruffled, though some students claimed later to have noticed his hands shaking. He spoke through an electronic bullhorn. Yes, he knew the police were on the campus. And rightly so.

"All of us are a bit uptight," he said. "The university is simply not prepared to deal with coercion and violence. We have a few security officers for parking and nightwatch duties, and that's the sum total of the university's capacity to defend itself against people who wish to impose violence on it. We operate under the idea that when men differ, they may sit around the table and talk. On an open campus, where ideas can be submitted to rigorous scrutiny and debate, the good ideas will float like cream to the top and the bad will go down the drain.

"But we get nervous when buildings are bombed or evacuated under threat of bombing. That's happened several times this year. We turn to the Eugene Police Department for our security force, which provides us with the same kind of protection that it provides the rest of its citizens."

An ovation from the crowd followed Johnson's talk. Was it out of admiration for his courage in facing the street crowd? Or did it show a lack of sympathy for the aims of radical students?

The radical students continued to operate under various names, SDS, Peace and Freedom Party, People's Liberation Front. Whatever the name, the faces were largely the same, and so was the rhetoric. They talked about the Man. The Man had begun to move on students, making arrests. Said a flyer: "At least ten of our black and white brothers have been arrested—*political* arrests, because students have dared to militantly challenge the power and the legitimacy of the corporate state's means of organized violence and oppression: the draft and the military."

The tone of the radical flyers had changed. Gone were the obscenities of the previous fall—the big blowup over obscenity had turned out to be counter-productive to their own aims, the radicals said. Replacing obscenity was the argot of the black ghetto: the Man, our Brothers. Even so, the black students on the university campus remained largely aloof from the excesses of white radicalism.

Though few would admit it at the time, a social class split separated the middle-class white radicals from the lower-class blacks. Rose Noel, a large-boned thirtyish woman who was an influential leader of the blacks, was singularly unimpressed by the antics of white radicalism. "It doesn't make sense to raise hell and destroy one who is trying to help you," she said. "Dr. Johnson is being honest with us. To us, smashing ROTC is not relevant. What's the use of tearing up the damned university? Hell, the university is suffering, too."

A lot of blacks agreed. If the government, in reaction to campus turmoil, should drastically slash funds, who would be hurt the worst? Surely not the "white cats" who could shave off their beards tomorrow, don neckties, and go to work for the very corporate power structure they claim to condemn. No, the chief victim would be the black student who can't change his color and who lacks the MCWASP's family financial backing and educational background. The first slashes would come in the special remedial education programs for "disadvantaged students," mostly of minority racial extraction.

The split between the radical whites and the blacks grew most evident at the observance of Malcolm X Day, February 21, the fourth anniversary of the assassination of the Black Muslim leader. White radicals demanded that President Johnson close the university for the occasion. Johnson refused, though he did urge students to attend the observance if they wished.

The white radicals lashed out defiantly. They called for a boycott of classes.

"Strike!" they screamed.

"Shut it down!"

The apprehension continued to grow. News reporters, including television cameramen, arrived on the campus to cover the forthcoming violence. Some professors removed important papers and equipment from their offices, just in case.

It was at this point that Patty Thomas wrote a letter to her parents in California, a letter that would represent a milepost in the presidential tenure of Charles Johnson.

Patty, a tall, blue-eyed freshman girl, the product of a private prep school, was scared. Throughout the fall and into the winter quarter she lived in a university dormitory wing that housed eighty girls. Half of them were of minority racial extraction, brought to the campus under the special programs for the "educationally disadvantaged." Hers was the only dormitory on campus with the fifty-fifty racial split.

It was the tensest dormitory on the campus. There had been "incidents." A knife had been flashed. A life had been threatened. For a time, a two-year-old infant lived in the dormitory with its unwed mother, a situation entirely without precedent in the university's history. A mood of apprehension had gripped the dormitory for weeks. Now, on the eve of Malcolm X Day, Patty's letter home captured some of the tension of the moment.

154

... There have been quite a few things building up in me and in the majority of the campus. And that is all the student unrest (in forms of the Black Panthers, Peace and Freedom Party, and SDS). They have really got us (including the administration) scared, which is hard to believe when they represent only 500 people at the most. But I'm including an article which has our acting president going along with the proposed day of tribute to Malcolm X. ... Though he says classes will meet, he also feels people should enter into the activities. ... The general opinion seems to be that these groups are using this Malcolm X Day deal as just an excuse to raise h—— and if possible get the university into an upheaval. ... Even if trouble doesn't exist tomorrow, the tense mood will keep rising until spring break. ... What it all boils down to is that it is very, very possible that we might have another San Francisco State on our hands very soon, especially since it has been reported that outside agitators have been arriving on campus and going to "work."

It is unbelievable what these people are asking for. ... When trouble occurs, like the blowing up of the ROTC building, the attack on the Navy recruiters, and the guy in the SU being jumped by 6 Black Panthers, the Eugene police are called in. And people want this to stop as they don't want to be subject to any means of law and order. If they break a rule or resist the draft it is just fine—they want political amnesty, too ... and the right to possess and use drugs without being subject to imprisonment—oh, sure I—

Patty apparently had a sudden change of thought and went on to another topic. To Patty's parents, the letter virtually exploded right out of its envelope.

Patty attended her classes as usual the following day, Malcolm X Day, as did most other students. Because of the black-white split, the campus emerged with two Malcolm X observances, one white, one black, separate and unequal. One was presented by the Black Student Union (moderate in tone and fairly well attended), the other by white radicals (sparsely attended). The BSU had dissociated itself from the increasing irrationality and paranoia of white radicalism and issued a formal statement saying so: The BSU was not calling for a boycott or strike; it would not support any activities "contrary to the beliefs and ideology of Malcolm X during our tribute to this Black and Shining Prince"—in short, a plea for moderation. One of the BSU members personally delivered the statement to the President's Office.

The day was moderate. The violence never came. "What a bore," complained one of the Portland newsmen. CALM PRE-VAILS ON UO CAMPUS, ran one headline. There was no strike. The white, middle-class radical students did not shut anything down.

Johnson had now made up his mind about the presidency. He wrote to his parents about it and about still another controversy—this one on the campus of another university, Oregon State.

March 2, 1969

Dear folks,

. . . Things have been going along here in their normal hectic fashion—the weeks seem to fly by and the days are never long enough to keep ahead of the ever-growing pile of things that need to be thought about and decided. . . .

Our presidential search committee has been busy at work finding my replacement, and some time ago they asked whether I would be willing to allow my name to be included as a candidate. I told them to look over all the outsiders first and then I'd let them know. The moment of decision arrived last week, after six outside candidates for the job had visited the campus—and I told them I'd be willing to be included. So I'm going to go through the regular committee interviews next week (met with the faculty section of the committee on Saturday).

I can't say I have much of a stake in the outcome—it was a hard decision to give up next year's sabbatical leave and to give up the prospect of book royalties from the next revision of the three texts. Not much economic joy in deciding to try for a position that will represent a substantial cut in income and that leaves little time for anything else, and is full of pressure and frustration. As a matter of fact it's pretty hard to figure out why I should take a crack at it at all.

I guess I find that being in a place where I can make decisions that determine the course of the institution is satisfying, along with the feeling that comes from being at the top of the heap in one's profession. But it won't really be much of a disappointment if they decide on one of the other candidates. The search committee will ultimately recommend three names to the chancellor, and the State Board of Higher Education will make the final decision. I've been in enough hot water during the last eight months and have made some decisions that have not set too well with many citizens around the state—so the State Board may prefer an outsider in the long run. But the decision is out of my hands now, so I can relax and at least not have to worry about whether to throw my name in or not. . . .

We're in the middle of a donnybrook over beards in athletics. The Oregon State football coach ordered one of his Negro varsity to shave off a short, neatly trimmed beard or be off the squad. This being the off season, and the black students feeling that coaches have no right to dictate such personal appearance matters—joined in an organized objection to the decision (very orderly and peaceful—but insistent). The football coach, joined by the basketball coach, made some rather dogmatic statements about rules are rules, and the coach had an absolute right to determine what an athlete wore and how he looked, etc., and the issue was joined. The black athletes at OSU agreed they would not participate in varsity sports—and set out to get support from black students at other Pacific 8 schools. This weekend Washington State and Washington played OSU without their black varsity players . . . we have 4 Negroes on our basketball varsity . . . and have two games scheduled with OSU this next weekend—one on national television. So we are embroiled in their trouble— not enough to keep on top of your own troubles—now we have to take on the troubles of a sister institution. . . . If our black athletes boycott the OSU game we will get walloped. . . . I'm afraid the OSU president is under such pressure from his coaches and outsiders that he's going to make the wrong decision. Oh, for the joys of the presidency when beards become the major educational issue of the day!

Love
Chuck

157

The distinct lack of enthusiasm for the presidency, as evident in this letter, might be seen as a necessary stance. He might, after all, not be offered the position, and he needed to prepare himself emotionally for that possibility. Further, the Presidential Search Committee took the view, tongue in cheek, that anyone who showed too much enthusiasm for so burdened a job in so turbulent an era was demonstrating a lack of mental stability that made him unsuited for the job he sought.

There was only one thing worse than overenthusiasm. That was to submit a formal application for the position—a fatal breach of etiquette roughly comparable to a teenage girl's act of calling boys for dates. The presidential hopeful must always wait to be asked.

In truth, men did seek the job, but they let it be known in more subtle ways, such as having a friend drop a hint to the search committee: "Dr. Blank is an up-and-coming young administrator who ought not to be overlooked." And if Dr. Blank *did* get a call from the search committee, he would, of course, express surprise: "Who, *me?*"

The University of Oregon's Presidential Search Committee compiled its list of 300 names in the traditional way: by soliciting suggestions from the faculty, administration, alumni, students, educational associations, and presidents and administrators of other campuses. At the same time at least 200 of the nation's 2,300 accredited colleges and universities were doing largely the same thing in largely the same way. The lists varied, each institution seeking the man uniquely suited to its peculiar needs, but they also overlapped. Some names turned up on everybody's list, notably that of John W. Gardner, the former Health, Education, and Welfare secretary, who remained prudently aloof from academia's siren call.

Each name was categorized, "A" candidates being judged as the top prospects, "B" as good back-ups. Then came the "more information needed" category, and finally the ignominious "scratch" file. "Local" candidates, members of the university's own faculty and administration such as Charles Johnson, remained in a special "holding" file, to be looked at later while the national search progressed.

In its earliest stages, faced with the massive list of names, the committee did not always need a rational reason for scratching a name. During the weekly meetings, the names of some of the nation's most prominent and promising educational administrators floated by, like a formation of ducks flying overhead. Sometimes a mere offhand remark by a member of the committee—"His wife talks too much"—was the salvo sufficient to send a man's career fluttering earthward, at least so far as the University of Oregon was concerned. By this—and by other, more rational, processes of elimination—the committee narrowed its list down to about twenty survivors, including Johnson.

Johnson remained quiet and aloof when the subject of his presidential aspirations came up. His office staff knew nothing; the secretaries could only guess at the significance of the visits by several members of the Search Committee. They did not ask, and he did not tell them.

Karen, his twenty-year-old daughter, was not so shy. "Hey, Dad, are you gonna be the permanent super-chief of this university?"

"I don't know, Karen."

Karen hoped that he would not try for the presidency, but she "knew" that he would if he got the chance. It was a challenge, and he could not resist a challenge. He was an ambitious man, achievement oriented, just like grandfather, though in different ways.

She also hoped that, if he did try for the presidency, he wouldn't get it. This, of course, was a thought that she could never share with him. Perhaps it was selfish on her part. But she felt that she knew her father pretty well, and she knew that his first love was teaching.

The presidency, after all, was too tension-filled, and he was too sensitive a man. They were a lot alike, Karen and her father. What bothered her, bothered him. And some of the problems of the presidency, the petty attacks from all sides, made her furious. The difference between them was that Karen could freely indulge in table pounding, tears, and even yelling at her best friend. Her father would never do that. He'd keep it all inside.

Karen also "knew" that her father would never be selected president of the university anyway. He was too much a middle-of-the-road man. Too open-minded. Too super-fair. A really cool guy, actually. It would be hard for her to marry, she once confided, because none of the guys she met ever measured up to him. None was ever so open-minded, so fair, so unprejudiced. "Like a question would come up at the breakfast table, and he'd reply, 'Well, I can't say a definite yes, and at the same time I can't say a definite no. So let's talk about it.' " And they would talk about it, and together they'd reach a decision.

But the community, she felt, would call that wishy-washy. Eugene was too conservative, too uptight about the problems on the campus. The rest of the state was even worse. Her dad wasn't going to call in the cops for every two-bit demonstration. He wasn't going to see student blood spilled if he could help it. He was too patient, too much the negotiator. "That man's patience," she once exclaimed with a touch of awe.

And Karen was pretty sure the community wanted blood.

There was this book she was reading. It was John O'Hara's *Elizabeth Appleton,* a novel about life at a small college in Pennsylvania. It was so close to "the real thing" that it frightened her. Elizabeth Appleton was the wife of the college's dean of men, John Appleton, the man considered the logical choice to replace the retiring president. But it was to his disadvantage that he was so logical a choice. He was, like Charles Johnson, a moderate and thoughtful man, no stirring intellectual but a skilled and judicious arbitrator. Like Johnson, he was considered rather unexciting, even a little bland.

Karen saw only two major differences separating the fictional Appleton from the real Johnson. Appleton's wife found him so unexciting that she found herself drawn into an illicit love affair; Karen certainly saw no analogy there. Second, though both men had learned to be more assertive, Appleton managed to explode with such ferocity that he once called his president a son of a bitch. Karen knew her father would never do anything like that.

Karen was not wrong about her father or about the community's lust for blood, as subsequent events would show. But she was wrong in her perception of the kind of president the university would select: the middle-of-the-roader. It was an unwitting move. The turmoil of the times dictated—and the search committee process supported—the selection of *men of low profile*.[1] It wasn't that the committee deliberately sought a middle-of-the-roader; it was merely a matter of survival. Like other search panels, Oregon's search committee had broadened its participation to include students. It had also empaneled three special groups—faculty, students, and administration—to interview each candidate so that no segment of campus opinion might be overlooked. Candidates selected by the Search Committee were then to be screened by the State Board of Higher Education, the group responsible for the final choice.

Which candidate seemed most likely to survive the subtle but deadly crosscurrents of opinion about the kind of man needed to lead the university into the uncertainties of the seventies?

The middle-of-the-roader, of course. The man who pleases everybody, and alienates nobody. He also excites nobody. The mediator rather than the polarizer, the listener rather than the rhetorician, the pragmatist rather than the visionary, the adjudicator rather than the aggressor, the task-oriented manager rather than the eloquent philosopher. It was a trend of the times, the result of the relatively new concept that who is represented on decision-making committees is more important than what is decided.

The university's Presidential Search Committee did not know, of course, that it was looking for such a man. The committee talked extensively about "criteria" for the man being sought as president. He would be a distinguished scholar, a man of attainment in his academic field, a man of statesmanship and integrity and good conscience, a man of financial acumen, a man of skill in communications and public relations, a man of vitality and good health, a man of middle age: roughly between thirty-five and fifty-five.

The committee began to crack jokes about its "criteria." The only man who seemed to fit, said one member, walked this earth some 2,000 years ago, and He probably would have to shave his beard before the board would accept him.

"Whoever our man is," said Chapin Clark, the committee chairman, a slow-talking Kansan of wry humor, "we'll know him immediately. He'll come walking on water, right across the Willamette River and onto the campus."

Each member of the committee knew what he or she wanted in a president. In the end it would be a matter of which flesh-and-blood candidates could attract the necessary majority to get his name on the list of three to five persons to be submitted to the State Board for the final selection. Most of them, inevitably, would be middle-of-the-roaders.

Past experience had shown that most public university presidents came from teaching backgrounds. A 1968 survey[2] indicated that the route to the presidency was first to become a dean, a provost, or a vice-president. Statistically the public university president was a man of fifty-four, with about eleven years of prior administrative experience and another seven years in his presidential position. He had been a full professor, he came from a business or professional family background, and he was a product of rural and small-town America (50% were born in communities of less than 2,500). The presidents came largely from four academic areas: humanities (25%), education (18%), social science (17%), and natural science (14%).

Other studies showed that the pace of academic administration had quickened. The turnover rate had increased. Where in 1960 the average presidential tenure was eleven·years, in 1969 it was seven and falling. This meant that presidential search committees were more active than ever. More persons were being courted with more ardor. And a lot of them were saying "No." They did not want to touch top-level university management in this troubled era and, with the demand for managerial talent at all levels never greater, they didn't have to.

This meant that the Presidential Search Committee had to push its romantic pursuits harder than ever before. No possible candidate, or "nominee," as the committee preferred to call them, should be overlooked.

The local or "inside" candidate—the man like Charles Johnson—always suffered some disadvantage in the process, however. He was like the girl next door: a little too visible to be as glamorous as the candidate across the continent. Indeed, the *acting* presidency was the least glamorous of positions. It was like trial marriage. Barring the occasional Hayakawa, the acting presidency seldom led to the permanent presidency at one's own institution. The odds were that the acting president would be discarded after the trial marriage, used and abused.

The "acting presidency" was in any event a relic of a less hectic era, when it could be assumed that a man who had achieved a college presidency would, barring such misfortunes as being caught at embezzlement or adultery, remain until retirement or death. In the latter case, an "acting president" would take the helm to keep the vessel hove to, while the search for a successor proceeded at a leisurely pace.

The leisurely selection process continued right into the fast-paced multiversity era. Each of the nation's 200 search committees built its list in the usual way, starting from scratch, duplicating effort, and relying to some degree on luck or romantic fantasy, as though fate would somehow bring the campus and its president together. Even after the process grew more unwieldy under the banner of broader participation, the romantic notions prevailed. If, for example, a college made an offer to Candidate #1 and was turned down, it must never let Candidate #2 know of the affair with #1.

It was romantic and unreal, particularly for 1969. Indeed, it was absurd that, in an era when campuses were splitting apart from burgeoning enrollments, student turmoil, and angry citizen reaction, committees should play such dainty drop-the-handkerchief games while someone—Charles Johnson and men like him—tried to hold everything together.

Such procedures as "grooming" men for the presidency, or keeping a systematic eye on the nation's college executive talent pool, or (God forbid!) employing an executive recruiting firm were considered authoritarian, unthinkable, and gauche, something corporate business might pull. It could and should never happen in the polite society of the university campus. Meanwhile the university, in terms of its management, grew as unwieldy as an elephant. And the student-faculty-public perceptions of it—as manifested in the presidential selection process—were every bit as keen as the proverbial blind men's descriptions.

The president was not, of course, the only administrator traditionally chosen by the search committee process. One U.O. committee, searching for a dean of a professional school, calculated that the process cost $30,000, including direct costs of $2,200 for telephones and transportation, and $27,800 in indirect costs, primarily the two and one-half man-years of time invested by faculty and students serving on the committee.[3] This committee was then turned down by both of its two choices for the job and wound up approving the appointment of its own chairman to the deanship. One of the two authors of a report on that committee's work concluded that "more research is needed" on college management recruiting—a not inappropriate use of that academic cliché.

Charles Johnson's first experience with a search committee came in 1957. Two members of a committee seeking a dean for the university's School of Business Administration, in which Johnson had been a professor for six years, visited him at his home. They asked if they might have his permission to present his name to the committee. Johnson, then thirty-six and deeply involved with his first book, declined. Later, at a party, he heard his friend and fellow business teacher, Mark Greene, comment, "Why would anybody want to be a dean? All a dean ever does is make sure the johns are stocked with toilet paper and the secretaries are stocked with carbon paper."

"Yeah," said Johnson, "that's about the way I look at it."

Johnson was not troubled again by a U.O. search committee until 1962. By then he'd assumed a minor administrative post, head of the Business School's eight-man Department of

Accounting and Business Statistics. He'd also been elected by faculty vote to the university's Advisory Council, entrenching himself as a member of the university's Establishment. He was re-elected to the Advisory Council and served the second year as its chairman.

By 1962 he had established himself as a broad-gauged man, a dependable leader, quietly impressive, scrupulously open-minded—so open-minded that a fellow Advisory Council member, Francis Reithel, a chemistry professor, was moved to remark: "Goddammit, Chuck, what you need are some good prejudices." A man without good prejudices, Reithel explained, is a man who might appear to be without enthusiasm and verve.

Yet the increasing complexities of educational management seemed certain to demand a man of Johnson's qualities one day, largely *because* of his lack of prejudice on a campus where opinions grew increasingly divergent. But it was a spectacle of some note to witness Johnson's selection as dean of the College of Liberal Arts. The college, after all, was populated by some of the most uniquely diverse and independent thinkers imaginable, a collection of prima donnas and dilettantes ranging from the molecular biologist to the classical linguist. What was the country boy from Wyoming, the accountant, the professor of business, doing in such esoteric and intellectually sophisticated company as this?

The explanation rested in the occult machinations of campus politics. As the search for a dean progressed, it became clear that the search committee and President Flemming could not agree on the suitability of several candidates. Flemming appeared to want an "inside" man, (i.e., a member of U.O.'s own faculty), the committee appeared to want an outsider. Flemming apparently had a particular man in mind, a man over whom committee opinion was sharply divided.

The deadlock was broken by a simple expedient. If the president wanted an "inside" man, perhaps one could be found. The chairman and the vice chairman of the search committee, Ivan Niven, a math professor, and Francis Reithel, the chemistry professor, met one afternoon in Niven's office. They

165

combed through the faculty roster, department by department, name by name. They stopped when they reached the name Charles E. Johnson.

Chuck Johnson?

He was the man everybody liked and respected and nobody detested. The man without prejudice. The dark-horse candidate. The compromise. The committee interviewed Johnson and reacted favorably. So did Arthur Flemming. There remained only one hurdle: Kester Svendsen, the brilliant, outspoken, irascible head of the English Department, a man with immense campus political clout. Would he approve? He was quoted as saying, "I never thought I'd see the day that you could turn to someone from the Business School for the deanship of Liberal Arts. But if it has to be, I can think of no one better than Chuck Johnson." With that endorsement, and with no other candidates on the horizon on whom the committee and the president could agree unanimously, Johnson's appointment was assured.

Johnson accepted the appointment, having by now tempered his harsh views on academic administration. To become a dean was no longer unthinkable. It was, he confided, a high honor to be chosen by one's colleagues for such a position—a little like the practice of "more primitive but no less uncivilized tribes who chose from among their members one to be sacrificed to the gods by being thrown into a volcano or burned at the stake."

It was as dean that Johnson gained his reputation for patient, calm, deliberative management; he was "unflappable." True, some professors within the college claimed to see in him a lack of creative vision and intellectual excitement. He was too much the captain of an airliner, a man of prudence and caution, forever monitoring his statistical instruments. Some professors would have preferred a pilot who flew intellectual loops and barrel rolls, so long as they were flown in the right direction. Typically, they seldom agreed on what that direction should be.

It was Johnson's calmness and open-mindedness—plus a conscious effort to block other supposedly less open-minded individuals from access to the presidential chair—that prompted the Advisory Council to endorse Johnson unanimously for the interim presidency in 1968. No other person was considered. When President Flemming, Chancellor Lieuallen, and members of the State Board added their unanimous endorsement, the appointment was official, without benefit of search committee.

The *Register-Guard* suggested editorially that the "acting" be erased from the title and thus have the search over and done. The only other person mentioned prominently for the presidency at the time was Robert D. Clark, the former dean who had become the president of San Jose State. Clark had wide faculty support.

But the search went on, and eventually Charles Johnson appeared before the committee. His candor never showed more dramatically than during the interview. He sat calmly at the end of the conference table, hands resting on the table, and he spoke without notes.

"If I were a search committee interviewing a candidate for the presidency," he said, "the first thing I'd want to know is, 'Why in the world do you want to be a university president?' It's a question I've asked myself many times. I'm not sure I can give you a convincing answer."

He talked of the satisfaction in being in a position of making decisions in an institution where the big social crosscurrents were being monitored. Whoever helped to chart the course of the institution had at least some small impact on the destiny of society.

He openly listed his strengths and weaknesses. He had no national reputation as an educational administrator, he said. "The name Charles Johnson is not going to shake any rafters in Washington." He also lacked flair in the art of political manipulation, he said.

"I recognize its importance," he added. "I know that a university president has to do a certain amount of politicking and buttering up and backslapping, but I frankly don't feel very comfortable in this role. It's not my strong point."

As strong points he listed three. He had the ability to be

"hard-headed but fair" in establishing budgetary priorities, he said. Second, he had had a good deal of experience and background in business management theories and practices. And third, he felt he had the ability to achieve rapport with various groups, the students, the faculty, and in particular the alumni and general public.

He talked of the presidency as the point where diffused and divergent ideas come together. The role of the university, he said, was "learning," which included teaching, research, and public service.

Yes, he said, responding to a question, he saw the need for "defining the lines of authority" in the university's administration. Yes, he saw the need for administrative reorganization. Yes, the selection of administrative staff was a crucial problem. No, he could not be more specific at this point, but he had in mind some kind of structure involving the appointment of several vice-presidents to whom he would delegate major responsibility.

One committee member said, "This may seem like an impossible question, but—"

"Don't apologize," interjected Johnson. "All the questions that come to the president's desk are impossible. If they weren't, they'd have been solved long ago."

"—I know you've talked about the grape decision many times before, but—"

Johnson spoke frankly. "I won't put up much of a defense for my administrative skill in handling that case," he said. "I'm sure a wiser head might have steered another course. There are several things I would do differently had I the chance to go that route again." He recounted the sequence of events, but he did not say what he would have done differently the second time around, nor was he asked. "I believe," Johnson continued, "that a university should go a fair distance in attempting to respond wherever it can to the desire of students to make personal commitments on controversial issues."

After he'd met with the committee and with the student, faculty, and administrative panels, the reactions came in. He was clearly the Number One choice of the administrative panel. He was universally the Number Two choice of the other two panels, but members of those panels expressed no unanimous agreement on their first choices.

The administrators saw in him the conscientious manager, calmly meeting the bizarre crises that beset the campus almost daily, basing decisions on principle and relevant evidence.

The faculty saw in him candor, decency, honesty, lucidity, empathy. He was efficient, sympathetic, tireless, sensible, and methodical. But such qualities did not outweigh what one professor called his "naïveté and lack of imagination." He had no particular "dream" he'd like to see implemented, said another. At least his grammar had improved, noted a third. He said he'd noticed only one grammatical mistake in the whole of Johnson's presentation, "and a fairly common one at that."

The student panel was largely noncommittal, a paradox to those who had read in the papers that the students were trying to take over the campus. The students preferred to write academic analyses of each candidate rather than express strong preferences. When the students did reveal choices, they placed Johnson a strong second to Harrison Scott Brown, a charismatic scientist from California. But out of the student panel came some unusually perceptive comments. One coed, for example, expressed the fear that Johnson, in his scrupulously open-minded procedures, might be "ripped apart" by the many vicious power factions operating on the campus.

The Search Committee itself seemed split on Johnson. Indeed, the committee seemed sharply split ideologically. At least that was the perception reported back to the State Board of Higher Education by the two members who served with the Search Committee, Elizabeth Johnson and Charles Holloway.

Charles Johnson, the committee generally agreed, had done a conscientious job. But in doing so, he had drawn down his bank account of goodwill. The public rancor over his controversial decisions would damage the university were he to be appointed. A further weakness was the self-admitted lack of clout in helping the university obtain federal grants.

It came down to an immense irony: the very decisions that made Johnson worthy of consideration—his courageous stands on free speech, individual rights, and due process procedures— made him so controversial that his appointment would be dangerous from the standpoint of public acceptability. But, as someone pointed out, he had made the right decisions. Was he to be punished for being right?

In the end the committee settled on the names of four candidates to present to the State Board of Higher Education:

Harrison Scott Brown, fifty-one, a charming and dynamic man, an author and nationally known geochemist at the California Institute of Technology.

Dale Raymond Corson, fifty-four, a low-keyed administrator from Cornell University, a physicist of national reputation, a provost at Cornell since 1963.

John Alpha (as he shall be known here), an administrator at a California institution of higher education.

Charles Ellicott Johnson, forty-eight, acting president of the University of Oregon.

Conspicuous by its absence was the name of Robert D. Clark, the former U.O. dean. Clark, born in March 1910, was almost fifty-nine, and the committee had been rigid in observing its age criterion: thirty-five to fifty-five or, "at the outside, perhaps fifty-seven for an outstanding candidate."

With each name went a lengthy commentary setting forth the committee's arguments in support of the candidate. Of Charles Johnson the committee said, in part:

DR. CHARLES ELLICOTT JOHNSON

In conducting a nation-wide search . . . the committee has been mindful of the unique qualities of its "local" nominee, Dr. Charles E. Johnson. . . . During the months that the search was continuing, Dr. Johnson has impressed the committee with his skilled and courageous administration under pressures that might have dismayed, even shattered, a lesser man. . . .

Dr. Johnson has . . . demonstrated a remarkable ability to cope decisively with a variety of problems, many of which he inherited on assuming office. He has worked effectively with diverse and occasionally hostile constituencies. To the extent that he has had exposure to these groups . . . he has demonstrated a unique ability to get them working together. . . . Unsolicited documents sent to the committee by various individuals and groups attest to the fact. . . .

The committee urges the State Board to take careful note of such testimony because the committee recognizes the fact that the public sometimes has reacted critically to unpopular decisions the president has had to make. . . . The committee is pleased with the manner in which Dr. Johnson has "matured" in office. Dr. Johnson has had to make more hard decisions—controversial decisions with great public visibility—in his eight months in office than have many presidents over a period of years. . . . The committee hopes that the State Board will not attach undue importance to the question of "outside acceptability." . . . Given time and exposure, Dr. Johnson could give much impetus to improving the university's image around the state. His record as acting president indicates a remarkable ability to bring order to the sometimes chaotic conditions of university life today. . . .

Twelve:
On the Beach

"Oh, by the way," said the acting president, leaning back in his chair with a smile on his face. His tone was casual, as though what he was about to say could be little more than incidental intelligence. Yet his family and colleagues had learned to recognize this opening as possibly the start of something big. He had used it in proposing marriage and in announcing an administrative promotion, and if he knew the world was coming to an end tomorrow, that probably would be the way he'd break the news.

He was talking with Bill Blevins, his staff assistant, a soft-spoken man of thirty-two who had agreed to work with Johnson through the interim year. Blevins and Johnson were alike in many ways, both intense, sensitive men beneath calm exteriors. Blevins's role was to monitor the presidential paper work, to unburden the president of minor details and tasks, to expedite presidential decisions, and, if possible, "to keep the students off the president's back," as Blevins expressed it.

With a background in student personnel work, Blevins had appropriated the latter role for himself. He knew Johnson enjoyed working with students. He also knew that, quite aside from the problems of militancy, students could overwhelm a president by their sheer numbers. It was Blevins who had intercepted a notoriously militant Black Panther who demanded to see the president immediately to arrange a personal loan— something he said he'd done earlier with Flemming. "This is no longer the super-financial aids office," said Blevins, sending the young man away. And it was Blevins who, confronted by the outrageous demand of a student group, had retorted with quiet dignity, "You're nuts."

It was Blevins who, among all the Johnson administrators, could get away with that kind of talk, even gain respect for it. Both Johnson and Blevins worked earnestly to see that the students—an element of campus society too easily brushed aside by busy administrators—got a break. Both men gained reputations for candor and honesty. Some student leaders began to look back on Arthur Flemming as something of a shrewd manipulator by contrast.

Johnson's "by the way" interjection did not seem, at the time, of earthshaking importance.

"Jeanne and I are going to the coast this weekend," he told Blevins. "We're taking Kylene along."

"That's great," said Blevins. "I'm glad you can get away, and I'm sure we can keep things from falling apart while you're gone."

"How would you and your wife like to join us? We're using Mark Greene's beach cabin. It's big enough for all of us."

Blevins was a little flustered. "Well, gosh, ah, we'd really enjoy doing that—"

"Fine."

"—Just let me check with Marcia and I'll get back to you. . . . I don't know, I mean, this is such a rare occasion for you to get away like this. Are you sure you wouldn't rather get away just with your own family? I mean we'd love to go, but—"

"We all need a break," said Johnson.

He explained that next week's meeting of the State Board would be held at Oregon State's Marine Science Center on the coast. It provided a unique opportunity for the two families to spend the weekend at the beach. Afterwards, Johnson would go on to the meeting while Blevins took everyone else back to Eugene. Then they would feel refreshed the following week, ready to tackle the nagging budgeting problems for next year. Some tough choices on financial priorities awaited his action.

But next week would be soon enough for that. For now he preferred to think only of the coast, the miles of sandy beach, the cozy evenings beside the fireplace within earshot of the Pacific Ocean's awesome roar. And for once there seemed to be no crisis imminent on the campus. This time the crisis was somewhere else—at Corvallis, forty miles to the north, where Oregon State University seethed in the wake of the coach's order that a black football player shave off his beard. It had touched off a tense racial situation in a tiny community that had not seen race problems before. Johnson was sympathetic, but it was still Oregon State's problem, not his.

"This is a perfect time to get away," said Johnson.

"Sounds great," said Blevins.

From all accounts, the situation at Oregon State was deteriorating. Leaders of the U.O.'s black students prevailed on Johnson to "straighten out those cats" at Oregon State. Johnson enjoyed relatively good relations with Oregon's 300-member black student population, partly the result of his "hair" decision, but also the result of Flemming-initiated programs to combat racism. As a result of black demands the previous spring, Flemming had appointed a committee on racism. Out of this came such innovations as the hiring of a black assistant football coach, a black financial aids director, and encouragement of special projects for minority groups. Johnson continued to encourage these programs, though he was candid with the leaders of the minority groups: the university was entering an era of declining financial resources. It was another of the financial problems that nagged at him through the year. Yet the blacks seemed reasonably patient and understanding.

They had less patience with the problems at Oregon State. Members of the U.O. Black Student Union declared angrily that their black brothers at Oregon State had "once again been

175

backed up against the wall by an overt display of white racism,"
and that they planned to support them "by any means necessary." They asked Johnson to intercede. What, asked Johnson,
was he expected to do?

Speak up, came the answer. Condemn racism. Call the Man at
Oregon State. Call President Jensen.

"Okay, I could really shoot off my mouth," said Johnson.
"But let's look at it from Jim Jensen's point of view. If I were
in his shoes, I don't think I'd want some other president
interfering and making things more difficult."

"But it's not just an Oregon State problem," Johnson was
told. "It affects blacks everywhere. It affects us right here on
our own campus. What they're doing at Oregon State is wrong,
and in the end this campus and all the others in the Pac-Eight
conference could blow up."

Johnson finally did call Jensen, sympathizing with the problem, offering to be of assistance. Jensen's response was cordial,
but he made it clear that Oregon State would try to handle its
own problems. Johnson put down the phone wishing he had not
made the call.

By midweek prior to the proposed beach trip, Oregon State's
blacks—about fifty of them—had dramatically walked off the
campus, vowing never to return. It began to look as if the
problem would spread. Black players from Washington and
Washington State had boycotted their basketball games with
Oregon State the previous weekend; now Oregon's four black
players planned to do the same at the two forthcoming Oregon-
Oregon State games, the first at Corvallis, the second a televised
game at Eugene. Militant white students, according to rumor,
planned to disrupt the televised game. A lot of "long-haired
freaks" were reportedly obtaining game tickets with the avowed
intent of leaving the game in protest. By Thursday, student
government had become involved. The student body president,
Dick Jones, planned to take charge of a "controlled demonstration" just prior to the game.

"If anybody can pull that off, Dick Jones can," Johnson told
Blevins.

"I'm wondering," said Blevins, "whether we should still try to go to the beach this weekend in the light of this basketball situation."

"We're going." Johnson was emphatic. "We get away from the campus so rarely, nothing is going to interfere with our going to the beach this weekend."

But the basketball problem still rode uneasily in his mind as Johnson left Friday for the beach with Jeanne and Kylene. He had approved the concept of a "controlled demonstration," with details to be worked out by a committee. He had done so over the protest of the athletic department, whose acting director, Norval Ritchey, made it clear that he considered it a foolish move. Athletics, he said, ought to remain aloof from political and social manipulation. Ritchey said he could not imagine a situation more potentially explosive. Sending a bunch of long-haired freaks out to demonstrate in front of an emotional crowd of eight or ten thousand basketball fans was roughly equivalent to dropping a lighted match in a gas tank.

"But what are the alternatives?" Johnson asked.

Cancel the game? Unthinkable. "We're determined to play that game," said Ritchey, "even if we have to play it at midnight or 1:00 a.m."

Let the irresponsible radical fringes take over? Johnson felt pretty sure, by the reports from student leaders, that this would happen, and it didn't take much imagination to picture the uncontrolled melee that might result.

The "controlled" demonstration made eminently more sense. Johnson obviously had more faith in the student body president than did the athletic department. If Dick Jones could lead a group of nonviolent demonstrators onto the floor, deliver a calm and rational message, and get them off before game time, it might demonstrate that student leadership *could* act responsibly. "Give me five minutes," Jones had said, "that's all I need." Johnson suspected that Jones had headed off student disruptions in the past, and he was equally convinced that Jones was the key to avoiding trouble this weekend. It was an example of what he'd been saying all along: give students responsibility and chances are they would live up to that responsibility.

The evidence through the year showed that, despite all the radical rhetoric, the majority of "active" students were interested in reform, not revolution. Most students, in fact, were apathetic; only 3,500 out of 14,000 had voted in the last couple of student elections, for example, even though some interesting issues were on the ballots. In one "referendum" (advisory poll), students had voted two-to-one to keep ROTC and military recruiting on the campus. A student political party with a "moderate reform" platform had made an almost clean sweep in the election for student senate positions, soundly defeating the radical Peace and Freedom movement.

At the beach, the acting president played tag with the surf, which ran heavy from seas still riled up from a storm a few days earlier. Waves crashed against offshore rocks with explosive anger, bursting into giant blossoms of spray. Clad in an old sweatshirt and pants tucked inside rubber boots, Johnson easily assumed the role of beachcomber. The group found two glass floats, prized possessions that had escaped from Japanese fishermen months, perhaps years, before and had floated across the Pacific with the Japanese current, finally to be driven up on the beach by the spring storms.

Kylene tossed a Frisbee to him, and he ran to catch it, a lumbering, heavy-gaited run, retrieving it from the surf. He flipped it downwind, and it sailed straight over the head of his wife, Jeanne, the intended recipient.

"Can we play games tonight?" asked Kylene.

"Sure," he said. He welcomed the opportunity to spend time with his twelve-year-old daughter, the slim and darkly exotic girl with the dimple in her chin, a straight-A student. He was proud of her grades; she was proud of his presidential status, especially when he brought home complimentary tickets to rock concerts on the campus. He gave the tickets to Kylene, and when her friends said, "Wow, where'd you get such great tickets?" she'd reply, "Oh, my dad's the president." He detested rock music, just as he'd always detested her Beatles albums. He said the Beatles sounded like a "truck full of empty milk cans colliding with a bus full of wild ducks."

"Oh, Dad!" she scolded. "Don't be such an old fuddy duddy."

Yet she did not feel the closeness to him that her older sister, Karen, felt. Her relationship with her father was largely superficial—he teased her about her excessively long telephone conversations and her raucous music; she teased him about his baggy pants and the way he piled the food on his plate at mealtime. He just put everything in a towering mound, and she could never understand it—the roast beef first, then the mashed potatoes, then the string beans, and finally the gravy. Any given mouthful might include a little of each. Kylene's habits were more dainty.

They played parlor games that evening, and later, after Kylene and Kara, the Blevins' five-year-old daughter, were asleep in the cabin's loft, Johnson excused himself. He said he was going to take a walk and make a phone call to check up on the plans for Saturday's game. "Chuck, do you have to?" asked Jeanne. "Yeah, I better go."

He called Charles Duncan and learned that Oregon had won the Friday night game, just over, by a score of 71 to 66. Wonder of wonders. The team had done it without using any of its black players, who were boycotting the OSU game. Duncan said the remaining white players seemed determined to win this one for their missing black comrades.

The rest of Duncan's report did not reassure Johnson. The demonstration for Saturday was still scheduled, said Duncan. The athletic department was still unhappy. "What about my pre-game warmup?" demanded coach Steve Belko. He was told he would have to give that up, but so would the Oregon State team. If the demonstrators didn't get off the floor by game time, as Dick Jones had promised they would, Duncan was prepared to read the trespass act and have the floor cleared by police. A riot squad would wait out of sight to be called on if trouble developed.

Johnson slept fitfully that night.

179

The conversation during the following day ranged pleasantly over a wide spectrum of trivia. They talked of the weather (clear and brisk and breezy), of travel, of camping, of children. They talked of the ocean's view from the cabin's big picture window. "It's spectacular," said Marcia Blevins, a tall, pleasantly attractive young woman.

Marcia Blevins projected an air of youthful enthusiasm and innocence. At first she was a little awed by the university president, but she found the Johnsons easier to talk to than she'd expected. Something about President Johnson brought her out, perhaps his country boy, pipe-smoking informality. She also liked the way Johnson paid special attention to her daughter, Kara. Yet at times she noticed that he seemed quiet and contemplative, too. When he didn't respond right away to her comments, she sometimes felt compelled to ramble on. When the conversation turned to the basketball game, she could tell that Jeanne Johnson was annoyed that such a problem should plague what had been planned as a carefree weekend.

"It just doesn't seem right," Marcia Blevins said. "I mean, here's this conservative campus at Oregon State where nothing ever happens, at least nothing you read about in the papers. They just go on their merry way oblivious to the problems of society. They could care less about losing all their black students. The football coach won't give an inch because he doesn't have to. Everybody will consider him a big hero, and the University of Oregon will somehow get blamed for the whole mess. Just wait and see. I suppose I shouldn't be talking this way, but it annoys me—"

Johnson was contemplative. "No, please go on. I'm interested in what you have to say."

"Well, the whole point is that this problem will go blundering on. One way or another it's going to come tumbling down on us, not on them. The Legislature and everybody else will pat them on their heads and say, 'Well done, Oregon State. You really know how to take care of those uppity black kids. Just throw them off the campus—that solves all the problems.' So in the end Oregon State will come out stronger in their narrow-mindedness than we do in trying to be understanding and conciliatory."

Both Johnson and Blevins remained ominously silent. She felt suddenly uneasy. "I hope I haven't said too much—"

"No, no," said Johnson. "You have some good points. You may be right."

"Well, it just doesn't seem right," she said. "We try so hard to work with the social problems, and all we ever get for our trouble is a black eye."

"Jim Jensen is under a lot of pressure," Johnson said. "In some ways the pressures are more intense over there because the position's more entrenched. Oregon State has always been the 'pure sister,' and heaven help her if that image of purity gets besmirched."

"Hey," said Blevins, "it's time for the game. Let's see if we can pick it up on the radio."

The game was in progress when they finally tuned it in. Oregon was behind and continued to lag behind, finally losing 66 to 57. Again the blacks did not play, and the radio announcer made occasional references to "the demonstration," but he remained agonizingly vague about it.

"I wonder if I ought to call," Johnson said.

"No, Chuck, don't," said Jeanne.

On Sunday morning—he hadn't slept very well again that night—he was up early. He walked to a nearby store and bought a copy of the *Sunday Oregonian*. Page one contained nothing about any campus demonstration, a good sign (the big news was the continuing earth orbit of Apollo Nine, the modular link-up mission). He turned to the sports page.

EUGENE (Special)—Oregon and Oregon State closed out their basketball season here Saturday afternoon with the Beavers winning the televised Pacific Athletic Conference clash, 66-57, but a noisy prologue by a mob of student demonstrators almost ruined the matinee show.

The protestors, clamoring for individual rights and shouting support of the Black Student Union boycott at Oregon State, assembled by permission of the University of Oregon Administration on the McArthur Court floor and heard Dick Jones . . . plead for human rights.

Although his talk drew some heckling response, he did complete it and then asked the protestors to leave the arena and carry their cause elsewhere.

But, after the sit-in had broken up, the floor was littered with smashed raw eggs.

A mop-up crew was quickly recruited and the floor eventually cleaned of the sticky mess, but judging from the mood of the 7,500 fans in attendance, it would have been hazardous for the demonstrators to return. . . .

Another story gave more details of what it called a "short but serious and orderly" demonstration by some 500 students; Dick Jones had been "hooted down" eleven times, but managed to speak: "We have gathered here today and sat down to show our black brothers our respect of human rights and black culture." No blacks were among the demonstrators. Jones concluded, "We are going to leave now in peace. We are going to leave anger here and be thankful for this lovely day."

Johnson put the paper down. He looked pale for reasons, as it turned out, that had nothing to do with the demonstration or the news account. He'd been feeling "kind of rocky," all weekend, he said. He'd taken aspirin earlier that morning with little effect. He wasn't sure he should go on to the State Board meeting. Jeanne, too, confessed that she had not felt well through the weekend.

"Bill, maybe I'll send you to the board meeting."

"I'll be glad to go," said Blevins, "except there's one problem. I didn't bring a suit. All I've got are beach clothes."

"Well, I'll go."

"No, you shouldn't go if you don't feel well. I'll be glad to go—"

"No, I may just go. You can take Ky back with you, and Jeanne can drive me to Newport for the meeting."

It was a meeting he didn't want to miss. Among the topics to be discussed informally that evening was the implementation of a policy on student governance adopted by the board last December. The whole gamut of questions about student rights, disruptions, and legal sanctions to be applied in the case of disturbances would be discussed. No doubt the University of Oregon—the "bad sister"—would be the center of discussion, particularly in the light of yesterday's sit-in. He'd better be there to defend his decisions.

"I think I'll go," he said.

He felt worse by the time Jeanne had driven him to the motel at Newport. He guessed that he had the Hong Kong flu. What irony. The flu epidemic ran through December and January. Why was he getting it now, in March? What rotten luck. Not only would he have to miss the board meeting, but if he didn't get back on his feet soon, the important decisions about the budget would be delayed. He could scarcely afford to get sick now.

They stayed overnight at the motel, with only a bottle of orange soda for supper. On Monday he felt worse. Jeanne felt a little better. She got him into the car about noon and took the wheel for the 95-mile drive to Eugene.

En route she noticed tears streaming down his face.

Thirteen:
Old Problems

He couldn't catch or throw nothing. His dad used to say, "George, take him over there and see if you can't teach him how to throw a ball so that maybe when he gets a little higher in school he'll be able to play on the team." I'd say, "Okay," and I'd take him over to the vacant lot. But it didn't work. He wasn't the athletic type a bit. He was sort of sickly, like I guess you'd say kind of fragile-like. He could never catch a ball right or bat very good. I remember I always had to take him on my side. We'd choose up sides for baseball or football. Nobody would want him to play on their side because he couldn't catch very good, you know? I just about had to take him on my side. So his dad, he'd be out there watching, so I'd make him feel good by heaving Chuck a pass once in a while. I don't think Chuck could see too good. I mean he wore pretty heavy glasses as I remember. He was a very good friend of mine.[1]

[GEORGE WHITE, 1971]

After he returned from the beach, Johnson was in bed for a week. He ran a high temperature, ate little, lost fifteen pounds, refused to see a doctor, and frequently shed tears. Mrs. Johnson assumed that the tears were symptoms of the flu, "a type of

185

flu that affects the nervous system," as she explained it. She was partly right; the tears probably flowed as a result of the flu, although they were not a symptom of it. They were a symptom of anxiety—a manifestation of stress seeping out through emotional defenses weakened by illness. They were, in a way, support for the psychoanalytic concept that when a person is tired, frightened, or ill, "old problems" return to haunt him because the emotional residue of childhood remains with him all his life.

One psychiatrist often dealt with this concept by asking his students at the medical school to look at a case history in a special way: "If you wanted to produce a person who has the kinds of self-attitudes that the patient has, how would you raise him? What kinds of learning and what kinds of experiences would you inject into his childhood?"

What kinds, indeed? Frustration was an old problem with Johnson. So was illness. So was anxiety accompanying the fear of failure. Now, in bed with the flu, perhaps the old bugaboos began to return.

His illness, at the very least, kept him frustratingly removed from the issues he knew were accumulating on the presidential desk: the "impossible" problems that only a president could handle. The fact that the State Board had its eye on him as presidential material made it no easier. It was important to remain at the helm of an institution that through the year kept drifting perilously close to the shoals of disaster. He was the one who knew where those shoals lay. Little time remained to accomplish the goal he'd set at the beginning—to keep the university moving ahead.

It could hardly be guessed, seeing the adult Johnson, that illness had ever been a problem. He took pride in his good health, as shown by his infrequent medical consultations, a mere half-dozen visits in sixteen years. But he had developed a stubborn perverseness in his character, often rising up to slay some personal monster by devious means. He reacted to his strict Methodist upbringing by attending church irregularly as an adult, then, finally, giving it up altogether. He reacted to his parents' drinking and smoking prohibitions by starting to smoke a pipe in college and drinking moderately through adult life, two facts he kept hidden from his parents. When they came to visit in later years, the pipe and the whiskey disappeared from sight. It was logical, then, for him to react to a series of debilitating childhood illnesses like the ninety-seven pound weakling signing up for the muscle-building course. He maintained a basic aversion to medicine and doctors; he believed that nature, given time, would cure all ills. As an adult he exuded a robust vigor through jogging, tennis, and calisthenics that belied his sickly childhood.

As a boy he had fallen prey to most of the childhood diseases circulating through town. A simple cold invariably brought him down with all its complications: bronchitis and even pneumonia. His towering height, his awkwardness, and his illnesses kept him from excelling in athletics, an activity that spelled success to a boy growing up in Montana during the thirites. But by the example and teachings of his achievement-oriented father, he could not admit to failure. Failure was for other families; the Johnsons did not fail.

This had been the attitude of Palmer Johnson, Charles's father, a robust man of boundless energy, self-educated, the fourth of nine children born to a pioneer farmer, Charles Marion Johnson, and his wife, Eliza. They had migrated to Wyoming from the Midwest. It was in Wyoming that Palmer met and eventually married Rose Ellicott, one of six daughters (there was only one son) of English immigrants who had farmed and run small businesses in Kansas, Colorado, and finally Wyoming. Rose was a tall (5'8") and pretty girl, though a little awkward, dark-haired, and blue-eyed. She was remembered for her even disposition, her reserve, and her sensitivity. "You could hurt her feelings quite easily," recalled her younger sister, Bessie, "but she'd try not to let on. She was sensitive to other people's feelings. She'd never say anything bad about anybody."

Charles was born in 1920. By the age of five—an age when children are said to have an unusually strong attachment to the parent of the opposite sex (the Freudian Oedipus complex) —Charles had adopted some of Rose's qualities: her reserve, her awkwardness, her even disposition. He was the little man who bravely faced adversity without complaint. He had also absorbed Rose's sensitivity to other's feelings. He worried, for example, about the back pains that accompanied Rose's second pregnancy in 1925.

It was less clear how he reacted deep inside to the tragedy of his mother's death from complications of childbirth. For the reaction was deep within, forever inaccessible to outsiders. She had gone to the hospital talking excitedly of the possibility of a "baby sister for Charles." She did not return. The baby, Barbara, whom Charles visited briefly in the hospital, lived for four days. Then she, too, succumbed to what Palmer Johnson later believed to be blood-type incompatibility from a transfusion of his blood that the doctor had given her.

When Palmer broke the news of the death to his son ("I probably said something like, 'Mama's gone to heaven, son'"), Charles responded with a simple, poignant remark. "Mama's back doesn't hurt anymore." And then he grew quiet.

He seldom, if ever, mentioned his mother again. His silence about her grew conspicuous down through the years. Charles remained noticeably quiet in the months that followed. He tagged behind his father "as though there were a hunger and loneliness in his heart," as Palmer wrote in a letter. Charles frequently asked for a "baby sister," and Palmer had to reply that he couldn't have a baby sister without a mother to care for her.

Charles's health turned worse. He lived with his father in a boarding house in Montana, and he ate all the wrong things: potatoes, gravy, and pastries, skipping fruits and vegetables. He grew increasingly frail. Once he was hospitalized with scarlet fever, another time with pneumonia. Concerned about his health, Palmer sent him to live during the summers with his brother, Kepler, who had married Rose's younger sister, Bessie. Charles continued to spend summers at the Kepler Johnson ranch in Wyoming where he played with his cousin, Vivian, four years younger than he. It was there that Vivian took note of such childhood traits as absentmindedness and a tendency to avoid confrontations. "We never fought," she said. "At least

Chuck didn't fight. I hit him over the head with a breadboard one time. All that happened was that the board broke in two. Chuck just laughed. Sometimes I'd yell at him, and then he just wouldn't play with me. I used to follow along after him saying, 'Oh, come on, I didn't mean it,' and he'd ignore me for a while and go off by himself until he got over it."

It was at the ranch that Charles, tall and awkward at age eleven, climbed atop a woodpile one day. He began a lecture to an audience consisting of a scattering of pigs and chickens and seven-year-old Vivian. The "Lecture on the Woodpile" would be remembered for its "orating, preaching, and wild gestures," if not for its substance. It was the first notice the Johnson family had taken of Charles's oratorical skills.

It was at the ranch that Charles also learned to milk cows, ride a horse, slop the hogs, and do other farm chores. There, too, he displayed one memorable outburst of anger when an old sow shook her head and flung some of the slop back in his face.

"You gosh darned pig, you—" he shouted. Vivian could not recall any other occasion when he so blatantly lost his self-control. The summers on the ranch were good for his health; he could drink four glasses of milk at a single sitting, and there was always more. Perhaps, too, Vivian temporarily represented the baby sister that had been denied him. Vivian adored him, eagerly awaiting his arrival each summer. She shed tears at his departure and, as they grew older, she was quite miffed when he began to spend more time with the older men at the ranch.

Palmer Johnson remarried in 1927. Charles's stepmother, Cora, a petite, reserved, fastidious woman from Kansas, was the product of a Methodist upbringing and a graduate of a fundamentalist Methodist college so strict that a classmate was expelled for having attended a dance. A college-trained dietitian, she was immediately appalled by Charles's emaciated appearance. Indeed, for the next ten years she would try desperately to help him regain his health through proper nutrition—frantic attempts inspired by the warnings of two doctors who had examined the boy: *If you don't do something about his poor health, you may lose him.* But Charles did not grow huskier, he merely grew taller. He remained frail and sickly and short-winded throughout his growing years, always frustrated by his failure to excel in athletics.

They hadn't been married a month before Charles began asking for a "baby sister." He fretted through Cora's pregnancy, and when, in 1929, a baby sister, Phyllis, did arrive, his joy overflowed. He rushed home from school daily just to hold her, freely spending his meager allowance to buy her gifts. Phyllis, in contrast to Charles, grew up robust and healthy; destined to become a medical doctor, Phyllis hardly ever got sick.

The family struggled through the Depression, during which Palmer Johnson ran a collection agency in Great Falls, Montana. There was plenty of work for a bill collector during those hard times, but little income. The family spent evenings at home reading and playing games. They reserved one evening each week for "family night" where the games ranged from chess to dominoes. Christmases were long on tradition and short on cash: Phyllis would remember them fondly years afterwards, even the time when the value of all the presents exchanged totaled only sixty cents. Presents were opened carefully and deliberately, with each ecstatic moment savored, and the process itself consumed the better part of Christmas Day. The hard part was facing school friends later: "Is that all you got for Christmas?"

Beneath his hard, driving exterior, Palmer Johnson harbored a sentimental streak, and the Christmas tradition was an example of it. Another, was his writing of verse, a trait picked up by Charles at the age of ten or eleven. Some of Charles's private, heretofore inaccessible feelings began to show up in writing.

JUST ME

I wish I had a bycicle,
Like other boys I see,
But even if they have one,
I'm glad that I'm just me.

Even though I'm not as fortunate,
As other boys I see,
And haven't got expensive toys,
I'm glad that I'm just me.

The verse represented a concept taught to him by the elder Johnson, something Phyllis later called the "yes-we're-different-be-glad" attitude. Palmer Johnson was also exacting and precise. He taught his son the value of money by giving him allowances from age seven on. Later, he showed Charles an elementary bookkeeping system so that he could keep track of every expenditure. Between April 30, 1936, and April 30, 1937, according to the figures, Charles had spent $142.00. His entire fiscal year emerged from the neat columns of figures on the big yellow ledger sheet, even down to the $0.25 budgeted for his annual supply of shoelaces (actual expenses: $0.45) and the $5.50 budgeted for cleaning bills (actual expenses: $2.25). He had budgeted $5.00 for "emergencies," of which he had two: one in July, "tore good pants" ($0.50), the other in November, "lost gloves" ($1.98).

Cora Johnson contributed to the boy's concern for people. In college, she had served with the race commission of the YWCA, and she later discussed with Charles the plight of some of the Negro girls in that group. One of them, a cultured and refined girl, had suffered a humiliating series of insults during a trip through the South. And Charles never forgot his Negro friend, George White, who displayed such a big-hearted concern for the gawky kid who "couldn't catch or throw nothing."

Perhaps it was George who inspired Charles to write his first book, *The One and Only* ("copywrighted August 25, 1933"), a few days before his thirteenth birthday. The book consisted of six typewritten pages sandwiched between cardboard covers. Its main feature was a short story entitled "Arnold's Chance," by Charles Johnson.

It was a childish story.[2] Yet it was a significant demonstration of its author's childhood concern for members of minority groups at a time when racial prejudice was not a

191

fashionable topic of discussion in Montana. The plot centered on a bigoted football coach who denies a talented Negro a chance to play on the high school's championship football team. Coach Freeman, goes the story, "used to have a prejudice against Negroes. A Negro in his mind was way below 'whites.' Since he has changed." At a crucial moment in an important game, Coach Freeman, beset by player injuries, has no choice but to let Arnold, the Negro, go in as fullback. Arnold makes six yards on his first play but gets up limping. He is assigned to take the ball again. "Oh, Lord," he whispers to himself, "help me to make it." He does make it, the game-tying touchdown, in one final, desperate leap, with the whole team putting its collective strength behind him. Arnold is knocked unconscious. The story ends: "When he came to a lot of noise was from the grandstand and Freeman was leaning over him. 'Did we win?' asked Arnold. 'Yes,' replied Freeman. 'Pug kicked over the goal.' 'God answered my prayer,' Arnold said joyfully. Coach Freeman had learned his lesson."

Whatever their concern for people, the Johnsons believed in striving to get ahead in life. Palmer vowed that his children would work for good grades and would go to college. It was his lack of a college education, he freely admitted, that kept the family poor. It accounted for Charles's meager allowance and for the family's lack of a car during the early 1930s. "Anybody could see," said Palmer in retrospect, "that if I'd had a college education we could have afforded anything." In his mind education was a means to an end, and the end was material affluence. He then dramatized his point when, during Charles's teen years, he studied the correspondence courses to become a lawyer and a CPA—and to become moderately wealthy.

Rising to the expectations of so talented a father may have caused Charles some strain. At least he showed some curious affectations as he grew older. Though he retained an element of reserve, he presented an exterior facade of increasingly light-hearted gaiety. His self-effacing humor had reached the point of adolescent clownishness. And his awkwardness had reached a point of seeming carelessness. He was accident prone to an alarming degree. He was constantly stumbling and falling, tearing his trousers or breaking his glasses, a point he once touched on through verse.

Oh how I hate to wear glasses
It ain't no fun at all
You have to be so careful
Not to stumble or to fall

And when you break your glasses
Your parents they have fits.
And throw their hands up in despair
And say, "There goes my 40 bits. . . .

The accidents became more severe. Once he thrust his bare foot onto a rusty nail. Another time, while helping a neighbor install storm windows, he fell off the ladder, and the window came crashing down over his head, leaving a nasty gash.

His parents' frequent moves to new neighborhoods further complicated his life. He was always the "new kid" in the block to be tested by the neighborhood bullies. He was no match for them (but he always got up smiling, according to one contemporary). Palmer Johnson told him, "There's only one way to stop this, son, and that's to defend yourself. Put up a fight. Let them know that this has got to stop." He tried to teach Charles the art of self-defense. Charles didn't like it, but he learned. Mostly he learned to avoid fights whenever he could. He became increasingly skilled in negotiation.

As he tried to avoid confrontation with his peers, he certainly avoided it with his parents. When he was late getting home one evening, he proceeded quietly to his room without dinner. His sister, caught in a similar situation, reacted quite differently. "Well, I'm late," she said boldly. "What are you going to do about it?"

The spanking Phyllis received on that occasion was a rare occurrence. Punishment usually took the form of "natural consequences." As a teenager, Charles once put a fifteen-dollar dent in the rear end of the family car when he backed into a pole. "Well, son," said his father, "when I make mistakes I have to pay for them—and I think you're going to have to pay for this one. If you don't have fifteen dollars now we'll pay for it on the installment plan." It took him most of a year to pay for the damage, but that, said Palmer Johnson, was lesson enough. There was no need to bawl him out.

Charles accepted this dictum without protest. On the surface, at least, he tended to take a mild view of such setbacks. He had few unshakably strong opinions on anything, unlike his father who once said of himself, "I say what I think is right and if you don't like it, well, you're wrong; that's all there is to it." Rather than confront directly so strong a parental figure, Charles Johnson, entering a period of adolescent rebellion, chose more subtle methods.

He started getting poor grades. It started in junior high school where he performed well for teachers he liked and shoddily for those he didn't. Palmer Johnson was appalled by this turn of events. Not only did he remonstrate with his son—*Why did you do so poorly? . . . You can do better. . . . You have to apply yourself more*—but he reinforced his expectations with hard cash: twenty-five cents for each "A" in junior high school, later raised to a dollar in high school. Charles Johnson's response was to come home, clutching his report card, with the cheerful comment: "Well, Dad, I saved you a couple of bucks today."

Cora Johnson applied pressure from another direction. Perhaps she had overreacted to the doctors' warnings that Charles might not survive to adulthood if he did not eat better and get more rest. She said as much in retrospect. But in an era when tuberculosis was a terrifying prospect and antibiotic drugs did not exist, the problems seemed awesome. She tried to get him to bed early, and she administered frequent doses of castor oil, which he hated ("If you'd quit giving me so much of this stuff, I wouldn't grow so tall"). She also tried to limit his involvement with the young people who were members of the Methodist Church's Epworth League.

That he inwardly resented her interference with his activities she had no doubt. She felt it was necessary for his health. The Epworth group had gained a reputation for teenage exuberance. The church that the Johnson family regularly attended represented a liberal branch of Methodist theology in contrast to the fundamentalism that Cora Johnson had known in the past. And the Epworth group was nothing short of radical. The young people pushed for reforms considered shocking to Methodists in the 1930s. They demanded the right to hold dances and roller-skating sessions in the church gym. Aided by a liberal minister ("Better they should do it at the church than somewhere else," he was quoted as saying), the kids won. It did not matter that few of them knew how to dance or that the dance program faltered for lack of interest after two or three sessions. Youth had fought for the good liberal principle and won.

Charles Johnson emerged as a leader in this group, though he was more a mediator than a pusher for reform. Among the reformist leaders were Burt Talcott, a charismatic star athlete destined to become a U.S. congressman, and his younger sister, Ann, slim, tall, attractive, who professed to hate athletics and who was, by her own account, a spirited and mischievous cut-up: "Always the first to throw the spitball."

The divergency of opinion within the league eventually reached the point that a more diplomatic kind of leadership was needed: Charles Johnson was elected president. He'd also been elected president of his senior class in high school. His peers saw in him two major qualities of leadership: his apparent ease in "talking rather than fighting," and his sheer persistence in assuming responsibility and in finishing whatever he started. The latter quality showed in other ways, such as his attainment of scouting's second highest rank, Life Scout. He was always nagged, however, by his failure to attain the highest rank, Eagle Scout, for lack of a single merit badge—one that required athletic abilities in swimming that were beyond his capabilities.

Charles Johnson did not serve in either of the two presidencies to which he had been elected. The Epworth League was, in the eyes of his parents, too active for Charles's frail health. Its parties and sojourns into amateur theatrics were keeping him

up late night after night. Perhaps there were other considerations: his faltering grades, his sloppy study habits, his slouch-
ing posture, his rumored indiscretions involving beer, his
apparent new interest in the opposite sex. His parents sought a
new environment for him.

Burt Talcott's cut-up sister, Ann, always resented what she
viewed as the sudden, inexplicable departure of Chuck Johnson
to the military academy in New Mexico. Not that she claimed
any special interest in him—kids didn't pair off much in those
days. It merely seemed unfair. Chuck Johnson seemed to enjoy
the good times of the Epworth gang; he certainly did not stand
apart from them. He could be as rowdy as the rest. Perhaps
there was truth to her brother's allegation that a "childhood
infatuation" existed between Charles and Ann, a possibility not
denied by her thirty-five years later. She saw him as "good
looking . . . clean-cut . . . a lot of fun . . . a clown." He certainly
was no athlete, and that was good. It infuriated her to witness
her family's adoration of the athletic exploits of her brother,
Burt, whom she alternately loathed and idolized with adolescent fervor.

Not much concrete evidence supported the inference of in-
cipient romantic interest unless one counted the inscription
Charles penned in Ann's high school yearbook in 1936: "To a
darned nice girl—even if you are a Talcott." Devious are the
ways of bashful adolescent boys, however. It was Ann who
received that first letter he wrote shortly after arriving at the
academy in 1937. It was she who agreed to an exchange of
photographs, she who kept up the correspondence through the
year, and she who kept his letters stored in a trunk for three-
and-one-half decades.[3]

Whatever its failure in encouraging romance, the exchange of
letters probably helped to ease his loneliness. At the very least,
Ann's letters were news from home. Perhaps they also gave him
a degree of status among fellow cadets, many of whom were
corresponding with some special Girl Back Home whose pictures they displayed with pride.

Ann sent Charles the picture he'd requested, along with a self-conscious note suggesting that he would surely wish to burn it the moment he saw it. He replied: "I received your letter and also the picture, both of which I enjoyed very much. Of course, I tried to burn the latter, but it must have been made out of asbestos because it just wouldn't ignite (catch on fire to sophomores). Thanks a lot and I promise not to burn them if you send some more. . . ."

If that was a subtle invitation to become more closely involved, Ann Talcott claimed later to have been too naïve to recognize it. She did not send any more pictures. She did continue to write. The letters she received back from him revealed something of an adolescent boy's quest for identity. For one thing, they showed a new interest in scholarship. He wrote of the discipline of the academy: "I am beginning to appreciate (strange as it may seem) the 2 hour night study hall. . . . I am afraid I would never study if left up to my own volition. I study twice as long and hard here as I ever did in G.F."

He made one final attempt to prove himself in athletics. "Believe it or not," he wrote, "I made varsity center on the high school basketball team here! I have been practicing about 1½ hrs a day, and I knew I had improved, but I sure didn't think I'd make varsity. The coach said he's got some of the best material this year he's had for a long time. . . . My only worry is staying on first string. I hope I don't do like C— did last year, be first string for the first game then drop until he only played every other game."

It was an impossible hope. Three months later he wrote that the team had gone on to great glory, winning nine games and losing only three, but that he could share precious little of that glory. "I think I will letter," he wrote, "but I won't have any extra quarters to spare, as I have been warming the bench most of the time."

He had failed again. But overwhelming his disappointment was good news, tucked at the end of the same three-page letter.

> Today I am a man! I was decorated last week with my first medal! It was the medal given for being on the Honor Society, the result of having a Semester Scholastic average of 92 or better. I can't help going around with my chest sticking out, but I guess it will wear off. One thing nice about this school is that very few medals are given and when you do get one it means something.

Charles Johnson had found his niche. Scholarship. What he lacked in physical vigor was compensated for by what he'd come to recognize as an extraordinarily keen mind and highly developed skills in speaking and writing. More important, the achievement was recognized by others and rewarded by something tangible, a medal. Several years would elapse before he would view the life of the mind as anything other than a means to an end. But henceforth his life would be one of achievement rather than of failure. He would go on to graduate cum laude from Minnesota, to rise quickly to the rank of master sergeant in the Army finance corps during World War II, to proceed through graduate school, to write books, to become a respected university professor rather than the spindly kid from Wyoming.[4] Not for a long time—indeed, not until he became a college president—would he encounter the kind of frustration that had plagued him through childhood.

Fourteen:
A Close Vote

He returned to work Monday afternoon, March 17, after being in bed a week with the flu. Did the mystical influences of "old problems," felt but not understood, accompany the acting president back to his desk that afternoon? It seemed likely, viewed in retrospect. Striking parallels existed betwen the frustrations of childhood and those of the acting presidency.

He had been urged to stay home for more rest, for he looked drawn and gaunt and pale. But no stepmother, not even a wife, would decide that for him. *He* would decide. Who, indeed, would dare to tell a university president that it was past his bedtime, that he must get his rest? He tried to resume his old pace.

Another frustration strikingly similar to those of childhood was the creeping black cloud of self-doubt. He had only to look at the letters, the growing pile of complaint letters, to confirm his worst opinion of himself.

It was a joyless world, the university presidency, not a place to be occupied by a man of faltering health and equally shaky self-confidence. Johnson returned to a desk laden with the fetid jetsam of the stormy seas of protest and reaction, curious, twisted documents, swept in from all parts of the state. The letters accumulating on his desk made very clear the view that he was not running the university right. Why did he do so poorly? He must do better. He must try harder. Viewed in retrospect, they must have been devastating letters, smashing through emotional defenses weakened by illness.

The letters talked about the basketball game demonstration, the controlled sit-in that he had allowed to proceed prior to the Oregon State game. True, a few letters congratulated him for allowing students to articulate a legitimate gripe on the race issue. But others warned that he was sitting on a powder keg. The letters expressed the usual dissatisfactions. Ninety-eight percent of the state was "fed up" with the permissiveness of the "present administration," which was furthering, even surpassing, the dreadful record of Arthur Flemming. At The Dalles, a historic little community on the Columbia river, a waypoint on the historic Oregon Trail, mention of the university was said to bring only ridicule. At Oregon City, the end of the Oregon Trail, petitions were circulating: "The conditions you are letting go on at a supposedly institution of higher learning is sickening," a point dutifully agreed to by 134 signers, not one of whom attempted to correct its wretched grammar. The solution, said the writers, was simple. Had the administration taken a *firm stand* on just one of the half-dozen "disgusting events" during the year, the subsequent event would never have happened. But when Coach Arnold—they would not forget Coach Arnold—had tried to take a stand last winter on the haircut issue, the administration did not back him because, in plain words, the administration did not have the *guts*. The black players who boycotted the Oregon State game should have been expelled. Anyone who objected should also be expelled. Blood should flow if necessary. We shall have to fight the anarchists and nihilists eventually; let's do it now and get it over with. Then the problems would cease, and the sovereign state of Oregon could rest in peace for all eternity.

The athletic department seethed in the wake of the basketball demonstration, having reached an "all-time low" in the words of its acting director. The department faced its own peculiarly hostile public: the athletic fan. One report indicated that every individual contacted for contributions for athletic grants-in-aid "was highly disturbed with the lack of direction and total permissiveness of our present administration."

Students exerted pressures in other directions. The Student Senate urged Johnson to cancel all athletic games with Oregon State until its problems of "intolerance and prejudice" were remedied; but the major thrust of student pressures had shifted. Now student leaders were holding mass meetings in support of a popular professor, the irascible and outspoken Arthur Pearl, whose seminars on poverty and on life-styles of the poor bulged with as many as 2,000 students. Pearl had an offer from a Midwestern university that he said he was "tempted to accept" unless the U.O. offered more support "for what I'm trying to do." His name was tied to programs for impoverished students, mostly of minority races. These programs struggled along on a diet of financial malnutrition in the face of tight budgets and vacillating federal support.

"What we want," said a Pearl supporter, "is a public commitment from the administration that's concrete and specific—something the students can hold them to." Students were showing increasing irritation at Johnson's candid response that the university funds were already overcommitted and that he was having a severe problem just making ends meet.

"That's a weak argument," snapped one student leader. "It's all a matter of restructuring priorities."

"Just what *are* the university's priorities?" demanded another student. How could the university justify its recent decision to install artificial turf at the football stadium at a cost of $300,000, but wouldn't spend "a few extra bucks to keep a man like Pearl?"

This grotesque imbalance troubled Johnson. But in plain truth, artificial turf was easy to "sell," and educational programs, particularly minority race programs, were not. Many citizens believed that the university's problems of student turmoil resulted largely from these very programs. Johnson, recognizing the imbalance, had made a special point of insisting that the $300,000 be raised from sources not otherwise available to the university. Specifically, $100,000 came from contributions by athletic fans unlikely to support any cause espoused by Arthur Pearl, $150,000 from local high school districts that contracted to play their football games at the university's stadium rather than build their own, and $50,000 in contributions from the stadium concessionaires.

Johnson was troubled by the plight of the minority programs, and he sought means of increasing their financial support. Once he even solicited the faculty to contribute a day's pay to these programs. But the faculty, like the community, was split sharply. In the face of student demands for the retention of Professor Arthur Pearl, some professors quietly wrote Johnson suggesting that Pearl ought to be wished well on his new job. One professor dreaded the day he foresaw unless the president stood firm: the day promotion of professors was decided in the streets rather than in the faculty committee rooms.

If there were ever a need for a skilled mediator it was now. But the answers, the decisions moved slowly, if at all. The paperwork piled up. For the first time, the office staff began to feel uncomfortable in Johnson's presence without quite knowing why. Partly, it was because so simple a decision as approving a committee appointment—something that required no more than ten seconds in the past—now seemed to take days, coming only after much secretarial prodding. Sometimes beads of perspiration broke out on Johnson's forehead, something they had never noticed before. His secretaries realized that he was smiling less. They had an uneasy feeling that perhaps they were at fault, that they were not performing up to his expectations. But the perceptive observer could detect the president's own expressions of self-doubt, scattered like seeds to the wind. After a particularly virulent meeting with a group of students, Johnson confided to Bill Blevins: "I'm not sure I'm cut out for this confrontation kind of thing." That seemed ironic. It had been Johnson's idea to make decisions in the atmosphere of the "controlled confrontation."

He felt a little more cheerful as he began to regain his strength. He was able to expand his working hours. He took to his home various documents, including the letter from Patty Thomas, the California girl who had written home anxiously about Malcolm X Day. Copies of her letter had navigated a number of channels before washing up on the president's desk, sent there by the president of the Oregon Dad's Club.

Johnson's attempted reply was significant quite aside from the fact that it would be his last attempt to reply to criticism. Its significance lay in his apparent dissatisfaction with what he had written. It lacked the vigor and facile tone of his earlier writings. Even the crossed out passages seemed to reveal difficulty in stating precisely his intended meaning.

Sorry for the delay. . . . I succumbed to the ubiquitous flu bug and have been out of commission for two weeks. . . . Let me say at the outset that I simple do not share his daughter's concern that the University of Oregon is in danger of becoming even a pale version of San Francisco State. Anything, of course, is possible in these times, but the evidence of ~~activities on this campus~~ in terms of the activities on this campus ~~is~~ points strongly to a sense of community and agreement as to the basic commitment among students, faculty, and administration that will simply not allow the small anarchist element to gain the upper hand. . . . The tone of apprehension in the young lady's letter about Malcolm X Day surprised me a bit; ~~it was certainly not shared by her ap~~ we certainly didn't view it as a crisis in any sense of the word. Frankly, I'm not much of an expert on Malcolm X. Since the event I have read several articles about him and find that while his early life and activities were hardly exemplary, in the later stages of his life he ~~became a considerable more fairly more respecable~~ gained more regard as an advocate for the rights of our black population. It ~~was, I~~ may have been, I gather, his move toward a more responsible and moderate position that brought about his assassination. In any case he has become one of the ~~symbols~~ heroic symbols of black students in this country, and I'm willing to respect their feelings on the matter.

He put the letter aside. It would remain forever unfinished. That, too, was significant; he detested leaving anything unfinished.

By the first of April he felt more vigorous, though he still had not regained his full strength nor the fifteen-pound loss of weight. But he impressed the nine members of the Board of Higher Education with his calm, confident demeanor on that day, the occasion of his final interview for the presidency. This board would make the final choice after interviews with the men suggested by the university's Presidential Search Committee.

Johnson told the board largely the same things he'd said to the committee five weeks earlier. He assessed his strengths and weaknesses; he talked of the problems of administration.

"The president, whoever he may be, has simply got to have more help," he said. "I've discovered that I simply cannot find the time to do all the things required of the president." He talked also of his plans for administrative reorganization, some kind of system of vice-presidents.

He made one remark that some members of the board found startling in its candor.

"If I were a member of this board considering candidates for the presidency, I think—all things being equal—that I would tend to prefer a man from the outside."   .

Perhaps he didn't say it precisely that way, though it was the way remembered and recorded in writing by the chairman of the board, J. W. Forrester, the newspaper publisher. Perhaps Johnson felt that all things were not equal. More likely he was merely continuing to be his ingenuous, candid self. The point needed no elaboration. His controversial decisions had soured much of the public. The new president ought to start with a clean slate, his bank account of public goodwill intact.

In contrast to his tranquil demeanor at the interview, Johnson appeared to be "visibly nervous," by one reporter's description, at a news conference afterwards. He perspired heavily under the TV lights. His hands fidgeted with a set of papers. He seemed intensely uncomfortable.

He was asked whether he had actively sought the position of

president. Johnson paused before answering. It was a naïve question. The reporter obviously didn't know the rules of the presidential selection; it was like asking the bride if she had actively chased the groom.

"I don't think being president of the university or any university has ever ranked as the strongest ambition in my life," he said. "But I will say that I am a willing candidate in that I go into it with my eyes wide open."

How would he feel if he were not appointed?

"Well, I think it would be half disappointment and half elation, although relief would probably swamp my disappointment."

It was a curious interview, and the most curious aspect was its very existence. Traditionally boards and search committees operated privately under the strictest security, with no public disclosure of individuals under consideration until the decision had been made. Among the reasons was protection of the stupendous egos of most men of presidential caliber, modesty being a rare virtue in the second-echelon administrative posts that most of them held. These men usually served in sensitive positions of high responsibility. Premature release of their names as candidates could cause them untold embarrassment for three reasons: (1) the likelihood of a public and political controversy surrounding their candidacy, particularly in this age of instant mobs; (2) the damage that might cripple their effectiveness on their home campuses (it was like an errant husband whose wandering eye suddenly becomes known to his wife); and (3) the irrevocable deflation of the egos of those not selected for the jobs. These reasons were so compelling that premature release of a candidate's name almost invariably resulted in that candidate's withdrawing himself from further consideration, like a woman spurned.

But the news media exerted other kinds of pressure. The sleuthing required to determine the names of the major candidates was well within the abilities of the greenest cub reporter. The candidates' identities were common knowledge on the campus. Plenty of "reliable sources" awaited quotation. A single mention of a name by a single medium could cause an avalanche of follow-up stories by competing media until several names were on the public record. To cope with such problems, the board had negotiated with the news media and reached a compromise. In return for media cooperation in keeping the names private, the board would specifically ask each candidate if he wished to acknowledge his candidacy publicly and submit to a press interview.

Of the four men under consideration, two did. The first, Harrison Brown, the geochemist from the California Institute of Technology, was an articulate intellectual of worldwide interests and activities. He had traveled throughout the world to promote scientific exchanges with other countries on behalf of the National Academy of Science. He had authored several nonfiction books of general interest, and he also coauthored a science-fiction novel. He was an editor-at-large for *Saturday Review.* Definitely a man of "high profile."

Charles Johnson, the middle-of-the-roader, the man without guile, was the other man to allow release of his name. "I can't see any reason not to," he said.

Dale Corson, the provost at Cornell, elected to keep confidential his interest in the position. He became the "mystery candidate," as some newsmen called him. Corson was deeply involved in a delicate and unsettled situation at Cornell where President James Perkins was under attack. The problems at Cornell were escalating daily, to culminate in the occupation of Willard Straight Hall by 100 black students. At the time Corson was interviewed by the board, April 1, the famous photo of the black students emerging from the building armed with rifles and bandoliers was a mere three weeks away.

The fourth man, "John Alpha," the California administrator, declined to be interviewed, removing his name from the list. It was an example of a growing disinterest among second-echelon men to try out for the first string. If beleaguered college presidents were resigning with acrimonious commentary about the savage demands of an utterly impossible job, other men were taking note of such comments. Many of them were diverting their careers to other directions.

In selecting one of the three remaining candidates, the eight men and one woman who comprised the Board of Higher Education were exercising an awesome responsibility at least equal to and, perhaps, greater than the board's financial responsibilities. (In earlier years when university presidents held great power, there would have been no hedging on that point.) It was a decision fraught with controversy and pressures, particularly now that two names had become public knowledge. The controversy centered largely on Charles Johnson. He was seen by many members of the State Legislature as the permissive administrator who always took the easy way out in the name of expediency. The legislators didn't hesitate to express these views to any board member who would listen.

The board, however, had zealously guarded its independence from political manipulations down through the years. Comprised of lay citizens appointed by the governor, with jurisdiction over all of the state-supported institutions, it had, indeed, been formed in 1932 largely to keep the variable currents of politics out of public higher education. Under the board policy, the legislature dealt, not with the budgets of individual institutions, but with that of the whole system. This gave the individual institutions and their presidents a certain aloofness from the harsh realities of politics. The traditional political pressures continued to exist in Oregon as elsewhere, of course: the threats of reprisals in the budgets, the demands for hard-line, no-nonsense administration, the resolutions of condemnation (one such resolution was proposed against Johnson's grape decision, but died for lack of support). The pressures in Oregon, were, however, a little more circumspect.

The legislature was in the middle of its biennial session at the time. Many legislators were alarmed by the announcement of Charles Johnson's candidacy. Republicans, in particular, saw weaknesses in his administrative policies for which even his rural charm failed to compensate. So did Governor Tom McCall. Beleaguered by pressures, he asked the board's chairman for "assurance" that the board would not appoint Johnson. Forrester declined to give that assurance. "There are nine members of the board who will decide on the presidency," Forrester said, "and at the moment I can't tell you who the next president is going to be."

The governor expressed strong reservations about the Johnson appointment, reservations based primarily on what he saw as the accelerating deterioration of public confidence in the university's administration. "With the kinds of problems we've been having," the governor said, "I just don't think it would be in the public interest to appoint Johnson to the presidency."

The major problem had been the grape decision, followed closely by general "permissiveness." The grape decision had also offended at least four members of the board itself, notably Ray Yasui, a fruit farmer. The board had held a private session with Johnson after his grape decision, and Yasui told the board that he had received complaints from people who felt Johnson had acted "hastily and perhaps unwisely in acceding to the demands of a particular group of dormitory students." The board, however, endorsed a resolution accepting Johnson's statement that the decision "was not intended to commit the institution to a partisan position." The vote was seven to two.

Now the board was being urged—indirectly for the most part—to appoint someone other than Johnson. The name of Robert D. Clark, the former U.O. dean, continued to receive prominent attention. Governor McCall had even gone to the trouble of checking some California sources on Clark's performance as president of San Jose State College.

"I know you don't like him," said McCall to California Governor Ronald Reagan at a conference in February, "but I'd like you to tell me something about Bob Clark at San Jose. . . ."

Governor Reagan promised to have his staff check up on Clark's performance. Soon Reagan's reply arrived. Clark was rated high for his academic leadership and community relations, but low for his permissiveness with students. McCall circulated copies of the letter to the Board of Higher Education.

Also mentioned as presidential material was an eastern Oregon attorney, Anthony Yturri, a Republican legislator, Phi Beta Kappa alumnus of the university, a hard-liner who had made clear to Johnson his dissatisfaction with the way the university was being run. It was Governor McCall who largely discouraged Yturri's candidacy, and the name never got as far as the Presidential Search Committee. Some also urged the appointment of Wayne L. Morse, the Democratic Tiger in the Senate, a maverick politician who had lost his bid for reelection to the U.S. Senate the previous fall. Others just as urgently argued against Morse's appointment. If there was ever a man of high profile, it was Wayne L. Morse.

The board, in any event, was unlikely to bypass its Presidential Search Committee. Whatever the faults of the search committee procedure, it did provide a nucleus of support among influential members to the faculty for the man eventually selected. Having helped to choose the new president, the committee members seemed obligated to support him when he arrived on campus. But disquieting reports reached the board about the search committee. Committee deliberations had not always gone smoothly. The two board members who served with the committee, Charles Holloway and Elizabeth Johnson, returned from committee sessions with reports of such schisms and cross fires that the board grew uneasy.

"I think there was a very definite effort on the part of certain segments of the committee to limit the board's ability to choose," said Charles Holloway, a Portland businessman. "Part of the committee was positive that it was going to have a president who would allow the faculty to run things—a hands-off policy. Some members of the committee were determined that they were going to get a certain guy, Harrison Brown. I saw this happen once before in another institution where the committee came in with only two names." Later, the board would insist on having no fewer than five names from which to choose from future presidential search committees.

In the end, the board's choice would be dictated less by a variety of candidates than by the variety of strong opinions about the kind of man needed to head a university moving toward the 1970s. It would be less a matter of whose educational philosophy prevailed, and more a matter of who could keep the campus reasonably intact through difficult times. The man who could do that was likely to be the man who could avoid offending the largest number of search committee and board members. He probably would be dependable, unexciting, and pragmatic, rather than glamorous, charismatic, and visionary. He would have the rigid discipline and dependability of the airline pilot rather than the cavalier spirit of the acrobatic pilot. Of the two men who best fit that description—Dale Corson and Charles Johnson—Corson had the advantage of an intact bankroll of public goodwill. When the discussion turned to Johnson the board split down the middle: he had made the right decisions, but he was too controversial.

Charles Johnson, awaiting news of the board's choice, seemed less sure of the merits of his own judgments, particularly his decision to become a presidential candidate in the first place. Occasionally he dropped a comment to Bill Blevins. He wondered at one point what he'd do if he did get the presidency. Shouldn't he bow out gracefully and return to teaching?

"I just don't know," he said. "I'm not sure I was ever cut out for this administrative role with all its pressures and its brushfire crises."

"You mean administration generally?" asked Blevins. "You obviously thrived on the deanship of the college."

"Well, that was a much different context. You're pretty much free in the academic context. You're free of all the other stuff, the distractions and the annoying little problems that eat away at you."

"That was a very positive experience, wasn't it?"

"Oh, yeah, I enjoyed that very much. But, you know, everybody grows. I'd had that experience in the deanship, and I thought this would be a natural progression from that. Now I'm not so sure. The classroom looks awfully good to me right now."

It was a brand of paranoia that besets many candidates for presidential positions at this stage. If being wooed for the presidency was like being wooed for marriage, the process had now entered a phase of awesome silence: sitting night after night by a telephone that never rings. Days passed, then weeks, and nothing happened. What was going on? If the board were enthusiastic about his candidacy, wouldn't it have communicated that right away? It's especially hard on the "local" candidate. He's like the girl next door. Every day she sees the boy who had given her such a rush. Now he has suddenly stopped calling. Why? What message could she read in his eyes, his facial expression? What inference was Johnson to draw, for example, from the comment of Charles Holloway, the state board member?

"Sometimes, Chuck, you first have to move sideways to move up," Holloway had said. He explained that a man with ambition to reach the top sometimes had to move to another institution to do so. Johnson nodded in agreement: well, he wouldn't feel too disappointed if he didn't get the presidency.

Johnson, inexperienced in the ways of presidential searches, had no way of knowing that the board was forced by circumstances into the position of the fickle lover, unable to say "no" to any one of the chosen candidates until a firm offer had been made and accepted. It was a common problem in presidential searches. What if the board had ended the paranoid speculations of Candidates Two and Three with a definite "no," and then was turned down by Candidate One? Could it then go back to Two and say that it was all a mistake, that you're the one, after all? Not likely.

The candidates had the option of withdrawing their names from consideration after a period of respectful waiting, of course. That was the course chosen by Harrison Brown.

The board continued its quiet endeavors, parrying the inquiries of the news media ("We expect to have an announcement at the next board meeting"). The board had actually made its choice already: Dale Corson, the man of low profile, the outsider with the intact bank account of goodwill. It was awaiting Corson's reply. Corson said he needed time to consider. Corson had decided to leave his provost's position at Cornell and was looking at several opportunities, including two firm offers: the one at Oregon and another in Washington, D.C. The problems at Cornell continued to fester. Corson, as the man who commanded the respect of many diverse elements, was becoming increasingly and frustratingly involved in those problems without commensurate authority (President James Perkins spent much of his time off campus, traveling in the institutional jet, making speeches, attending meetings). Then the Cornell Board of Trustees elected to reorganize the central administration, giving Corson appropriate authority for managing internal affairs. It removed many of his frustrations.

Oregon's Board of Higher Education grew impatient for Corson's answer. Facing the deadline for an announcement at the next board meeting in late April, the board asked Chancellor Lieuallen to "pin this man down: yes or no."

Corson's answer was no.

"I came to the conclusion that I would do better to continue with a set of problems the nature of which I at least knew," Corson explained later. Eventually he would assume the presidency of Cornell after the resignation of President Perkins.

With Corson, Brown, and "John Alpha" out, only Johnson remained as a candidate. Did the board wish to appoint Johnson? Or did it want to try to find someone else? Chairman J. W. Forrester asked for a vote.

The vote was five to four against Johnson.

With the board evenly split, the swing vote against Johnson was actually that of the chairman, Forrester. It was Johnson's own comment, Forrester said later, that had swayed his opinion: *all things being equal, the university might benefit more by having an outsider as president.*

Yes, Forrester agreed at the time, it made good sense. "I'd been tending to think that way right along, though my thoughts hadn't crystallized. Then when Johnson made that remark, I was persuaded. I remember thinking to myself, whoever we get, he's got to be one hell of a guy to be as good as Chuck Johnson."

The promised announcement did not materialize at the next board meeting. The Presidential Search Committee was asked to return to its work and provide additional names for the board to consider.

Johnson knew nothing of these events, of course. Bill Blevins approached him later with a bit of incidental intelligence he'd picked up from a student leader.

"I understand," said Blevins to Johnson, "that the announcement of the new president has been delayed."

"Oh?" said Johnson. He returned to the papers on his desk.

Fifteen:
Crossroads

Johnson's within one vote of the presidency. It was whispered rather than shouted, but within some segments of the legislature it almost equated with Paul Revere's cry, "The British are coming!" The news could hardly contain itself once it had leaked out of the boardroom, trickling down the legislative hallways and gathering into a flood of alarm among the anti-Johnson elements. These consisted primarily of two groups: (1) representatives of agricultural districts offended by the grape decision, and (2) hard-line disciplinarians offended by what they called weak-kneed permissiveness.

Even the defenders of Charles Johnson and the University of Oregon encountered tough going against the devastating impact of stories suggesting that men were hanging around the women's floors in the dorms preying on naked females in the showers, that somebody's daughter had returned unexpectedly to her dormitory room to find her roommate in bed with a boy, that hippies were fornicating in the darkest recesses of the campus, that nice girls were unsafe on the campus pathways after dark, that nude men had been seen running around the girls' dorms. How could one support a presidential candidate who allowed those kinds of excesses?

The Board of Higher Education, whatever its claim to political independence, scarcely needed direct advice from legislators to realize that the appointment of Johnson was fraught with political danger. The board's chairman, J. W. Forrester, had participated in one private negotiating session with several members of the Joint Ways and Means Committee—the key committee for budgets—and had emerged shaken, with an earful of remonstrances about the "goddamned University of Oregon" and the trouble it was causing. It was unlikely, then, that the board would change its five-four vote against Johnson. (Some board members would later claim that they weren't voting *against* Johnson; they were merely voting *for* someone other than Johnson.) The Johnson tenure had represented unparalleled disharmony. True, it was no worse than on many other campuses across the nation. Perhaps Johnson could not be blamed for having caused it; indeed, he might even be credited with having prevented a worse situation.

Still, his appointment would be risky. Some began to wonder whether *any* open-minded, sensitive scholar-teacher could survive the terrors of the presidency in so tumultuous an era. Board members began to notice signs of fatigue and anxiety in the presidents of both universities.

President James Jensen of Oregon State University shared with Johnson that haggard look during the throes of the football-coach-bearded-athlete controversy. Jensen had placed the issue in the hands of a human-rights committee, but neither side seemed willing to retreat from its entrenched position.

The board members saw a likeness in the two presidents: Both men exhibited a sensitivity for people and for human rights. But they saw one major difference: Jensen did not hesitate to speak his mind forcefully, at least in private.

Johnson did not speak so bluntly. Johnson was unflappable.

True, he did show other, more subtle, signs of anxiety. He continued to express self-doubt. He doubted his ability to handle the increasingly strident confrontations with the students. (Dick Jones, the student-body president, had all but disappeared from sight during the spring quarter, and Johnson sorely missed Jones's calming influence on students.) Johnson confided to Ray Hawk that he was not sleeping well at night, that he often awoke around three in the morning and, unable to return to sleep, went to his den to read (usually light paperback fiction, such as Arthur Hailey's *Hotel* or Don Berry's *Trask*). Johnson also told Hawk that his hitherto moderate drinking habits were beginning to escalate. "I never thought I'd see the time," Johnson said, "when the day's most important event was the predinner cocktail." Johnson's colleagues were also concerned about the president's increasing tendency to perspire heavily in tense situations. Orville Lindstrom, the university's director of fiscal affairs, took particular note.

"Chuck, take my advice and see a doctor," said Lindstrom. "I used to break out in cold sweats like that just before I had my heart attack."

Colleagues showed concern in other ways. Ray Hawk continued to divert the angry letters of complaint to his own office. Embert Fossum, the alumni director, decided that Johnson had had enough of hostile alumni meetings. He began to take Hawk to the meetings to represent the president.

"I'll be glad to go anytime," said Johnson when he learned of the plans for substituting Hawk.

"No," said Fossum firmly. "I think you need a rest."

But Johnson did not rest. He did not see a doctor. He continued to observe an increasingly busy spring social calendar and honored every social engagement as though duty bound, cutting further into his ability to cope. Gradually, he seemed to melt into the background of social conversations. His humor all but disappeared, often reduced to nothing more than an occasional soggy wisecrack. Once, at a small dinner party at the home of psychologist Leona Tyler, he fell asleep at the table.

The full impact of these manifestations of anxiety and fatigue eluded even his family and closest associates. Only later would they be pieced together. Colleagues who knew about the perspiration did not know of the sleepless nights; secretaries, uneasy about his seeming indecision on trivial matters, did not know of his droopy demeanor at dinner parties; his wife, accustomed to his occasional "quiet spells," did not know of the problems that haunted him, the confrontations, the budget, the seeming inability to "move the university ahead." Nor did she know of the awesome similarity between the frustrations of the presidential year—ill health interfering with accomplishment in the face of an inner compulsion to achieve—and the frustrations of his childhood.

Actually she knew little of his childhood; he hadn't talked much about it. He had not mentioned it to friends. His colleague and friend Glenn Starlin, noticed through the years that whenever a group started reminiscing about the Good Old Days—"Remember when you could go to the movies for a nickel?"—Johnson turned silent. He laughed at the funny stories his friends told, at the lies and exaggerations of childhood exploits, but Starlin could recall no instance of Johnson contributing a childhood recollection of his own.

Just as the fast-moving Epworth League in Great Falls would not hold still for the spindly, short-winded teenager, neither would the university hold still for the infirmities of a chief executive. Now, in the spring, the problems came from all sides and at an accelerating pace, ranging from the usual (budgets, personnel problems, legislative relations) to the bizarre: the murder of a beautiful brunette coed whose body was found in the trunk of an abandoned car. Now, as the spring term progressed, the president became embroiled in a series of hostile confrontations over the university's newest statewise issue. Shacks.

First obscenity. Then hair. Grapes. And now this—*shacks.*

There they were, tar-paper shacks, right in the middle of the sprawling front lawn of the Student Union, alongside the most heavily trafficked corner of the campus, Thirteenth Avenue and University Street.

First there was just one, a crude tar-paper and pasteboard shack. It appeared mysteriously one morning. No one seemed to know how it got there.

First the one. Then three more. Then finally six. Then plans for another forty.

216

What was it all about?

The shack builders, it turned out, comprised a loosely amalgamated group of students and nonstudents bound by one common interest: poverty. The shacks, they said, were educational. They would "teach the public about the misery of poverty." One of the shacks housed what was said to be an impoverished family from somewhere out in the county and was headed by a woman who cooked meals over an open campfire. On one occasion, somebody anonymously called the fire department which responded with a huge pumper to extinguish a tiny campfire. A confrontation developed between students and the fire department. The fire *was* illegal, after all, and after considerable discussion a compromise emerged allowing a fireman to douse the fire with a small hand extinguisher.

The major confrontation, in the conference room of Johnson Hall, was not so easily settled. The shack builders arrogantly issued demands for increased support of educational programs for the poor. They said they wanted an immediate answer, right there, at the meeting. The administration must stop fooling around.

"The university," stated Demand No. 1, "must state specifically and unequivocally how it plans to maintain and expand its commitment to solving poverty on campus and in the community."

And after all the demands had been read, the students' document added the final twist: "The university must be relevant to human misery or it has little reason to exist."

A leader of the shack builders, a middle-aged nonstudent, vowed that "the only way I can be chased off this campus is to go out in shackles or dead."

Johnson replied patiently.

He was sympathetic, he said, but the power of decision in this and any other university rested in more than one man. He certainly could not give an answer in mere minutes. The budget was fully committed, he said. The answers would have to await further analysis and study.

The students grew impatient and abusive.

217

"We are not interested in more kinds of analysis of the administration," one shouted. "We want the administration to get serious. We want an answer. *Now!*"

If the shacks proved nothing more, they demonstrated the wide gulf between youth and age. On Saturday, the day following the meeting with the students, Johnson met with a group of legislators, members of the powerful budget-making group, the Joint Ways and Means Committee. Some of them were as hostile as the students. They dropped dark hints that the legislative appropriation for higher education was by no means "automatic." Some members insisted that Johnson had acted unwisely. He should have destroyed the shacks immediately.

Johnson replied patiently.

He said the university has had a long tradition of student involvement in decision making, a delegation of authority he could not grant and then suddenly and capriciously withdraw, even if he wanted to. He said he had asked the appropriate student committee—the Student Administrative Board—to take action. The committee, after many traumas and vacillations that resulted in the resignations of two members, one of them the chairman, finally agreed to set a deadline for the removal of the shacks two weeks hence.

In any event, Johnson added, he failed to see the problem.

"To me," he said, "the shacks aren't any more unsightly than the Homecoming signs that students erected in front of the fraternities and sororities back in earlier years."

"I'm not in agreement with you on this," snapped one legislator, Representative Philip Lang of Portland, a Democrat. "This is an administrative responsibility of *your* office to take care of them. As I see it, you failed to do it."

"I'm sorry to hear you say that," said Johnson calmly. "I guess we differ. I think I'm discharging my administrative responsibility in a proper manner."

Shacks. What nonsense. "The whole thing has been blown out of proportion," he confided later to Bill Blevins.

Another brush fire. Why all the fuss?

Because the shacks were an *affront*, symbolically and actually, said the governor of Oregon, Tom McCall. "It's so far beyond our ken that when you bust your butt and pay more per person for higher education than any other state in the union,[1] you now have your beautiful state grounds absolutely *desecrated.* It's an affront to have the shacks there for even an hour. Are we now to have our campus *festooned* with these things?"

McCall drafted a form letter to answer the many complaints he'd been getting from citizens: ". . . The eyesores should never have been allowed to mushroom in the first place although some see the structures as serving a useful symbol calling attention to the plight of the poor and the disadvantaged students whose educational subsidies are threatened."

The public was outraged again. Why?

Perhaps it was because of the timing. The shacks appeared on campus at the same time the frightening photo of the gun-carrying blacks emerging from Willard Straight Hall at Cornell received wide attention. Perhaps it was the last straw, the culmination of everything that had happened on the campus through the year. Perhaps it was merely symbolic of youth versus age. Students on campus saw the shacks as something of a lark, something fitting (in the perverse view of youth) with the spring scene: newly flowering shrubs and trees, coeds newly emerged from winter coats wearing ever shorter skirts, tighter pants, and lower-cut blouses. Best of all, the shacks got the Establishment uptight.

As a means of putting students in touch with poverty, however, they failed. Eventually they came down, largely for lack of support from the very people they were supposed to benefit: members of impoverished minority groups. The black students and the Mexican-American (Chicano) students had been cool to the idea all along. "Why build these shacks and put them in front of all those college kids?" wondered Jesse Estrada, the president of the Chicano Student Union and the son of a migrant farm worker from Idaho. "The students don't even know what the hell they are. They don't know what it means to live in something like that, and we can't tell them."

So the shacks came down, and everything came out all right

in the end. It was time to move on to the important business of the university, among which was the matter of the presidency.

It was now assumed that Johnson had lost the presidency, had lost it, by one rumor, because of the shacks. The rumor alleged that the board had arrived on the U.O. campus intending to appoint Johnson, but it had been so offended by the shanty-town that it changed its collective mind. Like so many rumors about the university, this one contained just enough logic to be plausible, even if doubtful. Johnson's fate *was* decided by the board in a conference room within a stone's throw of the shacks. But the rumor was vigorously denied by Chancellor Lieuallen ("I never heard of anything so absurd") and by other board members. It could never be documented either way, of course, without the ability to read the minds of individual board members.

The presidency was quickly settled once the Presidential Search Committee sent along the names of two more nominees. One was the president of a small private college in the Midwest. The other was Robert D. Clark, the former U.O. dean of faculties, a one-time speech professor.

Clark, who observed his fifty-ninth birthday in March, seemed the classical stereotype of the scholar: quiet, soft-spoken, bespectacled, almost frail-looking. Even his tiny wisp of a moustache appeared timid.

Clark was imaginative, creative, well-read, and spoke with the quiet eloquence of the professor of speech and with the erudition of a man whose immersion in books was total and unequivocal. Reading, he once said, was the one pleasure he would not sacrifice to the great, demanding god of college administration. He had plunged with such fervor into the writings said to have helped to spawn the New Left movement on the campuses, that he could quote more widely, and, often, more accurately, the words of Marx and Mao and Herbert Marcuse than the most ardent of campus revolutionaries.

His frail appearance belied an inner resilience that made him a man of presidential caliber rather than an obscure scholar. It was Clark's calm demeanor that kept San Jose State College from exploding into the violence of San Francisco State. All but a few of his colleagues at San Jose agreed on that. It was Clark, they pointed out, who calmly and courageously walked into an angry crowd of 2,000 students who had come to witness the protest against the employment recruiters of Dow Chemical Company because of its alleged complicity—as manufacturer of napalm—with the war in Vietnam. Clark picked up a bullhorn and calmly engaged the protesting students in debate while the recruitment interviews proceeded within the building. When the debate had ended two hours later, so had the interviews. Everybody went home.

At Oregon it was clear that Clark had extraordinary support from within the faculty; it was said to have been only his age, four years beyond the search committee's upper limit, that kept him off the first list of candidates. The board extended Clark an offer to become the president of the university, and he accepted.

Chancellor Lieuallen promptly phoned Charles Johnson with the news.

"An excellent choice," said Johnson.

The board's announcement of Clark's appointment came at a press conference in the Chancellor's Office, on the top floor of Johnson Hall, at 10 a.m. May 2. The scene was directly above Charles Johnson's office. Johnson was out of town, addressing a Rotary Club meeting in Grants Pass, a community in southern Oregon 135 miles away.

As the session proceeded, one reporter asked Lieuallen whether Clark was the "mystery" candidate whose name had been kept confidential among the three candidates the board had interviewed early in April. The chancellor replied that the board had actually received a total of six names from the Presidential Search Committee. He left out a lot of details about the conduct of the presidential search process, details that might have filled a volume. Fortunately, the reporter elected not to pursue the point further. Other questions followed, and the chancellor answered smoothly.

How soon will Clark arrive on the campus? ("Sometime this

221

summer, depending on his ability to wind up his work at San Jose.") What will be his salary? ("$32,500 plus $2,000 expenses.") How seriously had Dr. Johnson's candidacy been considered? ("Very seriously. But in the end the board concluded that the significant quality of Dr. Clark is his capacity to bring harmony to a diverse community.") Would the chancellor care to appraise Dr. Johnson's performance? ("When the board appointed Dr. Johnson they gave him the full prerogatives of the president because they did not want any lag in leadership of the university. That is exactly what Dr. Johnson did. He has behaved as president and not as an acting president or caretaker.")

Two days later Charles Johnson wrote a letter to his parents.

4 May 1969

Dear Folks,

I'm afraid to look back at the calendar and estimate the time since I've last sent a letter your way, but there's no time like the present so here goes.

The major news at this end is that the U. of O. presidency is settled, and I will soon be off the hot seat. The board chose Robert Clark, who is current president at San Jose State College in California, and it was an excellent choice. Clark was formerly on the faculty here as a speech professor, then dean of the College of Liberal Arts, and finally Dean of Faculties before leaving for the San Jose post about 5 years ago—he will be coming back to a situation he knows well and his five years of experience will stand him in good stead. I find that whatever disappointment I might have experienced in not being offered the post is pretty much swamped by relief at the prospect of moving out of what has become an increasingly pressurized situation. Although I found the first six months or so of my experience very interesting and for the most part enjoyable, I really have begun to feel the strain during the last couple of months. At first I thought it was simply the aftermath of the siege of the Hong Kong flu and I expect that may have had something to do with it, but I had begun to seriously wonder whether I would find this kind of assignment satisfying over the longer pull of five or ten years. If the nod had gone to me I would have plunged in and given it the old college try, but I don't find myself particularly unhappy at the prospect of turning over the job to someone else. For about the first time in my life during the month of April I have found that I couldn't turn off the worries and the problems at bedtime, and have been spending sleepless nights with sufficient frequency that I'm sure I haven't been operating at top efficiency. But the enjoyment goes out of a job pretty fast under these circumstances and I was beginning not to look forward to a longer term steady diet of that sort of experience. In any case I'm glad the issue is settled and now I can begin to think about where we go from here. . . .

To Palmer and Cora Johnson, one aspect of the letter stood out: its lack of humor. The sleeplessness was another point of concern. Was it merely coincidence that the month of April—the period of sleeplessness he mentioned—represented precisely the period during which the presidency was being decided?

The letter plodded heavily through several speculations about his future. He might take his sabbatical leave next year. He might return to the deanship. He might return to full-time teaching. He just didn't know.

"I suppose that this is one of those career crossroads that comes to each of us," he wrote. "I'll have to admit the course doesn't seem very clear at the moment, and the decision is probably not going to be an easy one. In any case I'm not sorry I took this five-year detour—it has been an excellent experience and I'm sure I have grown in capacity as a result of it, no matter where we go from here on."

The letter ground on, two single-spaced pages in all, laden with personal notes of family life: Karen "safely past the 21 year milestone—we had a birthday party for her involving several of her sorority sisters"; Kylene's straight-A record in junior high school ("She enjoys getting out Karen's record in the 7th grade and making odious comparisons. . . . Karen of course claims that school was much tougher in her day."); Craig's experiences in the Army in Korea ("The recent incidents in Korea put them on alert several times . . . but so far no shooting war in his area."); the hectic social life (". . . a schedule of luncheons, teas, etc., that seem to reach some sort of climax during the spring term of the academic year"). And then at last the letter was at an end.

Well, it's getting late and tomorrow will be a busy day so I guess I'd better see if I can shove aside all the upcoming problems and get a good night's sleep in preparation.

Much love,
Chuck, Jeanne and grandkids.

Sixteen:
To Get Away

Around the middle of May, several students from the university's political science department conducted an attitude survey of sixty-seven members of the Duck Club, a sports booster group in Eugene. How did the club members, mostly business and professional men, feel about the University of Oregon?

They were not happy with it. More than half (56.7 percent) expressed dissatisfaction with "general conditions" at the university. When asked to name one aspect of the university that displeased them, they most frequently cited the university's administration, describing it in such terms as "weak," "permissive," "inept," and "acquiescent." The fact that the university's athletic fortunes had been in a slump for years, at least in football and basketball, bothered them far less than the administration's apparent inability to control the abnormal surge of student discontent. The survey only confirmed statistically what everybody "knew," including "The Administration" himself.

Charles Johnson's dissatisfaction with his own performance was based on different reasons, however. "Due to financial difficulties, there were a lot of areas where we couldn't move," he said, assessing the year. "I don't know if I've been able to move the university very far this year."

The remark, quoted in newspapers, implied a sense of personal responsibility, as though only a president could move a university ahead—or fail to do so. The term failure crept into his conversation a lot that spring. His frustration over failure showed in a journalistic interview in mid-May. The editor of the university's alumni magazine[1] had asked for an interview covering the "problems and accomplishments" of the year. When he finally managed to get an appointment around six one evening, he found Johnson standing behind his desk dressed crisply in gray suit and white shirt, but exhibiting less-than-crisp demeanor. He looked preoccupied. He did not smile. He spoke in staccato bursts. He blurted out his first remark with almost childlike abruptness.

"I'm not sure this is a good time to interview me. This thing is beginning to get to me."

"Oh?"

"I haven't been sleeping well at night."

"Well, the problems have been tough ones through the year, and I suppose—"

"I've always admired Flemming for that."

"For what?"

"He could make a decision and forget about it. Live with it and sleep with it."

"And you can't do that?"

"No." Johnson turned and stared out the window toward a view of a tranquil, grassy quadrangle flanked by attractive old buildings. "When I started, I said I'd keep the university moving ahead. I haven't done that."

"Well, wait a moment. Don't you think you're being unfair to yourself?"

"What do you mean?"

The interview had changed. Johnson asked the questions: the editor delivered the opinions. "Well, I mean I don't see how you could expect to move the university ahead with all the problems such as the downturn in federal support and the uncertain

226

mood of the legislature. You've had to make a lot of unpopular decisions. The legislature and the public haven't understood the complexities involved."

"Why do you say that?" Johnson sounded like a teacher trying to coax a wayward student into sharpening his answers. The editor struggled through a complex metaphorical explanation: the university was the elephant being described by the proverbial blind men. Johnson seemed not to understand.

"I guess I'm not making much sense," said the editor. "What I mean is, it's like losing brownie points in public goodwill for making unpopular decisions. They may be necessary decisions, but you always have to pay the price in brownie points."

Johnson stood silently behind his desk, eyes fixed on the carpet. The silence was devastating.

"Do you mind if I ask a few questions?" said the editor. "Or would you prefer that I come another time?"

"No, go ahead." Johnson sat down behind his desk.

"Of all the decisions of the year, which do you feel has cost you the most brownie points?"

"I don't know. What do you think?"

"I suppose the grape decision. . . . You said earlier that if you weren't appointed to the permanent presidency, relief would probably swamp your disappointment. How do you feel about it now?"

"That's about it."

"What do you plan to do now?"

Johnson brightened. "Take a sabbatical. Perhaps go back to school to retool myself to get back into the classroom. I've been away a long time. Five years. I've been out of touch. But with some concentrated effort I think I can get ready for the classroom again."

"Does this mean you plan to leave administration entirely?"

"Well, I haven't made up my mind about that."

"Do you think you might be interested in the presidency of another university?"

"I don't know. I've had a couple of opportunities to be a candidate at other universities."

"And you turned them down?"

"I wrote and told them I wasn't interested. Right now administration doesn't strike me as a very attractive prospect. I can't say how I might feel about it a few years from now."

Though the conversation did not reach print per se, it did serve as the basis of an article on "the world's most thankless job," that of the acting presidency: "Charles Johnson deserves a long ovation from alumni. . . . Any man who puts himself through the presidential meat grinder—all in the spirit of public service—deserves that much and maybe a lot more."

Of course, *all* presidents had difficulties during the height of the New Left-radical-revolutionary-hippie-black power-drug culture movements on the campuses. In time, the New Left would disintegrate like an exploding skyrocket. The hippies would be accepted by society or retreat to communes (or cut their hair and go to work), and many revolutionaries would enter into Establishment endeavors. Some would look back and say, "It was all a game."

But the nation, meanwhile, continued to place impossible demands upon the men who served as university presidents. A president was expected to be sensitive to other people's feelings while being insensitive to his own. He must not confide his personal insecurities to anyone, especially not to those who might use them to advantage, as some inevitably would. He must understand. He must feel. He must be in tune emotionally to everybody's hangup but his own. He must have a gut reaction. He must not retreat to abstract idealism or pull that old game of appointing an ad hoc committee—not when millions were starving in the ghettos, dying in Vietnam, or rotting in jail as political prisoners. And if, by chance, he cannot align himself wholeheartedly with the paranoia of the moment, then he is much more useful as a target. And the *acting* president is the best target of all, a figure of limited power to be fired upon with impunity and with minimal risk of administrative retribution. He is expendable.

When Johnson was passed over for the permanent presidency, his personal problems multiplied. It was not solely because of

228

disappointment or fatigue or sleepless nights or the lingering aftermath of the flu (he'd still not regained the fifteen pounds loss of weight). After these came the most devastating blow of all. He was no longer important.

The first dramatic crack in the unflappable exterior of Charles Johnson came in late May, about three weeks after Robert Clark's appointment as the new president. Jeanne Johnson, taking note of her husband's tensions and his tendency to break out in cold sweats, had obtained a prescription for a mild tranquilizer, Valium. She delivered it to his office, but he was in conference. She left it with Janice Medrano, an administrative assistant, with instructions to make sure he took a pill at the first opportunity. During a break in Johnson's appointment schedule, Mrs. Medrano walked into his office with the pills and a glass of water.

"Mrs. Johnson said to make sure you took one of these right away," she said.

"Okay."

"I brought a glass of water," she said.

"Okay." He made no move. She stood by his desk, tending him like a mother holding a spoonful of castor oil.

"Dr. Johnson, your wife said—"

He snatched up the vial, dropped a tiny yellow tablet in his hand, and gulped it down with a swig of water.

"Okay, I took it!" He shouted the words.

For the first time, Mrs. Medrano heard Charles Johnson raise his voice. She fled in tears.

She had no way of knowing that he was crying, too. Jeanne Johnson had heard them more than once: muffled sobs from behind the closed door of the bedroom in the evening. She said nothing to him about them. He was a hard man to reach when problems were on his mind. He did not tell her about those problems. She did not ask. Occasionally he dropped a remark such as, "Well, guess I'd better go out and struggle with that darned budget some more." When she replied that surely the university's budget problems were no worse than anybody else's budget problems, he did not respond. And when he asked her to make a note on their social calendar for June 3, the date of a reception in his honor sponsored by the university's Faculty Club, his tone was casual. Only later would he confess his intense feeling of irony. *A reception in my honor? To honor me for what? For failing to move the university ahead, as I'd promised?*

The presidential paperwork moved slower. It formed a gigantic reservoir of documents stacked all over his desk and on the table behind him. Some of it drained off into briefcase loads taken home to form another gigantic pool in his den. Even the simplest of decisions took days. Janice Medrano once approached him with a list of committee appointments for what she assumed would be a rubber stamp approval. He stared at the list for several minutes while she stood self-consciously beside his desk. He fumbled with his pipe, thrusting it unlit deeper in his mouth.

"Do you want me to check with you later?" she asked.

"Yeah, check with me later." By mid-afternoon, several hours later, the list still lay on his desk before him. He had taken no action on it. His mind seemed to be a thousand miles away. It left her with an eerie feeling. Others on the office staff felt acutely uncomfortable in his presence, and, not knowing what to do, they tended to avoid him. He obviously wanted to be alone, they concluded. They left him increasingly by himself.

With such pain involved in minor decisions, how was he to cope with the major ones? And what about the most major of all—at least the most potentially volatile—the decision on the student "incidental fees" budget?

For three years a trend had been underway to give student government more autonomy over the spending of student activity fees, or "incidental fees" as the university called them. These were extratuition fees assessed at the rate of $25 per term per student, some $1.2 million annually. The money helped to finance such extracurricular programs as intercollegiate athletics, the Student Health Center, the Student Union, the campus newspaper, and various student government activities.

Johnson saw nothing wrong with this trend. Give students fiscal responsibility, he always said, and they'll measure up. And when the student leaders tested him by suggesting that they might come up with some "drastic changes" in financial priorities, he did not discourage them. The president, he said, should not try to prejudge. He must have all the facts and the arguments at hand first. He did, of course, have the authority to change the students' recommended budget, even to veto it if necessary.

The student leadership tended toward radicalism. The student body had just elected, by a thirty-eight-vote margin, an avowedly radical president, Kip Morgan, the young man under federal indictment in connection with the draft board disruptions the previous January. The election result disappointed Johnson. "Oh, boy," he said grimly when he heard the news. "Only thirty-eight votes."

The increased authority granted student government to allocate the student fee money did not appeal to the directors of two departments in particular: the Student Health Service and the Department of Athletics. They did not relish the idea of testifying before student-run budget hearings. They did not share Johnson's faith that students might rise to the responsibility rather than furthering their own myopic political ends. Indeed, the students might at any time arbitrarily and capriciously decide to eliminate a department's entire student fee budget.

They were not surprised when it happened. Student government promptly voted to eliminate the entire student fee support, $238,000, for the Department of Athletics.

The department was outraged. Its acting director, Norval Ritchey, fired off a letter to Johnson pointing out that the Student Fiscal Committee had voted three-to-two to eliminate all support of athletics. Of the three members voting against athletics, he said, two had not even bothered to attend the meetings at which the department attempted to justify its budget.

"That shows how 'responsible' they were," he said.

The students relented and restored $100,000 to athletics, but only as a reserve against emergencies.

With the funds saved from athletics, the students proposed

several educational and social reform programs: an ethnic studies center ($75,000) for study of and scholarships for minority racial groups, a "center for the study of conflict management" ($30,000) for research into "peaceful methods of social change," a visiting professor program ($18,000), and a university ombudsman ($10,000) who would help students cope with institutional bureaucracy.

Now the proposals had reached Johnson's desk. What would be his decision?

He was noncommittal.

"You obviously are putting me in an extremely difficult position," he told a delegation of student leaders. "When you take this kind of radical action, with the likelihood of extreme reactions from alumni and sports fans, you're really creating problems for the university. Frankly, I don't know how I'm going to deal with this. But I'm interested in your ideas. I want to hear more about them."

The students explained that with limited funds available, and with the need urgent in these social action areas, they wished to change the priorities.

"I'm not as confident as you are," Johnson said, "that you can attack the Athletic Department without really affecting the university in ways that would alienate certain friends of the university. A lot of people identify with the university through athletics. Athletics, you know, are a means of support for other kinds of programs."

The students said that they were not attacking the department. The new program would, of course, require a new system whereby students would pay to attend games rather than attending them for free. Some West Coast universities, notably Stanford and U.S.C., had already gone to such a system. Washington, California, and U.C.L.A. had begun to move in that direction. The students also offered to help campaign for private contributions for athletics. They did not doubt the success of such a campaign: look at how fast the department had raised the money for the Astro-turf.

Johnson told the students that they had offered some "compelling arguments" and that he would "look into the situation more closely in the weeks ahead."

The problem gnawed at him. Funds for minority group programs had been a special pet project with him. His sympathy for them seemed somehow at odds with the professed ability to be "hard-headed" on budget priorities. He started a letter to Chancellor Lieuallen to inquire about state policies on student ticket sales. He put the letter aside unfinished. Other problems, other tough decisions awaited his attention. Among them was the Morris Yarowsky affair.

Yarowsky, a charming, witty, and urbane man of thirty, a mod-looking, iconoclastic Establishment-baiter, was the darling of a new generation of hip art students. It was he who had gained wide notoriety for himself and the university with the "destruction art seminar," the one involving such funky happenings as the girl shaving off an eyebrow and the guy smashing a ringing alarm clock with a sledgehammer.

Soon after he joined the faculty in 1965 on a one-year "visiting professor" appointment, Yarowsky became a colorful figure with his pipe, his heavy moustache, and his black hair drifting down over his ears. He delighted his admirers with his offbeat views and his provocative antics such as an exhibition of pictures entitled *Diseases of the Mouth*: vivid, grotesque renditions of oral malformations painted with the aid of medical texts. They so offended the departmental office staff and the then Dean Walter Creese that the staff demanded their removal. The demand was refused by the student-faculty Exhibitions Committee. The paintings stayed.

Yarowsky, a graduate of Dartmouth and the California College of Arts and Crafts, had had his visiting professorship renewed in 1966 and 1967. Then, in 1968, he was given a "terminal" contract, meaning he would not be rehired.

His own department was ambivalent about him; in a departmental meeting the tenured faculty voted 8-0 against another visiting professor appointment, but had voted 5-4 in favor of retaining Yarowsky in the department if additional funds were allocated for a new permanent position. There was scant chance of that, considering the university's precarious financial position.

So Yarowsky was leaving. His adoring students rose to his defense.

The storm broke at 3:35 p.m. on Friday, May 23. The day was warm, the presidential office a little stuffy. A half-dozen art students had come to see Johnson during his "open hours," a two-hour block he reserved on Friday afternoons to see students without appointments. An additional hundred Yarowsky supporters waited in the outer office. Soon they grew impatient. At 3:35 the entire mob surged into Johnson's private office, surrounding his desk, sitting on the table and window sills behind him, leaving him and his desk a tiny island in a sea of angry humanity.

"We're getting tired of this fucking runaround," shouted one student. "We're sick of taking this shit. The students are getting fucked over by this university."

"I want you to tell me," said Johnson calmly, removing his pipe from his mouth, "what shit you're talking about and in what ways the students are getting fucked over."

Tom Ballinger, a professor of art education, witnessing the dialogue, felt a surge of pride in the president's cool demeanor. This is really tremendous, Ballinger thought to himself. Here's the acting president of the university talking to the kids at *their* level of communication. Johnson had thrown the students off guard. Had he attempted to ignore their coarse language or been embarrassed by it, he might have lost the day.

Yet Johnson perspired heavily in the heat and tension as students continued to hurl invectives. He calmly and candidly explained the decision not to rehire Yarowsky. The "visiting professor" position normally rotated among several persons, as many as three a year, so that the students might benefit from contact with a variety of artists in residence. Yarowsky had, in effect, usurped the position over the past four years. Now it was time to pass the position around to other young artists. This was no attack on Yarowsky, Johnson said. In fact, if the Art Department were granted funds for an additional permanent faculty position, the job would probably go to Yarowsky.

"Okay, let's give the department the money," a student said. The answer was simple and poignant. Only two days earlier Johnson had issued a directive "freezing" all vacant positions as a result of the legislature's apparent vacillation in funding higher education. Thus if a professor resigned, he would not be replaced. It would hardly be fair, with some departments actually losing faculty positions, to add a new position in Art.

"Why don't you just go up to the legislature and ask for more money?"

Johnson's patient answer was a lesson in elementary civics, not to mention relevance. The political realities precluded such an act. Procedures must be followed. Budgets went from professors to department chairmen to deans to presidents to the chancellor to the governor and then to the legislature.

"None of your excuses make any sense," snapped a student. "For years now there's been a student mandate to give Yarowsky a permanent position."

"Surely Yarowsky is not the only contemporary artist you could bring in," said Johnson.

"But the faculty won't keep radical people in here. They don't like radical people."

"And we kind of dig it here," said another student, clearly counting himself among the radical element. "I'm not threatening, but I can tell you this, that ultimately we're going to have real problems around this university. If you use your fist against a wall and it doesn't give, you wonder why. So the next time you go back with a sledgehammer. That's what's going to happen to this university unless you listen to us once in a while."

"Unless you do something for us," said another student.

"You're an insensitive man," added another.

Johnson turned quickly to see who had made the last remark—it was an *Emerald* writer—and swung back again without responding. The heckling came with increasing intensity, and he found it difficult to respond to one comment or question before someone else fired another volley.

"Yarowsky does not have a job," someone said.

"We told Mr. Yarowsky a whole year ago that he would not

be rehired," Johnson said. "Surely he should have another job lined up by now."

"Students are never permitted to recruit faculty. The students' kind of people are weeded out before they ever get to consider hiring faculty."

"Students will have a say in who the next visiting professor will be," said Johnson firmly. "I'll make that commitment to you right now."

"Well, how about Morris Yarowsky?"

"Is he indispensable?" snapped Johnson.

"He doesn't have another job."

"I can't believe that if he is as good as you say he is, he doesn't have another job. I'd have thought he'd be in great demand all over the country if he's that good."

The tone was uncharacteristically argumentative for Johnson. The sarcastic edge to his comment surprised even a few students. Perspiration continued to pour down his face, occasionally spotting his glasses. The crisp white shirt he'd put on that morning was now drenched.

"If you're so interested in bringing fresh wind into the Art Department," Johnson said, "the visiting professorship is a good way to do it. But after four years, Yarowsky is not exactly fresh wind."

The argument raged on. The Department of Fine Arts, students asserted, was unresponsive; it was stale. It would never try to find another Yarowsky; the whole process of faculty selection was bound up in "dirty dealing and under-the-table shenanigans." Even worse was the Museum of Art, they said.

One of Yarowsky's students had completed a "terminal project" of sculpture pieces. Such projects, by long-standing agreement, were to be exhibited in the university's Museum of Art. But the director of the museum, Wallace Baldinger, refused to allow some of the student's exhibits to be shown including a sculpture depicting a nude woman, legs apart, with worms crawling out of her vagina. Students called this a "glaring example of censorship."

Johnson disagreed. "The museum director," he argued, "is

like the editor of a literary magazine. He has the obligation to edit the art displayed in the museum in accordance with the dictates of his taste. It's no more an act of censorship than an editor's rejection of a manuscript would be."

As the time edged toward five o'clock, the students gave no indication of leaving. Johnson literally became imprisoned in his office. The president's colleagues began to wonder at what point, if the students didn't leave, they should call the police. Should they convene the "crisis committee"? Rumors hinted that the students might try to keep the president there all night if necessary.

Morris Yarowsky appeared at the door of the President's Office at precisely 4:50 p.m. He'd spent all afternoon, he confided later, strolling the campus, wondering what to do. Students had told him they planned to stay in the president's office for days if necessary until they got satisfaction. It probably wouldn't do any good, Yarowsky decided during his stroll. The university would simply call the police and have the students evicted. Hell would break loose on the campus, and it wouldn't make a particle of difference so far as his job was concerned. If he had any hope of regaining his job, he concluded, it would have to be through legal action.

Now he strolled into the President's Office, looking crisp and fresh in a shirt and slacks. All heads turned toward him as he spoke.

"It's ironic now that I'm leaving the department that you're all here today," he said. He explained that he'd come "to ask you to drop the issue about me at this point. I don't feel honorable or benevolent about this. I think it's unjust, it's ironic, but the battle is lost. . . . I appreciate your support, but nothing is going to happen because the university is unresponsive. I'm out of it—press on with the bigger battle."

Charles Johnson rose from his chair for the first time since the students had jammed his office. He extended his hand to Morris Yarowsky. "Thank you, Morris. I appreciate your coming." The two men shook hands. They had never met before.

Thus ended the confrontation. Most students drifted out. A few stayed to argue about the museum's "censorship."

It was only one of several spring crises that had taken an obvious emotional toll on the acting president. During the weekend after the confrontation with the Yarowsky supporters, Johnson spent considerable time staring vacantly into space. He sucked on a dead pipe. He forgot the content of conversations occurring only moments before. During one conference with Tom Ballinger and Charles Duncan about the museum's "censorship" problem, Johnson sat quietly and grimly, saying nothing. His eyes appeared to focus on some faraway object.

He displayed a similar demeanor at the dinner party at Duncan's house that same evening. Some of his long-time friends were there with their wives—the Glenn Starlins, the John Hultengs, the Gene Scoles (he was the new dean of the law school).

The party was a little tense, the men trying too obviously to be lighthearted. But how else to bolster the flagging spirits of their friend Chuck Johnson? If he could just hold out for three more weeks.

That was the answer, of course. Three more weeks and it would all be over. Glenn Starlin issued an invitation to all present to join him at his cabin on the shore of Priest Lake in Idaho where he planned to go the moment commencement was over June 15—just three weeks away.

Three more weeks. Did he really have the time to take a vacation? A lot of decisions remained to be made.

"I'm not sure I can get away," Chuck Johnson said.

"Tell you what," said Glenn Starlin, tongue in cheek. "We'll call it an *educational conference*. That way it's in the line of duty, and Chuck will *have* to be there to represent the university."

Starlin proposed calling it the "Ecumenical Convocation of Select Officers and Administrators in Higher Education." It would be a "three-day simulation of campus confrontation crises."

"An insightful look down the road ahead," added Hulteng.

They were men of words, these professors. As they played

238

with the clichés of academia, the event assumed an awesome glow. The conference, they decided, would be a "meaningful, relevant and timely approach to a multitrack involvement with some of the most urgent and perplexing problems facing higher education in contemporary society."

It would be designed to stimulate the "participative interlinking groups in an orbital overview of the problems now being encountered in the management-by-objectives field, with particular references to synoetics and heuristics. . . ."

"Synoetics? Heuristics?" A smile cracked Johnson's lips.

"All right," he said abruptly. "I'll be there." He turned to his wife. "Jeanne, clear the calendar for the whole week after commencement. We're going to get away."

On the calendar later that evening, Jeanne Johnson drew a line through the entire week of June 16. They were going to get away.

In fact, they were not even going to wait. Memorial Day was at hand, and, he insisted, they were going to the beach. They had not gotten away since the beach trip last March, the weekend he caught the flu.

"By the way," he said in a casual tone to Bill Blevins, his assistant, "Jeanne and I are going to the beach this coming weekend. How would you and Marcia like to join us?"

They agreed. Plans called for the Johnsons to stay at a motel; the Blevins would take their small travel trailer to a nearby camp. They would drive separately and meet at the motel around noon on Friday.

The Blevins had been at the motel for several hours before Johnson arrived with his wife, his daughter Kylene, and Kylene's friend, Betsy Acheson.

Johnson entered the room and looked around.

"What?" he said. "No fire?"

"Fire?"

"Yeah. You've been here all day, and you don't even have a fire going in the fireplace?"

"To tell the truth," confessed Blevins, "it never occurred to us."

"Well, we've got to have a fire," said Johnson firmly. "I'll

239

build one." He set the fire carefully, placing kindling over crumpled newspaper, and touched a match to the paper. The paper burned but the wood did not ignite. He put more paper in and tried again, without success. He tried a third time, and failed.

"Don't bother, Chuck," said Jeanne. "It's not that important."

"No," he said, "we've got to have a fire. The darned wood's wet."

He went to his car outside and found a hatchet. He worked patiently, splintering the kindling into tiny pieces. He crumpled more newspaper. He put the splinters over the paper, then painstakingly laid larger pieces of wood over the smaller until he'd built up a complex pyramid. Now he was ready.

"Darn, I'm out of matches."

"Let's see," said Blevins. "What we really need are those big kitchen matches back at the trailer. But that's three miles away."

Blevins searched through his car. He finally found a book of matches and handed them to Johnson.

Johnson lit a match, but it went out before he could get it to the paper. He lit another. He watched transfixed as the paper caught hold, igniting the tiny splinters. The fire soon crackled cheerfully.

"There," he said triumphantly, enjoying the warmth of the fire. Perseverance, as always, had paid off.

The weekend went well. By tacit agreement, the men avoided talking about the office. They played horseshoes (Blevins beat Johnson badly), they played beach golf, they played tag with the surf. Johnson and his wife took a long, quiet walk on the beach together.

That evening they played a parlor game, Acquire, a complex investment game. The game dragged. Johnson, as the "banker," was inattentive; sometimes he had to be reminded two or three times to pay out or collect money.

"I wonder," said Blevins, "if we should just flick it in and go to bed."

240

"No," said Johnson, "let's finish. We've got to finish."

They did finish eventually, and the Blevins left for their trailer.

The families compared notes the next morning. "Did everybody sleep well?" asked Marcia Blevins cheerfully.

"I suspect Jeanne didn't sleep very well last night," said Johnson. "I tossed and turned all night long."

The Johnsons were visiting the Blevins at their tiny trailer parked at the camp. "I'd like to take a look at that trailer," he said.

He entered the trailer and lay down on the small bed.

"Well Jeanne, this looks as if it might do the trick. I think I'd really enjoy a trailer like this. What do you think, Jeanne?"

"I think you'd have a tough time wedging your big frame into that little bed," she said.

"Well, we might just take up camping again," he said. He sat up on the bed. "We used to do a lot of camping with the tent. I never liked that tent. It was such a hassle getting it up and taking it down. But now something like this—"

He patted the bed and tapped the walls and peered into one of the cupboards.

"—this is the life."

Later that Sunday, Mark Greene, Johnson's friend and fellow business professor, came roaring up on his motorcycle. The Greenes were staying in a nearby cabin over the weekend.

"Hey, how about letting me try that motorcycle?" said Johnson.

"Sure."

Johnson roared off. Ten minutes later he returned, wearing a big grin.

"Well, how was it?" asked Greene.

"Great."

"Well, Chuck," asked Greene, "when are you going to take your vacation? What are you going to do when Bob Clark comes?"

An awkward pause ensued.

"I'd better stay on," Johnson said glumly.

"The trouble is," explained Jeanne Johnson, "we don't know when Bob's coming." There had been talk of Clark's arrival in July, then August, then not until September. There had even been a hint that he might not arrive until January.

Later, Blevins asked Johnson privately, "Have you heard anything for sure?"

"No. But I wish it would be as early as possible. I just don't know, Bill. I just don't know if I can last."

"Maybe you ought to make it clear to the chancellor that *you* have plans to be considered, too," said Blevins. "Maybe you should make it clear that this date of arrival doesn't revolve solely around the wishes of the new president."

Johnson grew quiet. Soon it was time to return to Eugene.

"I wish we could stay," said Marcia Blevins. "It's a darned shame to have to go back."

"Yes," said Charles Johnson, repeating her words precisely, "it's a darned shame to have to go back."

Seventeen:
The President is Missing

A shame, indeed, to return to the campus. It was now "dead week," the week before final examinations. Some students viewed finals as yet another symptom of fascist repression. But most merely worried about them, cursed them, and then submitted willingly enough to their repression. Even the *Emerald* ceased publication during dead week in order that its harried staff might catch up with the term's academic work. And so the students grew silent.

From the presidential point of view, the final confrontations of the spring were spelled m-o-n-e-y. Spring was budgeting time. It was decision-making time. It was when presidents stayed indoors struggling over long columns of figures, being hard-headed about priorities. They were oblivious to the beauties of the balmy outdoors such as the mini-skirted coeds nimbly dodging traffic on East Thirteenth Avenue, or the gigantic rhododendrons now laden with delicate-looking purple and white blossoms.

Johnson, by judicious husbanding of financial resources, by freezing vacant faculty positions, and by scraping up nickels wherever they fell, actually was ending the year with close to a

$50,000 surplus. Even last winter's snow disaster, which cost the university an unexpected $34,000 in grounds maintenance costs, had been taken in stride. But when the budget office informed him of the surplus, Johnson did not shout in glee. He only seemed to stare uncomprehendingly. No, he said, he had no plans for spending it or for restoring any of the frozen positions.

"But if we don't spend it," said Don Schade, the budget chief, "we'll lose it. It'll revert to the State System's general fund."

Johnson had next year to think about. The chancellor's office had agreed to equalize the imbalance in graduate level student-teacher ratios between the university and Oregon State. It meant the university would be allocated twenty-seven new faculty positions instead of five. The jobs of twenty-two tenured professors whose NSF grants expired this year were safe.

Yet gloom gripped the presidential suite. The legislature, in the session just ended, had declined to authorize construction of the university's new administrative services building, even though the State Board had given it a high priority. It would have replaced Emerald Hall, an ancient World War II wooden structure hauled in to accommodate "temporarily" the influx of veterans in the mid-1940s. The university was still temporizing with it in 1969.[1] The legislature had also placed enrollment ceilings on graduate students and on nonresident students, and both actions placed a damper on the university's rapid expansion.

Since the university enrolled more graduate and nonresident students than the other institutions in the state system, many professors saw the ceiling as a none-too-subtle slap at Acting President Johnson and the University of Oregon. At the very least, it effectively eliminated the university's "overrealized enrollment" financial bonanza each fall.

The nonresident enrollment ceiling would eventually be seen as a foolish move, even by some who originally supported it. The legislature apparently intended to place a moratorium on higher education's rapid expansion, which threatened to outpace the state's ability to pay. But in the crass world of higher education finance, warm bodies—and parental checkbooks—were what counted. The out-of-state money was tantamount to new industry, smokeless industry. Almost a third of the university's new undergraduate students came from other states, particularly California, and they paid $999 in tuition (vs. $339 for resident students). If through the enrollment ceiling some 200 were denied admission, as seemed likely by the calculations of the director of admissions, the state would lose almost $200,000. It would have to export a lot of Hood River apples to make up for that loss.

Whatever the impact of such problems, Johnson seemed more plagued by the "incidental fees" question. He could not get away from it. He would (as he confessed later) think about it the last thing as he tried to get to sleep and the first thing in the morning.

It was a wretched dilemma. If he sided with the students and allowed almost $150,000 to be siphoned away from intercollegiate athletics in favor of student-run social action projects, he'd probably draw the wrath of politically powerful alumni and athletic fans. The university could scarcely afford to lose still more support. The other alternative loomed equally disastrous. He told the student leaders that they had presented "compelling arguments" for their projects, particularly the ethnic studies program, an area chronically undernourished. If he now denied them their idealism, could he live with himself? He might not only invite their disrespect (and possible violent confrontations), but he would also undermine his own philosophy of allowing students to assume responsibility.

A third choice existed, of course—to do nothing at all. That would be the easy way out. But it would be the worst choice of all. It would leave the mess for his successor, Robert D. Clark, to clean up. No. No self-respecting president could do that. As he said when he assumed the presidency, "No decisions will be postponed during my administration."

So he wondered how to cope with this latest "impossible

problem." He slept poorly. Small wonder he dreaded returning from the beach.

Charles Johnson was not alone, of course. In presidential offices all over America that spring sat college administrators who desperately preferred to be somewhere else. The college presidency represented a perilous no-man's-land in the crossfire of campus battles from San Francisco to Cambridge. There would be no letup until long after the cathartic convolutions that followed the deaths of four students at Kent State University a year later.

The Kent State affair would become known as a campus tragedy, and it would cause students throughout the nation to shout, stomp, march, riot, trash, and generally raise hell in righteous indignation against the violent repression of Amerika the fascist state. In January of 1969, no mass demonstrations followed the tragedy of Courtney Smith's death from a heart attack in the midst of a crisis at Swarthmore over demands from students. That college presidents might also be considered victims of fascist repression apparently was beside the point.

And Douglas Knight's resignation from Duke University in March 1969 caused scarcely a ripple of national notice. Knight resigned a job so marked by "savage demands" that it had become "nearly impossible." He explained that many of the problems of the university president were of a "frankly irrational nature"—such as when "Irrational Group 'A' wants to get at Irrational Group 'B'. . . . Unless you're surrounded by a very understanding group of trustees, students, and faculty friends who recognize the irrationality when they see it, you can be destroyed by it."

In April, the executive secretary of the American Council on Education, Charles Dobbins, voiced further concern about college presidents. Too many of them, he said in a speech at Atlanta, "were quietly letting it be known that they no longer can endure the mental and physical punishment to which they are being subjected by faculty and students alike." And how many talented young educators, he wondered, were turning away from academic administration because of the "adversary relationship" between the president and his constituencies?

Taking note of such problems, a small group of professors and administrators at the University of Oregon began to feel vaguely uneasy about an upcoming social event. These men were members of the executive committee of the University of Oregon Faculty Club. In spring the Faculty Club presented its annual "Faculty Follies," which included a skit poking fun at the university president.

Arthur S. Flemming had been a favorite target. He had an element of pompous dignity and aloofness about him that was easy to mock, yet he gave no indication that he found such parodies personally offensive. Past Follies had mimicked such Flemming foibles as his habit of mispronouncing the word "recognize" (rek-a-nize), his view of problems as "opportunities," and his use of cliché-infested platitudes ("I rekanize the opportunity to make a firm commitment to relevance").

To subject Charles Johnson—the man who seemed to smile less and less that spring—to such scorching treatment seemed inhumane. It would be no fun for anybody, least of all Charles Johnson. So the executive committee began to seek other means of injecting fun into the life of a beleaguered president.

Fun. That was the key word. Whatever else happened, the executive committee wanted the president to have fun—"to isolate him from his problems briefly in a 'fun setting,' " in the words of law professor Chapin Clark, a member of the committee.

So, in Committee Room "D," upstairs at the Faculty Club, the executive committee formed plans for a reception to honor the president, a social event that, as it turned out, would be the most memorable in the university's history.

The Faculty Club occupied an old, white, wood-frame house, half-hidden behind overgrown shrubs and rangy trees. The scene resembled a backwoodsy setting for a Gothic horror novel rather than the center of a modern state university campus.

Yet it had always been in the center. Built by a pioneer

scientist named George Collier, the little house—it was considered a mansion in its time—had served as the home of five of the university's ten presidents. When the demands of presidential living outgrew the Collier House, the Faculty Club acquired it.

The old house was, in some ways, the most curious of the eighty-nine buildings that comprised the campus proper that spring. Curious because it now seemed tiny and grotesquely out of place: a doll's house surrounded by giant brick-and-mortar monoliths. Curious, too, because it seemed to be a tranquil, bucolic sanctuary, a paradox on a campus anxious to be "relevant," anxious to chart a significant course through socially troubled waters.

It was for another reason, however, that the Faculty Club decided to hold its reception away from the campus. A state policy discouraged the serving of alcoholic beverages in campus buildings, and that included the Faculty Club, Number 81 on the university's building inventory list. The reception was moved to the Laurelwood Restaurant, a mile away. The setting was equally bucolic: the Laurelwood overlooked the cool, verdant hills of a nine-hole golf course. The date was set for Tuesday, June 3, from eight to nine-thirty in the evening, the late hour dictated less by fashion than by election laws that prohibited the sale of liquor while the polls were open. This was the date of a special election to establish a sales tax in Oregon, a measure that would be soundly defeated.

There now remained one further detail in the planning. How should the inscription read on the gold-plated desk set that was to be presented to the president as a "token of appreciation"? Arthur Litchman, a journalist, president of the Faculty Club, found this an arduous task. What can you say about a battle-fatigued combatant who's gone through the hell of the campus wars and survived? Litchman settled on the following, which the executive committee approved unanimously.

DR. CHARLES E. JOHNSON
ACTING PRESIDENT U. OF O. 1968-69
A YEAR OF CHALLENGE AND ACHIEVEMENT
U. OF O. FACULTY CLUB

A year of challenge and achievement. Later some professors would complain that the phrase sounded "chamber of commercy." But no one could deny that the year had been a challenge.

Achievement?

The day of the reception was warm and pleasant. Litchman, bearing his inscribed gift wrapped in tissue, arrived early at the Laurelwood, along with Professor Chapin Clark of law, Professor John Sherwood of English, and Embert Fossum, the alumni director, all members of the Faculty Club's executive committee.

At the start, the party assumed a festive note, a drama staged against a backdrop of colored lights which added an exotic touch to the dimly lit lounge. The first guests alternated between the bar and the large table of hors d'oeuvres. Some guests moved out to the glass-enclosed balcony which offered a spectacular view of the golf course below and of Spencer's Butte looming greenish-blue in the background.

The evening moved on. It was eight-twenty.

"Where's the Guest of Honor?"

Where, indeed? By eight-thirty people were conversing in hushed tones. This was not like Chuck Johnson, the most punctual and conscientious of men, to be late for a party, particularly one in his honor. By a quarter to nine the colored lights now seemed to cast an eerie glow. A feeling of unease fanned through the 150 people present. Rumors spread quickly.

"I hear Chuck's been detained by a group of angry students. He's been with them for three hours now."

"I understand they dropped cigar ashes on his rug."

"If Chuck has been with the students for three hours, he's doing too damned much listening."

"Oh, but you know Chuck. He'll sit there and take it as long as anyone's there to sock it to him."

Monitoring such bits of conversation, Professor Ed Cykler of the School of Music decided that he should mention the telephone conversation he'd had with President Johnson that noon.

"It was very strange," Professor Cykler confided. "We had a luncheon meeting of the Advisory Council this noon. Chuck

249

was supposed to be there. When it got to be twelve-thirty and he still hadn't shown up, I called his office. He answered the phone himself. I asked him if he planned to come to the meeting. He said, 'No, I don't see any reason for coming over.' He didn't make any effort to explain why. I thought he might have had some people with him at the time and that he didn't want to say anything in front of them. But later I found out that he was alone at the time. Even more strange was the way he talked. His voice had a kind of vague, far-away quality to it, almost as though he were talking from way off somewhere."

Guests now remembered another telephone call taken on the house phone earlier that evening by Charles Duncan, dean of the faculties. Duncan motioned to a colleague, Ray Hawk. The two men casually stepped outside and promptly drove off in Hawk's car.

Law professor Chapin Clark remembered Duncan's comment as he put down the phone. "He said something like, 'The man has taken too much.' I wonder what he meant?"

Speculation grew more ominous. The president had been kidnaped. He had had an accident. Students were holding him captive in his own office. There was a riot on the campus. The administration building was on fire. The computer center had been smashed. How easily and quickly, that spring of 1969, the most bizarre of spectacles seemed not only plausible but quite likely. Some people began to leave the reception, furtively, to drive by the campus to see if everything was all right.

By a quarter to nine the sun had set for the day, leaving a slightly yellowish glow on the western horizon. The "challenge and achievement" presentation was scheduled for this time. Just then Charles Duncan reappeared at the reception. He sought out Arthur Litchman and some of his Faculty Club colleagues.

"I think you should go ahead with your party," he said. "But I'm sorry to say that Chuck and Jeanne are not going to be able to make it tonight."

"What's wrong?" asked Litchman. "Trouble on the campus?"

"No, I've just come from there. Everything is quiet."

"Then what's the problem?"

"Ah, Chuck isn't well. He's ill. And Jeanne doesn't want to come to the reception by herself."

It was true enough, Duncan told himself, as far as it went. He guessed from Litchman's look of concern—was it disbelief?—that he hadn't been very convincing. But he couldn't bring himself to tell them that the president had disappeared. Simply vanished. Wherever Johnson was, Duncan told himself, things obviously were not right with him: he was ill.

Duncan left quickly, before more questions could be asked. He had no answers. He knew only that the president had left his office around six. At eight Jeanne Johnson called Duncan at the reception. "Have you seen anything of that man of mine?" He detected a slight edge to her voice. "No, not since this afternoon. Why? What's up?" She said, "Well, he's not home yet, and I know people are waiting at the reception, and I was just wondering. . . ." Her voice trailed off. Duncan felt an immediate sense of foreboding. This was not like Chuck Johnson. This was serious. Duncan and Ray Hawk drove to the president's office on the campus. They inspected the office and found no leads to his whereabouts. Their feeling of apprehension grew. They pieced together what they could remember of the president's day, which had been routine, though busy.

A meeting at nine with several professors to review the case of a man who had been turned down in his candidacy for a doctor's degree in education. The candidate himself was present. Johnson upheld the departmental decision and wished the man well in whatever new ventures he might undertake. A calm meeting.

A meeting at ten-thirty with a group of black students. They had come to discuss possible changes in the leadership of the minority-race educational programs. It was a noisy meeting, Hawk said, but probably not "threatening" to the president. The blacks had split into two factions and were arguing among themselves. The president had been merely a bystander to the battle.

A meeting at three with Duncan on faculty business. Strictly routine.

A meeting at four with Hawk and Gerald Bogen, a young man just back from the Peace Corps, to talk about Bogen's reassignment in the university administration. Bogen left around five, and Hawk and Johnson talked together for another hour.

"We talked about a lot of minor things," Hawk recalled. "Budget items, some details about tomorrow's faculty meeting, and I don't know what else. I looked at my watch and it was not quite six. I said, 'Chuck, I think we'd best be getting on home because we have a party tonight.' Chuck looked a little puzzled at first. Then he said, 'Oh, my gosh, that's right.' I said, 'Yes, I'm sure that Jeanne would appreciate your getting home to freshen up a bit. After all, you're the Number One man up there tonight. You don't want to be late for your own party.' Then I left, and that was the last I saw of him."

They learned from Bill Blevins that Johnson did leave his office shortly thereafter. He stopped at Blevin's office, located adjacent to his own.

"He poked his head in the door," Blevins recounted. "He said, 'Is there anything I should be aware of before I go home?' I said I didn't have anything at the moment. I asked if I should call him at home if anything important turned up. He said, 'Yes, why don't you do that—anytime up to about eight. I've got that awards thing tonight at eight.' Then he left. I guess that must have been around six."

As their feelings of foreboding grew, Hawk turned to Duncan. "Chuck," he said, "I think this is a matter for the police." Duncan agreed.

Now, at nine o'clock, three hours after the president had last been seen, there still was no word. The police had transmitted a radio bulletin asking patrol cars to watch for a "missing vehicle," a pale green 1968 Plymouth sedan, license "E" four-one-five-seven-eight. The dispatch discreetly omitted mention of the driver's name, Charles Johnson. No use prematurely alerting the news media, which monitored the police radio frequencies.

When he left the reception after advising Litchman that the president and his wife would not attend, Charles Duncan headed his car for the Johnson house. The ten-minute drive gave him time to collect his thoughts, consisting mostly of ominous reflections on the past few weeks.

All the signs were there in Johnson's demeanor, Duncan decided, the preoccupied looks, the hesitant strides as he walked, the forgetfulness, the unproductive shuffling of papers. No one incident had seemed particularly alarming at the time. In retrospect, the cumulative impact of them seemed frightening indeed. And now this. *The man has taken too much.* Damn! Duncan shuddered a little as he drove across the Ferry Street Bridge spanning the twilight-darkened waters of the Willamette River. He remembered a meeting held two weeks earlier, another of those abusive, angry confrontations. Only this time the abuse had been hurled at Duncan rather than at Johnson. Afterward, Johnson told Duncan, "I don't know how in the world you kept so calm. I was about ready to blow my top."

That seemed strange, now that Duncan thought about it. If Johnson was ready to blow his top hearing a colleague suffer strident abuse from militant students, what must he have felt the many times he heard it directed at himself? Chuck Johnson was always the unflappable one. Calm. Patient. A man who kept his cool while everyone else exploded. Indeed, Johnson had not raised his voice in anger once during the ten months he'd been acting president, so far as Duncan could recall.

And now this. Damn!

Eighteen:
Pent-up Thoughts

"Daddy's going to be all right, isn't he?" It was Kylene, the youngest Johnson daughter, the only child still living at home. Kylene had sensed the anxiety in the household, and she could not get to sleep. "Daddy's coming home, isn't he?"

Jeanne Johnson tried to hide her own anxiety and tried to be reassuring. "Of course he's coming home," she said, and she believed it.

It was midnight before Kylene dropped off to sleep. By then all the people had left the Johnson house except Ray Hawk, who stayed to monitor the calls to and from the police. Two officers of the Eugene Police Department had been detailed to work on the Johnson case. They'd checked bars, motels, hospitals, ambulance services, and other police agencies. They had cruised through parks, overlooks, and viewpoints in search of the missing Plymouth. They'd turned up nothing. Around 1:00 a.m. they drove by to talk with Mrs. Johnson in person.

She was at a loss to explain the disappearance. This was not like Chuck, she said. He'd never go into a bar alone or to a motel or off somewhere without telling someone. And he knew he had the party.

Sometimes, the officers said, people do stranges things in times of stress. Did he have a close friend, someone in whom he might confide—pour his heart out?

No, she said, not really. Chuck was a loner, basically. His closest friends had been at the house this evening. And if the question implied "another woman," that, too, seemed unlikely, she said, if only because his mind was too preoccupied, his time too limited.

The most logical explanation was an accident. He had a reputation as a careless driver. But an accident surely would have been reported by this time. What could have happened? She did not know.

The officers left and the house was silent. As Hawk and Mrs. Johnson sat in the living room a lot of pent-up thoughts chose this moment for release.

"This," said Hawk, breaking the silence, "has been a very rough year for Chuck."

"Yes."

"I keep wondering about today," he said. "I've spent nearly twenty years of my life as a student of people. I think I know people pretty well. But when I left Chuck at the office this evening, I saw nothing in his behavior that left me with the slightest degree of alarm. He seemed tired, yes. But I saw nothing alarming there."

"Chuck has been tired and preoccupied lately," she said. "The whole year has been like walking on eggs, always afraid of that fatal misstep."

"He's worried about that darned incidental fee question. It's sending him straight up the wall."

"Yes," she said, "and I think he's disappointed in the outcome of the student elections. I think he would have preferred a less radical group of students in office. And yet, he's always said that both classes of students are healthy for a university. He says some of these conservative kids are just as wrong in their viewpoints as the noisiest radicals. He says you've got to mix them together in a university and let the ideas flow. That's his favorite statement. Let the ideas flow and the good ones will rise like cream to the top. I don't think he's disillusioned about students. I think the outside pressures have been the most trying. The taxpayers. The alumni. The politicians. They won't leave the university alone to solve its own problems."

"Chuck always said he was no politician."

"And he was totally honest in saying it. Politically you don't tell the governor that he's probably wrong. You don't tell an influential alumnus that he doesn't know what he's talking about. The alumnus can be obnoxious and drunk and totally out of order, but you have to talk to him. And Chuck will do it. He can talk to anyone, drunk or sober. But it's disillusioning to him that in order to get money for the university or to keep on the good side of those kinds of people you have to placate them. This is not his strong point. He really prefers the academic side of things."

"Chuck is a man who doesn't get much release from emotional tension," Hawk said. "I can only marvel at how calm he's been in the middle of openly hostile groups. Yet he's a sensitive man, more than he'll admit. The hate mail, for example—I think it bothers him more than he'll say."

"People probably think he stays calm at the office and then comes home and takes it out on the family. Well, if anything he's been kinder than before. Of course, he's been more withdrawn than usual, and I think he's lost a night or two of sleep. Things have hit him hard in the last few months. I don't think he's ever quite bounced back physically from the flu."

"I wondered for a time," Hawk said, "how he felt when the board passed over him and named Bob Clark as the permanent president."

"I think he meant what the papers quoted him as saying," she replied. "He said relief had swamped his disappointment. I'm sure he approved of Bob's appointment. All year long he'd been saying, 'I don't know why they're overlooking Bob Clark. He seems like such a logical choice.' "

Hawk said, "A few days after the board announced Bob's appointment, I walked into Chuck's office. I said, 'Chuck, I feel that we've let you down.' I was kind of emotional about it.

Chuck looked at me and leaned back in his chair. I said, 'Those of us who worked most closely with you were certainly pulling to see that when the board selected a new president, you would be that man. I think you should have had a chance for this. I think you have the timber to make a great president. I don't think we've given you the kind of support that would make you look good in the eyes of the board.' Chuck just about expostulated his response. 'Oh, no, don't feel that way at all, Ray.' He said he'd been thinking quite a lot about himself lately, where he might go from here."

"We've talked about that," she said.

"Chuck said that while he might have wanted the presidency at one time, he'd come around to a different view now. He said, 'It's come to my mind that the only place where I'm going to be happy is back where I started—in the classroom.' Chuck said he got an inquiry from Colorado State not long ago; they're looking for a president. He said it was almost a joy to write and tell them he's not interested."

"But we're not sure where to go from here," she said. "He doesn't want to go back to the business school and try to build the accounting department up again. He doesn't want to be an administrator, and he doesn't want to leave Oregon. What now? Stanford is the only place he thinks he might like as well as Oregon. I guess he's pushed a lot of this from his mind now. We have a sabbatical leave coming up. We've talked about going to England. Maybe some opportunity will turn up during the year."

"I think Chuck is bothered less by whether he wants to be a college president than by how much *longer* he has to be one," said Hawk. "There's been some talk about Bob not coming to take over the presidency until January. Chuck and I talked about that today. Chuck shook his head and said, 'I don't know, Ray. I just don't know if I can last.' I'm sure he's been counting the days and hours until Bob gets here and he can get out from under the pressure."

They were silent again. *The fun has gone out of the college presidency,* she thought to herself. Who said that? Not Chuck.

Yes, now she remembered. It was James Jensen, the president of Oregon State University. During the Rose Bowl trip last January, the men got together, both smoking their pipes out on the balcony of the hotel room. "You know, Chuck," Jensen said, "the fun has gone out of the presidency. It used to be a lot of work and there were a lot of problems. But it was fun, too. That's not true any longer. The fun is gone." It was only a few days later that Jensen announced his resignation to take a job with a Rockefeller Foundation-financed project in Thailand.

It was dark and still at three-thirty in the morning when the car drove up. Jeanne Johnson had retired to the bedroom; Ray Hawk had been napping on the playroom sofa. Both awakened to the sound of the car. It slowly eased along Palomino Drive and pulled into the wide cement driveway of the Johnson house. The driver did not turn out the headlights. His footsteps clicked heavily and unevenly along the walk to the front door. Chuck, Mrs. Johnson thought to herself, would have come in the back door.

She ran quickly to the front door. She opened it and felt an overwhelming surge of relief.

Standing there was her husband.

"Am I home?"

He seemed unsure. He wobbled unsteadily on his feet, then slumped against the door frame, his legs askew.

"I'm home, aren't I?"

"Yes, of course, Chuck."

He seemed strange and distant, and for a moment she thought, with relief, that he'd merely been at a cocktail bar after all.

"Of course you're home, Chuck."

He acted as though he might have been drinking. He seemed childlike and helpless. His deep voice had lost its tone of self-assurance. It must have been quite a night, she thought. His trousers were torn at the bottom and caked with mud up to the knees. His hands and face were laced with tiny scratches.

"I had to come back. . . ."

She put her arm around his waist and guided him to the

bedroom. She doubted now that he'd been drinking. He always held his liquor well. The vagueness in his demeanor, the curious, glassed-in look in his eyes—these suggested something else. She thought of the tranquilizer pills.

"I couldn't do it. . . ."

Little of what he said made sense to her. His talk was incoherent, tumbling out in bits and pieces like parts of a jigsaw puzzle to be assembled. He spoke of driving, of a lake, of walking in the trees, of getting lost, of his love for his family.

She asked about the tranquilizers.

"I don't know," he said. "Look in my coat pocket.'.'

She looked. The tiny yellow Valium tablets were in a plastic vial in the pocket. They were all there, so far as she could tell. She doubted that he'd even taken one.

"We missed the party, didn't we?"

The remark startled her. He'd spilled it out almost as if the reception had suddenly occurred to him, almost as if he thought they might still make the party if they hurried.

"Yes," she said. "We sure did."

"I'm sorry. I feel bad about that."

"It's not important," she said. "What matters is that you're home and you're all right."

"Well, it was nice of them to do this. I'm sorry we missed the party."

She wondered how he might explain all of this. Would he be embarrassed facing those who had planned the reception? That would have to be worked out later. His demeanor still puzzled her, and she agreed with Ray Hawk who, witnessing the homecoming, suggested the family physician be called. Dr. Charles Williams said he would be there in half an hour.

Hawk, meanwhile, stepped outside to look at the car. He turned off the headlights. By the garage light he could see that the car bore no dents or scratches. But it was very muddy and dusty. On the front seat Hawk found a charge slip for gasoline purchased by credit card from a Chevron station in Oakridge, Oregon, on June 3, 1969. It was signed by Johnson in his usual scrawl.

The president, then, had driven at least as far as Oakridge, a logging community of 1,500 on the western slope of the Cascade Mountains, forty-five miles southeast of Eugene. That would account for ninety miles. But by the dirty condition of the car Hawk guessed that Johnson had driven on back roads, too. Hawk didn't know it then, but a subsequent check of mileage records would show that Johnson had driven almost 200 miles that night. That was sufficient to have driven to the high mountain lakes—Crescent and Odell lakes—about eighty miles to the southeast. At this 4,800-foot elevation banks of snow lined the roadsides, even in June.

It was four-fifteen and still dark when Dr. Charles Williams drove up. Williams, a slim, bald man, almost as tall and rangy as Johnson, found his patient sitting up in bed. To Williams's professional eye, Johnson's appearance—the pale skin, the grim set of his mouth, the weak, sighing respirations—seemed to spell out physical exhaustion. His heart, lungs, and blood pressure were normal. Williams asked what had happened that evening. Johnson said he could remember very little of it.

"I remember getting in the car on the campus," he said. "I was driving along when something told me, head for the hills!"

"A small voice was telling you that?" the doctor asked. "Or were you saying that to yourself, or what?"

"Well . . . I just don't know. I just don't remember. I do remember being by a lake. I remember walking, getting out of the car and walking."

"Walking along the shore?"

"No, I think I was going pretty much cross-country. I remember going uphill. Climbing and going through brush. I walked quite a ways. Finally I decided I can't do this to my folks. To my family. I had to come back."

Can't do what? Dr. Williams did not ask that question. He assumed that Johnson meant running away. By the daily papers, he knew there was a lot for a university president to run away from. The University of Oregon campus seemed to be in a continual uproar.

"You've been under a lot of pressure lately, haven't you?"

the doctor asked. "You've been working long hours with a lot of people trying to tell you how to run the university?"

"Well—" Johnson paused. "I just can't seem to make decisions."

"How do you mean?"

"It's the darndest thing. I can't make up my mind. I just can't seem to make up my mind. I get a new problem every day. It's not solved, and then the next day I get another unsolvable problem. I just can't seem to make decisions."

The man was pushing himself too hard, Williams thought to himself. Or the job was demanding too much of him. In many people, the resulting stresses brought a variety of somatic complaints: headaches, stomachaches, ulcers, rashes—all anxiety-produced ailments. Johnson had none of these.

"Do you think you can ease off on your work load?" Williams asked. "Shift the responsibility to your subordinates and stay home for a while?"

Johnson hesitated. "I don't want to give up. But I suppose I have been working too hard. Maybe with a day or so off I'll be all right."

Dr. Williams thought it might take more than a day or so. While it seemed a simple case of overwork, it remained, in another sense, very complex. Johnson had driven off somewhere for nine and one-half hours and could remember almost nothing about those hours.

Amnesia. A fugue state. Fugue, a French word meaning "flight."

Johnson's hazy description of the night's events reminded Williams of a case described to him years ago by a psychiatrist. The patient had been plagued by frequent fugue states: mental blackouts accompanied by "flight." The patient said he could feel the blackouts coming. Each time one came, a little voice kept saying something incomprehensible. It sounded like *con-radd-staw-fur, con-radd-staw-fur.* The voice repeated it in a kind of electronic monotone *con-radd-staw-fur, con-radd-staw-fur.* It took two years of psychotherapy to unlock its meaning. It turned out to be the name of a German soldier the patient had killed in hand-to-hand combat during World War II. Konrad Stauffer.[1]

Dr. Williams gave Johnson a sedative, Valium, to help him sleep. He explained about the fugue: a mental condition where the mind, pushed to emotional extremes, simply blocks out reality and the patient literally takes flight. The mind substitutes a more pleasant pattern of behavior. Last night, driving to the tranquility of a mountain lake and taking a walk through the woods might have been more pleasant than going to the reception. A fugue, one psychologist said, "is a caricature of a vacation."

"You just go along," Dr. Williams told Johnson, "doing your best to cope with the problems. All of a sudden the mind goes on automatic pilot, and you don't know what you're doing. You have amnesia. But you can still function. You can drive a car or carry on a conversation. But a completely different system of the mind has taken over, a second personality, you might say. And these two personalities don't speak to each other. In a fugue you usually don't remember the past. When you come out of it you usually don't remember what happened. The fugue can last only minutes or it can last for hours, even months."

Johnson accepted this explanation impassively. He asked no questions. Williams said he would be back that afternoon. As he left, he noted a paperback book lying on the nightstand beside the bed: *Confrontation.* What irony, the doctor thought to himself.

In his office later, Dr. Williams found time to reflect further on the Johnson case.

The fugue, it seemed to him, was a quaintly old-fashioned reaction to stress. He had not seen many cases like it. What he did see were ulcers and heart attacks and strokes. He recalled that Sigmund Freud used to write about the fugue as part of a mental condition he called "hysteria." Freud used the term to mean the appearance of symptoms that had no base in organic pathology. It was in the mind. Hysteria came in two dimensions by Freud's definition: "conversion hysteria" and "dissociative hysteria."

Textbooks contained many classic examples. A man developed paralysis in both legs after his wife had left him for another man. The paralysis apparently was the result of a suppressed desire to pursue his wife and kill her and her lover. A woman lost her sense of smell when her son began to drink excessively and came home with the odor of alcohol on his breath. Two examples of conversion hysteria.

The Johnson case seemed to fit the "dissociative" side of hysteria. This included the fugue, amnesia, sleepwalking, and occasional extreme cases of "multiple personality": two or more fully developed personalities in the same person, the kind made famous by the book and movie, *The Three Faces of Eve.* The hysteria symptoms were said to be more common among women than men.

To Dr. Williams, they seemed rare in either sex in 1969. Perhaps that was because of increased public sophistication. People no longer accepted such bizarre symptoms when "it's all in your head." Tranquilizers and other drugs made it possible to head off trouble before it became serious. But Johnson, Williams, recalled, was wary of medicine.

He pulled the Johnson folder from his records file. It was a skinny folder, covering seventeen years of medical history of a man who seldom sought medical attention. Indeed, the friendship between Williams and Johnson had developed from a mutual interest in tennis, not from professional visits. The record contained little more than notations of minor irritations treated. Sinusitus in 1952, a boil on the neck in 1953, a back pain in 1955, a bad cold in 1961, a tennis elbow in 1966. In 1966, Johnson requested a thorough medical examination believing that, at age 46, he ought to be "looked at." A questionnaire, filled out as part of the examination, revealed a more or less typical medical history: childhood bouts with scarlet fever and tonsilitis and, later in the Army, with a tropical virus called dengue fever. He'd worn glasses to correct myopia since the age of nine. He was troubled by a persistent buzzing and ringing in the ears, and his hearing was slightly below normal. He had varicose veins but they did not bother him. Notes on the examination revealed his weight to be 201 pounds, blood pressure 112 over 70, pulse 88, temperature 99, chest expansion 39 to 41. He was, the doctor concluded, a man of good health who played tennis weekly, who did back exercises for half-hour periods three to five times a week, who seldom took medicine, and who lived a life of moderation. One cigar and four or five pipefuls of tobacco a day. A weekly average of six ounces of whiskey, six ounces of wine, and thirty-three ounces of beer.

Dr. Williams chuckled when he read the last entry. He suspected Johnson, in listing such precise figures, was practicing a little tongue-in-cheek humor, or perhaps even subtly protesting against the meddlesome nature of questionnaires.

The major question was the heart. In 1951 a doctor in Berkeley, California, told Johnson that his electrocardiogram showed signs of a now-healed posterior myocardial infarction—a heart attack. Johnson had gone to the doctor complaining of chest pains after having slipped and fallen on some icy steps. The Berkeley doctor had called it an "abnormality," rather than a heart attack; the doctor had even offered to write a letter certifying the absence of a heart attack should there be any problem in obtaining life insurance.

Dr. Williams had a new electrocardiogram made on Johnson's heart. He concluded that the term "heart attack" would be an overinterpretation even though he did find small Q-waves in two limb leads. The Q-waves were about one millimeter high. To be significant in a man of Johnson's size, they would have to be about four millimeters.

Dr. Williams now turned to the part of the questionnaire dealing with emotional health. He glanced through the questions and Johnson's answers.

Did you have a happy childhood? *Yes*, Johnson answered.

Do you have a compatible spouse? *Yes*.

Do you have difficulty making decisions? *No*.

What frustrations do you have? *No major ones.*
Do you regard yourself as being successful? *Yes.*
Do you withdraw or fight back when you are hurt? *No.*
Are you aggressive or retiring? *Neither.*
What conflicts do you have? *None.*
Are you a perfectionist? *No.*
Do you have periods of excessive depression? *No.*
Do you feel life is not worth living? *No.*
Have you ever had a nervous breakdown? *No.*
Have you ever seriously considered suicide? *No.*
Have you ever been under the care of a psychiatrist? *No.*
Do you regard yourself as being well adjusted? *Yes.*

These and other questions were routinely answered to suggest a well-adjusted personality. Williams knew, of course, that people are often defensive about their emotions. Johnson, a man who tended to keep his feelings to himself, might be more defensive than most. It was ironic that people could accept certain types of emotion-based complaints—an ulcer for example—as a badge of prestige. It showed a man was diligent and hardworking in the pioneer American ethic. But other symptoms—the problems that were "all in your head"—represented a mark of shame. Perhaps that was because people did not understand mental aberrations as well as they understood the physical, and they were frightened of things they did not understand.

Dr. Williams put away the file. He was satisfied that the record contained no hint of previous psychological disorders. Nor did it contain any organic explanation for what had happened. It merely confirmed his earlier belief. The fugue episode was the result of a job so pressure-laden and traumatic that it simply overwhelmed the emotional defenses of this man. Now a new question arose. What could be done to help Charles Johnson cope with the presidential burden for the remainder of his tenure? Should he return to the job at all? The answers called for assistance beyond what Dr. Williams felt he could deliver. They called for psychiatric help. If the patient agreed, he planned to ask a psychiatrist at the University of Oregon Medical School, located a hundred miles away in Portland, to see him.

Nineteen:
A Test
of Manhood

The life of the university moved on, of course. The faculty, holding its regular monthly meeting that Wednesday, the fourth of June, passed a resolution commending Acting President Johnson for "outstanding leadership" in the face of "severe financial constraints" and "restless pressures for change and reform." The public affairs office continued to assemble the details of commencement 1969, scheduled for Sunday, June 15, less than two weeks away. Rumors persisted that black students might try to disrupt the ceremony.

Questions remained. Would Dr. Johnson preside at commencement? Would he deliver the president's traditional "charge" to the graduating class? Or should a substitute be secured? Ray Hawk promised that he would consult with Johnson at the earliest opportunity. Other more immediate problems pressed in on Hawk that morning. What about the news media? The failure of the university's president to show for a reception in his honor was surely news. It would be a miracle if it escaped attention.

At Hawk's direction a statement was prepared indicating that the president had been ordered by his doctor to stay home and

267

rest after having been "overcome by fatigue." The *Register-Guard* discreetly played down the story with a brief item on page 2 of Section B under the headline, REST ORDERED FOR U OF O ACTING CHIEF.

> Charles Johnson, acting president of the University of Oregon, has been ordered by his physician to remain home to rest after being overcome by fatigue Tuesday, his wife said Wednesday.
>
> Johnson, who had been scheduled to attend a reception in his honor Tuesday night, was overcome while driving home from his office, according to his wife.
>
> After working late, Johnson began driving to his home at 250 Palomino Dr. in the Willakenzie area before going to the reception. But en route he was apparently overcome by fatigue and stopped his car, Mrs. Johnson said.
>
> When he failed to arrive home as scheduled, Mrs. Johnson said she became anxious and notified police. But Johnson, in the meantime, drove on home after resting for some time in the car, she said. His physician was then called.
>
> Johnson has "been working evenings and weekends for a long period," a university spokesman said. There was no indication of how long Johnson will be gone from his office.

It seemed an adequate explanation, one that would not embarrass the president or his family. But at the Faculty Club, in the historic little house half-hidden among the trees and shrubs, word began to get around. The president, professors told each other in hushed tones, had suffered "some kind of nervous breakdown." John Hulteng, the journalism professor, typed a letter to President Johnson, addressing it to his home.

He wrote that he was "embittered" by the president's collapse "because I know the kinds of pressures that have focused on you and your office all year from righteously ill-informed taxpayers, impatient militants, and a faculty all too willing to pass the buck on up until it stopped at your office. . . . You made decisions carefully and surely after laying out the evidence and arguments with a surgeon's kind of precision. . . .

You explained those decisions to a variety of constituencies, including some of the most inherently hostile and antagonistic around (I was on hand for some of those confrontations with the alumni, the editors, the Malcolm X celebrators). . . . I'm so very, very sorry that the unreasonable demands of an impossible office and an unprecedented era have worn down a truly good man. . . ."

Professor Hulteng reflected later on the irony of timing. Johnson's collapse, on June 3, 1969, came precisely a year after announcement of his appointment: June 3, 1968. The earlier date was the occasion of the dinner party at the Starlins' house, the one at which Chuck and Jeanne Johnson had talked so excitedly about the year ahead as interim president.

Now the talk was different. It was often incoherent. What was one to make, for example, of Johnson's remark upon returning home that evening? *I decided I just can't do this to my folks. I had to come back.* Had he contemplated suicide? The question was asked two days later in the office of a psychiatrist, Dr. Agnar A. Straumfjord, associate professor of psychiatry at the University of Oregon Medical School.

Dr. Straumfjord, at 40 a stocky man with a round, pleasant face and light brown crew-cut hair, exuded a friendly amiability not unlike that of Johnson himself. As director of the Student Health Center, he occupied an unpretentious office on the second floor of the Clinical Laboratories Building, just down a narrow corridor from the Otolaryngology (ear, nose, throat) Department.

It was here that Charles Johnson, for the first time in his life, paid a professional visit to a psychiatrist. Dr. Straumfjord greeted him at the door of his office and motioned him toward the large black leather chair that dominated the office. The doctor had arranged his office so that his desk faced a wall. When talking to a patient he spun his chair around so that he might face the visitor directly with no desk as a barrier to communication. Jeanne Johnson, who had driven the car to Portland, sat in a straight chair adjacent to her husband.

Dr. Straumfjord perceived Johnson to be, as he wrote in his

notes "a tall, well-developed, neatly dressed man wearing a business suit. His affect today is appropriate, his mood neither elated or dejected. He appears of above-average intelligence, and is oriented in all three spheres.[1] There is no evidence of thought disorganization."

The doctor perceived a certain reticence in Johnson, however; he answered questions fully, but he never warmed up to the idea of talking about his personal problems. He volunteered nothing. The doctor guessed that Johnson was seeing a psychiatrist somewhat under duress.

He did not know about Johnson's life-long aversion to doctors. If Johnson avoided doctors who dealt with the body, what was he to think now about a doctor of the mind? Perhaps the visit was a blow to his self-esteem. He certainly had made his share of wisecracks down through the years about "having my head examined." Now it was a reality.

After an exchange of pleasantries, Dr. Straumfjord opened with what he called his "standard question," calculated to be "nonthreatening" to new patients.

"How does it happen that you're here to see me today?"

Johnson recounted the evening's events like an accountant delivering a fiscal report. He'd been having troubles with forgetfulness and indecisiveness for several weeks, he said. He really couldn't explain the flight to the hills, nor could he remember anything more about it than the flashes of memory he cited to Dr. Williams earlier. At one point, Dr. Straumfjord asked the question. Had he, at anytime during the flight, contemplated suicide?

"Yes," Johnson answered candidly and calmly. "It crossed my mind as I was out there. But I thought, 'This just doesn't make any sense at all.' I decided I had to come back."

Dr. Straumfjord felt reassured. Johnson did not attempt to cover up his thoughts of self-destruction, nor did he attempt to dramatize them. They merely formed part of the recitation of events of the evening. The doctor had learned to worry more about patients who vented some more intense feelings about the subject of life and death or avoided talking about the subject altogether.

Johnson answered other questions in a similar matter-of-fact tone.

When had the problems of forgetfulness and indecisiveness begun?

"I think it must have been about six weeks ago.[2] That's when I came down with the Hong Kong flu."

Things had begun to disintegrate at that point, Johnson continued. He tried to carry on with the work while in bed, weak and feverish, but he could accomplish nothing. He did not see a doctor. After a week at home he returned to the office for half-days. He felt pretty shaky. A lot of work had piled up, and he tried to get to it. But he was losing ground and he knew it. It was just one impossible problem after another, and none of them ever seemed to get solved. He just couldn't seem to make the necessary decisions to get the paper moving off his desk. On top of that, he'd had a substantial loss of appetite, he'd lost fifteen pounds and never regained them, and he wasn't sleeping well—all of which he felt had caused some loss of efficiency in his performance as president.

What was the nature of the sleep disturbance? How would he characterize it?

"Well, it seems to be a matter of mulling over the problems of the university. I just lie there and think about the decisions I have to make. I just can't get them out of my mind, and yet I can't seem to make up my mind. I can't seem to make the necessary decisions. Then when I do finally get to sleep, I sometimes wake up early, maybe around three or four in the morning. That's when I go back to the problems of the university again, mulling over the decisions that I've got to make, and I can't seem to get back to sleep. Sometimes I go out and read."

What was the nature of the decisions?

A variety of problems, Johnson replied, mostly in the area of budgeting.

Could he give one specific example, please?

"Yes," he said, "there's one problem in particular. There's a group of activist students who've given me some new ideas for projects to be financed out of student activity fees. Because of circumstances, I find it hard to respond, yet I *want* to respond.

It's a hard decision, and I haven't made up my mind yet. I just don't know what I'm going to do."

What about exercise? Was he getting regular physical exercise?

"Not much since I got the flu." He said he used to jog and play tennis several times a week. But since the flu episode, he'd had neither the stamina nor the time, he said.

At the end of the hour-long interview, Dr. Straumfjord recorded this note for his files:

IMPRESSION

Situational adjustment reaction with depression. I think it is likely that Dr. Johnson suffered post viral asthenia following his bout with the flu. That he had been chronically fatigued and has been in a vicious cycle of increasing fatigue, decreasing performance, and increased anxiety, etc. I have recommended that he not return to his office before the first of the week, that he attempt to shift responsibility to his subordinates, that he attempt to get himself involved in a program of progressive increasing physical activity and that he return on June 9 for reevaluation.

Dr. Straumfjord explained to Johnson that asthenia is a "generalized weakness" that is common after a virus infection. Men whose jobs demand a high level of performance are particularly susceptible. They often get up in the morning feeling pretty good. Then, after a couple of hours, they become exhausted, unable to continue. The body, weakened by the illness, simply could not keep pace with the demands of a determined mind.

"What you have, then, is a vicious cycle," the doctor continued. "The less able you are to perform, the more distressed you become. The more distressed you are, the more depressed you get. The more depressed you get, the harder it is to make decisions. You're being dragged lower and lower. So some kind of break in that cycle would seem to be the appropriate action to take at this point. Do you think it would be possible for you to remain at home away from the job for a while?"

Dr. Straumfjord was conscious of their respective positions—you don't *order* a university president, you suggest.

"Well, yeah," Johnson replied, "there isn't anything urgent just at this moment. I've got some decisions coming up before too long, but for the moment what I can do is meet with some of the people I work with and let them take over most of the responsibilities."

Dr. Straumfjord found in Johnson what he called a "compulsive and perfectionistic" personality, a man whose determination and drive had simply outpaced his body's capacity to respond. It was not unusual. Like any college president, Johnson would not have attained his high position without having demonstrated a high level of performance. His job, his work, his level of performance—these were important to him. Dr. Straumfjord felt that Johnson should be encouraged to reengage himself into his work after he had built up sufficient stamina. It should be a gradual thing, as his health permitted. Dr. Straumfjord, reassured by Johnson's calm demeanor, did not believe suicide to be of imminent concern. The case required careful monitoring, however, lest matters become worse. The doctor gave Johnson his phone number and urged him to call should problems arise.

The "fugue state" should not unduly concern him, Dr. Straumfjord told Johnson. "The fugue state, of itself, means little more than preoccupation. It's a little like driving home with a preoccupied mind and not remembering where you've been. I do that myself sometimes."

Just as the body has limitations on its endurance, he continued, so has the mind. It has "defenses" against being engulfed by emotions, just as the body has defenses against disease. When the mind, for example, becomes overwhelmed with the unpleasant task of making crucial decisions, often with inadequate information, amid the strident and often-irrational pressures of special-interest groups, one of the mind's defenses is simply to block everything out. Get rid of all the unpleasantness. Hence the amnesia or fugue.

That a fugue should be triggered by a reception in Johnson's honor puzzled Straumfjord a little. He did not discuss it with him, but he guessed that Johnson simply did not consider himself worthy of the honor and found it hard to accept.

The most dangerous aspect of the fugue, he told Johnson, was the highway hazard. If a fugue should overtake him while driving, he could be as menacing as a drunk driver. Therefore he should leave the driving to his wife. He continued the prescription for Valium, the anti-anxiety drug. He suggested that Johnson resume his physical exercises.

"That's a very acceptable form of getting rid of tensions and frustrations," he said. "Just go beat the hell out of a tennis ball. I've always felt that a big canvas punching bag ought to be required equipment in every executive suite."

Johnson's second session with Dr. Straumfjord, on June 9, was more relaxed and open than the first. The doctor seemed now to have established that delicate and fragile quality necessary to a successful psychiatrist-patient relationship—trust.

Johnson voluntarily discussed his feelings of "inadequacy" in his job. He said he was tortured by the belief that he had not measured up to the level of performance that the job demanded of him. He said he had failed in a number of presidential endeavors, particularly those requiring crucial decisions. He was even now failing to cope with such issues as the incidental fees question. He just could not make up his mind about that, nor could he see any compromise solution.

The comments surprised Dr. Straumfjord a little. Others would judge Johnson to be a very adequate person; Dr. Straumfjord himself felt a little in awe of him. Now he was confessing his own feelings of self-doubt. It was typical, of course, of the "compulsive personality." Such people often set impossible goals for themselves. Dr. Straumfjord recorded in his notes:

> Dr. Johnson is doing somewhat better. He has been quite active over the weekend, has been participating in sports activities, has avoided responsibilities of work. On Sunday, June 8, he again felt himself to be somewhat anxious and a bit depressed, particularly as he anticipated meeting the

demands of his work. At the present time he says he feels overwhelmed when he considers all the things that he must do and the confrontations that face him which he feels inadequate to deal with. He admits that there are no solutions to some of the problems that he is facing, but that he cannot disregard his feelings of responsibility in facing the next few weeks.

Johnson's apprehensions and doubts about himself contained a vagueness typical of patients overwhelmed by what they consider insurmountable problems. Such feelings are often accompanied by an element of irrationality. Clearly the patient ought not to judge his performance on the basis of the weeks since the flu; hadn't the doctor made it clear to Johnson that postviral asthenia was a real and deadly thing for anyone who attempted to maintain his usual fast-paced life? It was a little like an airliner trying to maintain speed and altitude with two of its four engines out.

Further, the patient ought not to apply standards of expectations to himself that he did not apply to others. He could forgive foibles and failures in just about everybody else, why could he not forgive them in himself? And, finally, the patient ought to look rationally at his own feelings and nail down those vague anxieties. Perhaps, looked at in terms of specifics, they were not as bad as they seemed.

"What would you say is the worst thing that could possibly happen to you?" asked Dr. Straumfjord.

Johnson paused for a moment. "I suppose to be permanently unable to function effectively in making decisions."

"All right. And how long do you suppose this problem is likely to continue?"

"I don't know."

"Do you think it's likely to be permanent?"

"No, I suppose not."

Dr. Straumfjord then asked Johnson to define specifically the priorities he faced in the immediate future and what he planned to do about them.

Johnson replied that among the most important at the moment was commencement. He must preside at commencement on June 15, less then a week away.

He had set a new goal for himself. To preside at commencement and deliver the ten-minute "charge" to the graduating class was a "test" of his ability as a man, Johnson said. He must perform. Dr. Straumfjord recorded in his notes:

> If he fails the test this means he is of no value, and if he passes the test this means that he is an adequate human being. We discussed alternatives available to him at the present time. He says he is unable to completely disregard his responsibilities and does not feel up to returning 100% into facing the situation. I asked him to find somewhere in between where he might function. He said he thought he would ask knowledgeable people to come to his house to discuss their situation with him.
>
> I have suggested that it may be helpful for Dr. Johnson to be seen also by Dr. Saslow. He is agreeable to this and this has been arranged for Tuesday, June 10th.

About 2 a.m. on Tuesday, June 10, Dr. Straumfjord's father unexpectedly died in Denver, Colorado. The doctor left later that morning for Denver. He would always regret this turn of events, quite apart from his own personal loss. It meant that Johnson would be confronted by an entirely new psychiatric personality in Dr. George Saslow, the chairman of the Department of Psychiatry at the Medical School. Straumfjord considered it bad practice to change psychiatrists in the middle of treatment. He had not intended this; he merely had planned a joint consultation, drawing on the background and knowledge of Dr. Saslow, one of the nation's most eminent psychiatrists. The fact that Saslow and Johnson were acquainted might, of course, ease the transition.

At sixty-two, Dr. Saslow was a handsome, durable man, articulate and urbane, a New Yorker by birth, the author of more than 100 scholarly articles for medical and psychiatric journals. Having known Johnson before, he was able to draw a contrast between this visit and the last time he'd seen Johnson, about two weeks earlier at the annual banquet of a private agency called the Oregon Research Institute. Both men served on the board of directors. At the banquet, Dr. Saslow observed, Johnson showed no signs of emotional distress. He looked well and cheerful, and he participated effectively in both the social and business portions of the meeting.

Now, in Saslow's office on the fifth floor of the Medical School's hospital, Johnson looked "much harassed, distraught, and troubled," as Dr. Saslow wrote in his notes. Johnson's conversation seemed weighted down by grim apprehensions about returning to the office and about his failure to solve the problems of the university. They discussed ways in which he might return to the office on a limited schedule. Could he, for example, limit his accessibility to students? Could he see every fifth student, or confine his student appointments to an hour a week, or otherwise curtail his contacts? They chuckled a little over that: there seemed to be no way.

Johnson continued to see his commencement speech as a "test" of his manhood. Dr. Saslow noted:

> We finally reached an agreement along the following lines. He could try going to his office on Wednesday, June 11th, for not more than a half day. He was to be driven there by his wife and returned home by her. His chief secretary was to limit his appointments. He was to continue taking Valium, to phone me each evening so that I could keep in touch with how he was doing. We arranged an appointment for Friday, June 13, in the afternoon. We left the question of his giving the commencement address himself or finding a substitute without a decision for the immediate present. We included some form of regular exercise each day.

Dr. Saslow saw in Johnson three major areas of disturbance. The first was his seeming inability to make decisions. The second was his apprehension about returning to the office after several days absence from it. The third was his feelings of inadequacy and self-condemnation.

He suggested to Johnson a technique for coping with these

feelings, one that had worked effectively with other patients, a technique called the "self-presentation." Once learned, it could be used at home, at the office, or anywhere he happened to find himself.

The self-presentation was a simple technique. Basically it meant spending five minutes of each hour facing directly and concretely one's "areas of disturbance" instead of allowing them to lurk vaguely and ominously in the background.

Johnson could not erase his feelings of failure by wishing them away or taking a drug. He could not conceal or deny them. But by giving them "controlled expression," Dr. Saslow explained, he might restrict them to a limited place within his life rather than allowing them to dominate it.

It was, in some ways, a personal, internal equivalent of Johnson's own philosophy for dealing with student unrest: the "controlled confrontation." For five minutes of each hour he would confront his own emotions. He would allow them to run rampant. He would let them spew out like steam from a ruptured boiler. Then, having reduced the emotional pressure to a safe level, he might proceed with his regular routine.

Dr. Saslow suggested that Johnson might profitably spend five minutes of each hour asking himself such questions as, "Precisely what does it mean to be a failure?" By directly facing such a question, he might become less sensitive to it. For now, the doctor urged Johnson to use the self-presentations in two areas: decision-making and the apprehension about returning to the office.

In the decision-making area, Johnson was to review for five minutes not more than three decisions that he must make and then decide on some step that would implement at least one of those decisions. He would then start this step during the next fifty-five minutes.

To cope with his apprehensions about the office, he was to spend five minutes during alternate hours experiencing as vividly as he could his feelings about returning. Then he was to resume his normal routine.

Many of Dr. Saslow's former patients testified that they

found the self-presentation technique effective. One woman had used it to cope with her intensely bitter and angry feelings about her former husband. By Dr. Saslow's directions, she was to go to the bedroom for five minutes of each hour and let the angry thoughts pour forth. Then each evening she was to telephone the psychiatrist and report her progress.

"I thought it sounded silly," she said later in a written comment. "But my high regard for Dr. Saslow, plus the fact that I would get to speak with him every evening on the phone, convinced me that I would give it a go. I did. The five-minute periods were filled with a tirade of A——'s injustices to me, how I hated him for everything he had done to me, how I wished him dead, castrated, mutilated, bankrupt, or even worse. . . ." She soon found that she could control her feelings. When A—— came to mind she could tell herself, *to hell with him—I'll fix him in my five minutes.* It became a very effective five-minute weapon, she concluded, useful anytime her emotions threatened to engulf her. After six days filled with five-minute anti-A—— tirades, she found that she could no longer muster up any feelings of anger toward him.

Other patients reported similar experiences. A woman with a weight problem spent her five minutes thinking thin whenever she felt hungry at nonmeal hours, and she reduced her weight from 165 to 128. The self-presentations on decision-making— concentrating one's thoughts to a few specific decisions rather than being engulfed by "all the problems"—had also worked effectively for some patients.

Charles Johnson appeared to be less enthusiastic. In his first phone conversation with Dr. Saslow, he said he found the self-presentations useful, not as a desensitizing device, but as respite from the steady working demands that he'd placed on himself. He had worked steadily for three hours that evening, taking time off only for the five-minute periods. He said that after consulting with two or three colleagues, he had decided not to go to the office at all. He would work at home instead, meeting with his subordinates in the evening.

Although Johnson worked diligently—at least he put in the

hours—his productivity was dramatically deficient. Everyone in the presidential suite knew it. The work had been piling up for weeks. The decisions simply didn't get made.

As a result, the running of the university was largely out of Johnson's hands during the period of convalescence. Chancellor Lieuallen had consulted with Ray Hawk and Charles Duncan, and they had agreed to form an ad hoc "co-stewardship" to run the university. Duncan would run the academic side, Hawk the administrative side.

The men agreed that Johnson should not be told of this arrangement and that it should not be publicized. They agreed to proceed quietly on the backlog of decisions and to keep in touch with Johnson in a way calculated to give him the impression that he was still in charge. They visited him frequently to ask his advice or secure his approval on matters they had already decided. They were, as Hawk admitted later, choosing very carefully the issues that they would take to him. They felt (and Dr. Saslow agreed) that it was important to his self-esteem that he feel he was still in charge. Yet the gentle deception also required that they confront him only with "nonthreatening" issues, to avoid disturbing what they felt was a highly precarious mental equilibrium. Thus they could take before him their list of recommended salary increases for deans and department heads. Johnson pored over the list and approved their recommendations. They discussed plans for commencement (they did not know of his intense feelings about his speech). They avoided mentioning the latest batch of acerbic letters and the grim report on the inaugural ball staged by the new radical student body president, Kip Morgan (the maintenance crew reported extensive damage to the floors and restrooms of the basketball pavilion where the ball was held; they also reported finding a lot of girls' underclothing in the dimly lit bleacher section).

The process worked reasonably well except for the incidental fees issue. Hawk could not soft-pedal it, much as he would have liked to. If he failed to mention it, Johnson asked about it. And each time the issue arose, Johnson's face clouded over with a look of grim preoccupation.

Hawk reported that he had discussed it with Chancellor Lieuallen. Out of the meeting came a chancellor's directive, dated June 5, advising presidents to "avoid any recommendations for major shifts in allocation of incidental fees" pending the outcome of a study undertaken by a new interinstitutional committee. The action had been calculated specifically to take the pressure off Johnson and the university, though it was, of course, justified on the basis of establishing a uniform policy among all schools.

Hawk did not tell Johnson about the reaction of the new student body leaders, Kip Morgan and Vice President Sonja Sweek, when advised of the chancellor's action through a letter from Hawk. They scrawled in angry red letters the words "NOT ACCEPTABLE" on the face of Hawk's letter and returned it to him.

Johnson gave no indication that he was aware of the deception, though through the week he displayed signs of inner turmoil. On two occasions, while sitting on the living room sofa with his wife, he put his head in his hands and burst out crying.

"I'm sorry," he said, tears streaming down his face. "I hate myself for doing this. I don't know why I'm doing this."

He grew more aloof and remote. He spent much of his time in the bedroom, behind a closed door. Sometimes he read paperback books; sometimes he merely lay resting. Once Jeanne Johnson lay down beside him. They chatted for a while and in the course of the conversation, she asked whether his failure to get the permanent presidency had really hurt him inside.

"No," he told her, "if I'd gotten the presidency I'd be in a lot worse shape than I am now."

Later they talked about the faculty reception they'd missed.

"I guess," he explained soberly, "that I just couldn't go out and face those people, knowing what they were going to say. They were going to say what a fine year it had been. They were going to shake my hand and tell me what a fine job I'd done. I

281

just couldn't face that. They don't know how bad things really are. They don't know what the troubles are or the decisions that still have to be made."

She asked about the psychiatrists. Were they really getting to the root of the problem?

"Well, I don't know." After a pause, he added, "I just wish they'd told me to stay home. I wish they'd told me not to go to the office at all."

She thought to herself, "Why doesn't he tell *them* that?" She'd sat through three interviews (except for one brief period when, at her suggestion, Dr. Saslow interviewed them separately), and not once did she hear him mention that point. Perhaps if he told them that, they'd understand the situation differently. When Dr. Saslow asked her, during their period alone together, "Don't you think he's getting along better?" she replied that she thought he was. She would conclude in retrospect that her husband was superbly skilled in hiding his real feelings.

Dr. Saslow had also asked her, "If Charles and I differ on what needs to be done, to what extent are you prepared to help us?" She replied that her husband was a "law unto himself," and that she was totally unprepared to exert any persuasive or coercive pressures.

Dr. Saslow did not seriously consider hospitalizing Johnson: it might have been a fatal blow to his self-esteem, and it seemed to be overreacting to a situation whose only bizarre manifestation was the single "conversion symptom"—the fugue state. As shown in studies, a person could have a single conversion symptom without having a full-blown case of "hysteria." Dr. Saslow's basic concept of treatment, then, was to desensitize his strong feelings against himself, to encourage him in such endeavors as the commencement speech but at the same time not put too high a premium on it.

In his second telephone conversation with Dr. Saslow, Johnson said he was less apprehensive now about returning to the office. He said he had been working on a number of complex university problems and seemed to be making headway. He said he did not think it necessary to keep the appointment for

Friday, June 13. "I saw no way of persuading him to keep this appointment," Dr. Saslow recounted later, "though I told him I thought it would be good for him to do it since it would mean that he and his wife would have participated in removing him from his office and work pressures for part of another day." Johnson said he'd begun to work on his commencement address and had it in fairly good shape. He said it was no longer important to him to demonstrate that he could do it as a test of his adequacy. He'd even arranged a substitute should he decide at the last minute that it was too difficult. Dr. Saslow asked him to call again on Saturday, June 14, the day before commencement.

Thoughts of the speech continued to plague him, however. Bill Blevins, visiting Johnson one afternoon, found him preoccupied with it.

"I think maybe I should give it," Johnson said. "I just don't know."

Blevins was equally uncertain. All week long the argument had raged back and forth in the president's office during Johnson's absence. Some argued that the pressures were too great, particularly with the rumored threat of a disruption by black students. Others contended that his appearance would be "therapeutic." It would allow him to end the year on a positive note and gradually to regain confidence. But in the end everyone agreed that Johnson himself would have to make the decision.

"I think you ought to do what will make you feel best," said Blevins. "You certainly should not do it out of some sense of obligation. If you think it might be too much of a hassle, perhaps you ought not to try."

"Well, I just don't know."

"We could make some adjustments in format, you know. If you decided not to participate, I know we could work out an alternative format. On the other hand, if you feel up to it, then I know people would be delighted to hear it. It's all a matter of how *you* feel, what *you* want to do."

"Well, I've got something here. It isn't much but it might just get the job done."

Blevins took note of Johnson's preoccupied look and the

perspiration breaking out on his forehead. He decided to break off the conversation about commencement addresses.

Other colleagues and friends dropped by occasionally, including Johnson's former neighbor, Max Risinger, the music professor. Ray Hawk and his wife, Phyllis, were there at the time, and the group chatted amiably, with Johnson mostly listening. Risinger told of his recent operation. "The old body's beginning to fall apart, I'm afraid," said Risinger.

"Max," said Johnson soberly, "I'd be just glad to trade you my body for your head."

Risinger remembered that comment when he heard of the strange event of a few days later.

Was it preoccupation over commencement addresses that precipitated this new incident? Perhaps it was sheer coincidence that it happened on Thursday, June 12, the evening Johnson was scheduled to give a commencement address at a local school, Sheldon High.

The speech had been cancelled when Johnson became ill, of course. But now it was Thursday evening, the time the speech would have been delivered. Just about the time the speech would have ended, Johnson returned from his nightly jogging exercises. Unseen, he picked up the keys to the Oldsmobile and drove off into the night.

Three hours elapsed and he still had not returned. Then, about three miles away, a night watchman at a construction project near the Willamette River heard strange squishing noises and stepped out of his office to investigate.

The scene was the construction site for a new branch store of the Meier & Frank Company, an historic Portland department store. The store was to become part of a complex of stores, all under a single roof, to be known as the Valley River Shopping Center, located on the north bank of the Willamette River about a mile from downtown Eugene.

It was the job of the nightwatchman, Larry Robertson, a young man of stocky build and quiet demeanor, to protect the construction from scavengers and other nocturnal visitors and to investigate and report any "suspicious activity."

The squishing noises coming up the parking lot from the direction of the river struck him as a suspicious activity.

Robertson stopped a tall, slim man, whose clothes were completely drenched. The man, wearing tennis shoes, cotton pants, and a light jacket, said he had fallen into the river.

"Could I have your name, please?" asked Robertson.

The man was reluctant to respond. "Isn't this a public area?"

"No, sir, it's not. It's a private parking lot."

The man staggered a little, but Robertson did not smell liquor on his breath. He was shivering in the cool night air. It was well past midnight.

"There's no crime," Robertson said, "but I should have your name, just in case. I have to write it in my report."

"Johnson," the man said.

Robertson immediately recognized him. "Are you President Johnson of the university?"

"Yeah." Johnson confessed his identity reluctantly. He didn't want to give his name, he said, because the incident might be picked up by the papers and result in unfavorable publicity for the university.

"Well, no need to worry about that," said Robertson. He said he worked for a private agency whose reports were not open to the public. Even the other agency personnel need not know. "I'll have to put something in my report, but I'll just put down that I stopped a man named Johnson. There are so many Johnsons in the phone book that no one will ever know it was you."

Robertson had read the news reports about Johnson's collapse from "fatigue." Now, as he looked at the president in the dim light of the doorway to his office, he concluded that Johnson was still suffering from some kind of peculiar malady. Johnson exhibited a distant, preoccupied demeanor. He seemed confused and disoriented. He said his car was parked somewhere upstream. He frankly didn't know how he got here. But now he planned to walk the rest of the way home. When Robertson found out where home was, he realized that Johnson had been walking in the wrong direction.

Robertson invited him into his office. It was warm there. He poured him a cup of coffee. He watched the water dripping off Johnson's clothes and onto the rug. Johnson's hands shook, and coffee occasionally slopped out of his cup and onto the rug. Robertson decided not to let Johnson walk on. He was frankly worried about Johnson's strange demeanor.

He called Mrs. Johnson, telling her that her husband was safe and suggested that she pick him up. But she did not have a car at home. Robertson called a taxi.

He put down the phone and turned to Johnson.

"The taxi will be here in a few minutes. By the way, I'm a student at the university myself. We probably know a lot of the same people. Do you know Ed Ebbighausen in Physics?"

Johnson brightened. Of could he knew Ed; he was an old friend. Johnson's demeanor changed abruptly and dramatically. He smiled a little.

"How are you getting along in the course work?" he asked.

"Oh, fine," Robertson said. "I'm really happy over the fact that I can study on my own now. . . ."

They conversed amiably for another ten minutes. Then the taxi arrived, and Robertson sent him off into the night, hoping he'd get home all right. He wondered if anyone else would ever know about this incident. He planned to keep it strictly confidential to protect the president from public embarrassment.

Twenty:
The Speech

Commencement 1969. The cap and gown, trimmed in royal blue, lay on the sofa. He was ready. "Gonna wear your cap and gown today, Dad?" Karen Johnson asked tauntingly. She knew that her father hated caps and gowns. He considered them too formal and too effeminate to suit a country boy from Wyoming. But she didn't push him too far; she felt dismay seeing how her father had aged over the past few months. He was getting old. She'd never thought of him as old before.

He'd probably tease her back, of course, later in the week when her grade report arrived from the university. She tried to prepare him for the shock: "Now, Dad, if my grades aren't the best, well, don't be surprised . . . you know how it is spring term. . . ."

Karen, who arrived home from the sorority on Friday bringing the Volkswagen with her, had always achieved adequate grades but seldom spectacular. Kylene, the youngest daughter, was the honor student.

Johnson wore a hard and fixed smile through the morning. Tense and preoccupied, he glanced frequently at his speech manuscript, typed by his wife the evening before. On Saturday he informed his colleagues that he'd made up his mind. He would preside at commencement and he would give the speech.

The events of Thursday night were brushed aside. He had not bothered to tell Drs. Saslow and Straumfjord about the incident, nor had he bothered to keep the "telephone appointment" with Dr. Saslow on Saturday night. The incident on Thursday night bore an uncanny similarity, however, to the episode of June 3 when he disappeared into the mountains. In each instance he had driven off, gone to water, taken a long walk, and returned dazed and confused with only a hazy memory of what had happened. This second time he had parked the car at a riverside park near the Ferry Street Bridge. From there he apparently hiked along the north bank of the Willamette River for more than a mile through dense underbrush. A journalist, retracing the route in daylight, found it impassable without either wading into the river or climbing up the bank to a nearby roadway.

Another fugue state. But quietly brushed aside. Perhaps it was his intractable aversion to medicine and doctors that caused him to ignore its significance. Within hours on either side of a fugue state he could be feeling fine and working at the height of his mental ability. At such a moment it would be inconceivable to him that he needed help. Equally important in his reasoning may have been the significance of commencement. He must finish the year by presiding at commencement and delivering the ten-minute speech. Nothing must stand in his way. Not even the threat of a disruption by black students could divert him. It was, after all, a test of his competence.

About 3,000 degrees would be conferred this day, bringing the total for the year (including the midyear commencements in September, December, and March) to 4,273 degrees, including 1,567 graduate degrees (1,273 master's degrees, and 294 doctorates).

Johnson fumbled repeatedly with his speech script. He was not satisfied with it, but he guessed that it would have to do. He did not know that another commencement speech was being written that morning for delivery to the same audience. Eight black students would be among the graduating seniors, and several of them had talked of moving en masse to the commencement platform at which two or three of them would deliver their own commencement addresses. They would tell the new graduates and their doting parents the realities of life for the black man. One of them, Ray Eaglin, ex-Marine, ex-football player, a man of tough exterior and sensitive interior, was writing such phrases as, "This is a very beautiful occasion, but there is hunger in the foothills. . . . There is racism in men's hearts. . . ."

Johnson's speech was less assertive. He had borrowed a few phrases from an earlier commencement speech, including some clichés: "We can't help but wonder what kind of alumni you will be five, ten, twenty years down the road." But where the old speech offered patent advice ("Avoid the loss of your passion and compassion . . . avoid rediscovering the wheel"), the new one questioned more than it asserted. It adopted the pedagogical tone of a teacher asking rhetorical questions to stimulate thought, but providing no answers.

The university's intelligence operations could not determine the exact nature of the rumored disruption of commencement, so it prepared for the worst. A squad of deputy sheriffs waited in a dressing room, out of sight, to be called upon in case of trouble. Ray Hawk positioned himself in the pressbox on the east side of the football stadium, where commencement was held, scanning the proceedings with binoculars, prepared to relay word by walkie-talkie radio of any possible trouble. Other deputies, both in uniform and in plain clothes, formed a phalanx guarding the commencement platform from a possible takeover.

It was something Charles Johnson had to get through, a kind of last hurdle. One more hurdle, and then there would be time to catch one's breath.

As the crowd assembled for the 2:30 processional, Ray Eaglin, wearing blue jeans beneath his commencement gown sought out his fellow black graduates. They should all sit together, he said, and move to the stage together.

One by one, they dropped out of the scheme. *I can't do it, my mother's here . . . count me out, my folks would flip . . . they drove all the way from California. . . .* And in the end, there was only Ray Eaglin. He had a reputation for being a loner anyway. It was he who wanted to build forty shacks on the front lawn of the Student Union to demonstrate the plight of poverty. He claimed to represent the interests of all blacks, but in the end he appeared to represent only himself. He had grown up in poverty in Beaumont, Texas, in a cabin lighted by kerosene lamps, raised as one of eight children by a mother who served a steady diet of biscuits and hoe cake. He never knew his father; he learned that he had died shortly before his birth. The events of his youth shaped Eaglin into a paradoxical figure: a tough exterior of an angry militant black, yet possessed of an inner sensitivity that prompted him to write more than 200 poems and ten plays. But the civil rights movements of the 1960s forced Eaglin to put away his pen. The cause required activists, not writers, so he turned activist.

In the dressing room where the faculty was donning caps and gowns for the ceremony, Charles Johnson sat alone on a bench, wanly acknowledging the greetings of colleagues. He displayed a wooden smile; he said he felt so-so, good enough, he guessed, to get through commencement if his luck didn't run out. The colleagues noticed his preoccupied demeanor and the taut muscles in his neck.

It was after the processional and the invocation that Ray Eaglin made his move. He got up from his seat high in the grandstand and began moving down the center aisle. Ray Hawk spotted him immediately from the pressbox.

"There's a man coming down toward the platform," he radioed to the officers across the field. "Stop him. Don't let him get to the platform."

They did not stop him. Hawk never understood why, but suddenly Eaglin was on the platform chatting with Charles Duncan, the dean of faculties, asking permission to speak.

"Why didn't you ask earlier?" Duncan said. "We could have put you on the program."

"Because we didn't feel that they would let us speak," replied Eaglin.

The discussion continued, and Johnson stepped back from the speaker's stand. "What's up?" he asked.

Eaglin stepped forward. "We're asking permission to give a short address to the audience."

"An address? You mean you want to speak right now?"

"Yes. But I can assure you that it's all right. We have nothing personal against nobody."

"Who is 'we'?"

"Black people. It's nothing controversial. It's very clean."

"Can you keep it short?"

"Yes. I guarantee you, we have not come to disrupt nothing. We have nothing personal. It's just a message to the graduates."

"What is your name?"

"Eaglin. Raymond Eaglin."

"All right," the president said. "All right."

Was this the rumored "disruption"? If so, it seemed mild compared to the grim predictions of the grapevine. Johnson moved back to the microphone.

"Mr. Raymond Eaglin"—he mispronounced it *Englin*—"a student at this university has asked permission to have the podium for a period of five minutes to made an address to the graduating class."

The announcement drew a scattering of boos and "no's," followed by applause.

"Perhaps you could ask for a show of hands," said Eaglin to Johnson.

"What?"

"A show of hands. Ask them if they want me to speak. If it's 'no,' then I'll leave."

"No," Johnson said firmly. He turned back to the microphone. His voice grew more assertive.

"I have decided to grant this request." (Applause.) "And I ask that you give him the courteousness of an audience."

Eaglin stepped to the microphone, and in a calm voice delivered his words.

291

"As of this moment," he began, "we are all under arrest. We are under arrest because we are perpetrators of crimes. We are symbolic of clear and present danger—the danger of ignorance, the danger of racism, the supreme danger of being forced into supporting an illegal war."

He talked about the war and about racism, sometimes stumbling over words. "It is said that the source of all trouble with student anarchists and student radicals is that their sibling days were not up to par, that well-intentioned parental toilet training somehow moved these kids to extremes. We understand par to be a chicken in every pot and two cars in every garage. Par changes from neighborhood to neighborhood. In *our* neighborhood par means rats in every house, disease in everybody, high rent for dilapidated houses, all the avenues of redress closed. . . ."

Johnson seemed captivated by the speech. When it came time later to deliver his own speech—the one that had caused him such anguish through the week—he appeared tortured by self-doubt.

"The young man who . . . ah . . . was granted the platform at the beginning of this morning's ceremonies in effect has given you a charge to the class . . . ah. . . ."

Would he discard his own speech? Abandon the whole thing? What would that do to his self-esteem? He stumbled on for a moment, ". . . ah . . . I was tempted . . . ah . . . in listening to his charge to allow that one to stand. . . ."

No one other than his wife and closest associates knew of the intense feeling about the speech as a test of his adequacy as a man. He could easily junk the whole thing. An easy way out. He plunged on.

". . . I have prepared a brief charge to the class, and I think I will give it to you now."

He read from the manuscript, stumbling over the beginning words. He talked of the inextricable tie between the graduates and their alma mater, and of the view historians might take of the year 1969 with all the "wonderful erudition of hindsight." He himself had only questions, not answers.

292

> Are the changes that are taking place in America today and that must take place in the days just around the corner a part of what will be viewed by historians as advance or retreat of civilization? Are we really faced with a living observation of what Alfred North Whitehead said when he said, "The major advances in civilization are processes which often all but wreck the society in which they occur"? Are your problems today growing at the rate which outstrips the capacity of the nations of the world?

They were questions that plagued him all through the year. The questions had also been asked, usually in more strident form, by militant-activist students through the year.

> The basic question, I suppose, is whether the university can adapt itself to the accelerating change taking place in the society in which it exists, whether it can accommodate to the demands being put upon it by all segments of society and still retain its basic and unique objectives, the nurturing, promotion, and fostering of the learning process.

Did he feel threatened by the new social forces? He talked of the paradoxes of modern life.

> There is the paradox of freedom. Having pursued freedom more successfully perhaps than any other nation, the country now finds that such freedom can lead both to civic irresponsibility and an unparalleled sense of a loss of personal freedom. The question you have hopefully been engaged in trying to answer and will attempt to answer in the days to come is *freedom for what?*

The question had always bothered him. All year long he'd been asking his wife Jeanne, "Freedom for what?" After having proven their right to distribute obscene literature on the corner of Thirteenth and University Streets did the radical students have more freedom or less freedom? And when they talked of freedom of expression in one breath and shouted down a speaker in the next, because they disagreed, just whose freedom did they have in mind? And what did they plan to use it for?

He talked of other paradoxes: greater knowledge so special-
ized that fewer people understand the world around them. Mass
communications that produce conformist thinking as opposed
to the independent thinking of the educated mind. And he
talked of change.

> If the new technology we have created can be as innovative
> as it is calculating, we may look forward to change at an
> even more rapid pace. The time span between techno-
> logical development and application is becoming startlingly
> short. Barely three years separated the invention of tran-
> sistors from their wholesale manufacture. The first manned
> space craft rocketed skyward in 1961 and by 1970 we will
> probably be on the moon. . . .
>
> Yet it is your generation that has forcibly reminded us
> that society is valuable not only in terms of its ability to
> attain some technological utopia, but in terms of the
> caliber of its people, their sense of justice and honesty, and
> their appreciation of duty, their self-restraint, and the
> excellence of their discourse and thought. And ultimately
> the ability of our society to survive will depend primarily
> on its ability to cure the ills of racial prejudice, poverty,
> decaying cities, crime, and all the other current socio-
> logical and political burdens on our mind and spirit.
>
> Your generation and ours must join hands to penetrate
> one of the biggest mysteries in American life today. Why is
> it that a can-do country somehow cannot grapple success-
> fully with its social problems?

Johnson closed with two quotations, one from Charles Dickens's
Tale of Two Cities: "It was the best of times; it was the worst
of times. . . ." and the other from Bertrand Russell who said on
his eightieth birthday: "I may have thought the road to a world
of free and happy human beings shorter than it is proving to be,
but I was not wrong in thinking that such a world is possible. . . . The world for all its horrors has left me unshaken."

The speech ended there, receiving no applause; Johnson
seemed to expect none. He immediately proceeded to the
introduction of the dean of faculties who would commence the
conferring of degrees.

The speech was over. He had delivered it. He had passed the
test. But with what grade?

After commencement Johnson stayed on the platform, posing with new graduates for family album snapshots. Then he walked to his car at a nearby parking lot. A colleague, John Lallas, director of Institutional Planning and Research, accompanied him. Lallas expressed a vast relief that the university had somehow made it—it had reached summer at last without a major explosion. Now the easy days of summer were at hand.

"Things are going to go better now," said Lallas.

"Yeah, John," said the president glumly, "but, you know, there are still a lot of decisions to make."

"Move them on. Don't make them all yourself. Move them on. Let somebody else grapple with them."

Johnson laughed, a hollow, sardonic kind of laugh. "That's what you'd do, huh? Move them on."

"Yes," said Lallas. "I would."

Johnson was quiet during the brief drive home.

Karen Johnson greeted her parents at the door. "Hi. How did it go?"

"It went really well," said Jeanne Johnson.

"Yeah," said Charles Johnson, "it went all right. A lot better than I expected."

He retired to the bedroom where he lay on top of the bed for half an hour. Then he arose and mixed Manhattans for himself and Jeanne. He joined the family on the patio.

Kylene handed him a gift-wrapped package. "Happy Father's Day," she said.

"For *me?*" he said. "Why would Kylene want to give *me* a present?"

"It's nothing, really," she said. "We just thought you'd enjoy having a few old rocks."

"Rocks? That's funny. It doesn't feel heavy enough for rocks."

"Well, they're small rocks wrapped in cotton."

He asked Kylene to tell him what was really in the package—come on, now, how about a hint?—a ritual they'd gone through countless times in the past, just as he had at home during those Depression era Christmases when family tradition dictated that each exquisite moment must be stretched out and savored. A colored shirt and tie emerged eventually from the package, plus a sweater from another package presented by Jeanne. He put the sweater on as the evening grew cooler, and promptly burned a hole in it with pipe ashes.

Karen's friend, Julie Keith, arrived later that evening in preparation for an evening on the town; they planned to hit a few cocktail lounges, Julie armed with fake identification papers to show that she was twenty-one.

"Hi, Julie." He greeted her with a wan smile, and she wished him well on Father's Day. "Well, thank you," he said. "I guess you're getting ready to go on your trip to Europe. When do you leave?"

"Tuesday. I'm all ready, except I couldn't find an AC-DC plug. I wanted to take my electric hair curlers."

"Hair curlers?" He laughed.

"Well, I decided not to take them after all."

"I should hope not. Why is it that women always have to take so much excess luggage?" He was teasing her again, just as he had so many times in the past, such as the time it was "Julie's fault" that the Volkswagen got stuck in the sand on the beach. But his heart wasn't in it this time, and he let the matter drop. He listened, eyes downcast, to Julie's excited chatter about the trip.

"First we're going to England, and we're hoping to get some tickets to the opera, and then on to Spain, and. . . ."

Later, over cocktails at the lounge, Julie asked Karen about her father. She was shocked by his appearance. He seemed so "strained . . . so tired," she said. Karen candidly retraced the story, the disappearance, the flight to the mountains, the sessions with the psychiatrist, and, finally, her intense relief that he'd gotten through the year without a major blowup. Now, with summer at hand, he'd undoubtedly get better, even though some difficult decisions remained. She worried a little, though, about his reaction to the sessions with the psychiatrists.

"I know it's not all that serious, but I can't help thinking how degrading it must be to him. How'd you feel? You'd wonder, am I cracking up?"

"Why doesn't he just quit?" asked Julie.

"Quit?"

"Yes. Quit his job. He's entitled to a vacation. Why doesn't he just drop it now that summer is here and go away for a while?"

"He can't. He's not built that way. He's got to revise the budgets and get everything ready for next year. He's not the kind of man who can walk away and leave things untidy."

"Do you think he was terribly bothered by not being made president?"

"I asked Mom about that, and she said he seemed relieved," said Karen. "But I wonder. In a way I think he probably was bothered. Until now he's been successful at everything he's done. His books, the family, his job. He's never experienced failure. When he took over the presidency, he did it exactly the same way he's done everything else. He gave it everything he had. And he didn't get anything back except a kick in the face. And when he didn't get the presidency, it was like everyone saying you haven't done a good enough job. I think he was troubled by the insult more than whether or not he got the job. But that's just my opinion. He'll never let on, of course."

June 16, the day after commencement. Back to the office for half a day . . . the beginning of the gradual reengagement process.

It was a sunny day. Everything pleasant lay on his desk, awaiting his attention. Everything unpleasant, threatening, or distasteful had been carefully removed to the desks of Ray Hawk, Charles Duncan, and Bill Blevins.

On Johnson's desk lay the memorandum from the faculty unanimously passed on June 4, the one commending him for his "record of achievement," in the face of financial constraints, restless pressures for change, and an intolerant public.

There, too, was the memorandum from the faculty of the College of Liberal Arts, his old outfit, thanking him for his "sterling leadership."

The pen and pencil set, scheduled to have been presented to him at the faculty reception the night he disappeared into the mountains, was there, too. It sat in the middle of his desk with its engraved message, *A Year of Challenge and Achievement*. He gave no indication that he noticed it. Most of his work that morning consisted of an unproductive shuffling of papers, but he said it was good to be back.

On that date, June 16, letters were being written to him, letters that began with phrases like, "All year long I've been meaning to write this letter to tell you what an excellent job you've done through the year. . . ." The letters would arrive in his office later in the week.

An excellent job you've done through the year. Looking back, it seemed almost a comical year. Dirty words. Hair. Grapes. Shacks. He wasn't laughing yet, but maybe he would later on. The anecdotes he could tell!

In an adjacent office a professor visited with Bill Blevins. They discussed the professor's idea for a new parlor game. It would be called "University President," and it would be a severe challenge to anyone who dared to play it. It would, for one thing, be the only game in which the players moved backward instead of forward. It was a game no one could win. You roll the dice, you move your player forward, you draw your penalty card. *Shanty shacks on your front lawn; go back three spaces. A coed yells an obscenity at the Mother's Club meeting; go back thirteen spaces. Long blond locks of hair creep out from beneath your star quarterback's helmet; lose one turn. A hostile alumna is keeping a tally of unmarried coed pregnancies; lose one goodwill point for each pregnancy. Your admissions director refuses to admit the daughter of your wealthiest alumnus; forfeit an endowment. A bosomy blonde coed burns her bra, and her blouse along with it, at the Free Speech Platform; go directly to jail.* With every roll of the dice, utter frustration.

And who knew the game of frustration better than Acting President Johnson?

"I'll bet Chuck Johnson could give us a lot of good ideas," the professor said. "With his sense of humor and his experiences through the year, he can probably tell us more about frustration than any man around. Why don't we talk to him about it? I mean later on, after he's licked his wounds and is back on his feet."

298

Twenty-One:
A Drive
in the Sun

I graduated from high school in 1968. I went to Lane Community College winter term, started in January. I bought me a new car and went to work for a garage. Worked there two or three months. I was supposed to be a mechanic, but they shuffled me around, put me in the used-car lot washing cars. So I quit and went to work in the woods. I worked for Crawford [Logging Company] for about two months, setting chokers, bucking limbs, and stuff like that. Then one day the foreman wanted me to drive truck. At the time, I was up there at Boulder Creek— that's up above the McKenzie Pass turnoff. I worked up there for about two or three weeks before I started driving truck.[1]

[ALAN RHINEHART]

Alan Rinehart, a tall, slim, slow-speaking youth of nineteen with a narrow, rather sad-looking face, was up at three that morning. It was June 17, a day that would reach ninety-seven degrees, the hottest of the year. In his new job as driver of a Mack B-61 logging truck, Rinehart reported to the company shop at four o'clock. There he picked up his truck and drove it empty into the mountains via winding, unpaved logging roads to a "landing" where it would be loaded with Douglas fir logs.

299

Alan Rinehart was part of Oregon's immense timber industry. It was logging and lumbering that formed the mainstay of Oregon's economy. It was the state's Number One economic asset, ahead of tourism and agriculture. In Lane County, of which Eugene was the seat, the industry provided jobs for 14,750 people with a $110 million annual payroll in 1968. Lane County was by far the most productive logging and lumbering county in Oregon. It accounted for roughly a fifth of the state's production which provided jobs for 72,300 Oregonians with a $547 million payroll.

The state income taxes paid by these people helped support public higher education in Oregon. And Boulder Creek, the site of the landing where Alan Rinehart's truck was being loaded by a machine called a "shovel loader," was mercifully far removed from the tensions of the nation's campuses. There on the moist western slope of the Cascade Mountains, the Douglas fir trees grew tall and straight. The loggers—the fallers and buckers and choker setters and 'dozer operators—expressed little understanding and even less sympathy for the "right on's" and "no way, man's" and similar arcane patois of the rich kids who tore up college campuses at taxpayers' expense.

By seven o'clock Alan Rinehart's truck, loaded with thirteen logs secured by chains, had begun the 75-mile, two-and-one-half-hour trip to the mill in Springfield. There the logs would be dumped into a millpond and, eventually, run through the mill to be sawed up into various measures of lumber.

Alan Rinehart planned to make two trips that day. An experienced driver could easily make three trips a day, making the last delivery just before sundown when loaded trucks were required to be off the highway, but Rinehart's inexperience had caused his boss to suggest a less demanding schedule for him. Rinehart had been plagued with problems in his new job as truck driver. On Friday, the thirteenth of June, his first day as a driver, he took only one load, as his boss had suggested, to permit him to get the "feel" of the truck and its handling characteristics. That was the day a highway patrolman ticketed him for a load in excess of the highway width limitations. That wasn't his fault; he had nothing to do with the way the truck was loaded—it was just bad luck. On Monday, the sixteenth, his second day as a driver, he had more bad luck—two flat tires. Now, on Tuesday, his third day, he hoped that things would go better.

That summer of 1969 was a busy logging season. Somewhere between 115 and 125 truckloads of logs would come roaring down the McKenzie Highway that day hauling mostly Douglas fir out of the mountains to the twenty lumber and plywood mills in the Eugene-Springfield area. From the upper-McKenzie River area where Rinehart was working, some 150 million board feet of lumber poured into the mills and eventually onto the lumber market during 1969. By the time the year was at an end, it would set a new record. The "board foot" was a unit of measurement peculiar to the lumber industry. A "board foot" was a slab of wood twelve inches long, twelve inches wide and one inch thick. An average-sized, three-bedroom home built to Pacific Northwest standards (i.e., almost entirely of wood), required about 10,000 board feet of lumber. Thus the lumber coming out of the upper McKenzie area during 1969 was, theoretically, enough to build 15,000 homes. The thirteen logs on Alan Rinehart's truck, now crawling down a winding, graveled mountain road at a little after seven o'clock, contained close to 5,000 board feet of timber, enough to build almost half a house. Those logs, worth about $600 at the lumber mill, weighed approximately sixteen tons. Counting the weight of the truck (twenty tons), Rinehart was responsible for guiding thirty-six tons of equipment down the mountain road and onto the McKenzie Highway to the lumber mill at Springfield.

It was about that same time that Charles E. Johnson, the acting president of the University of Oregon, tuned in the "Today" show on television and glanced at the previous day's edition of the *Register-Guard*. His own picture was on the front page: it was about the incident with Ray Eaglin. The story and the photo were spread across five columns in the middle of the

front page under the headline PROTESTER ARRESTS
AUDIENCE. It was a dramatic photo of Eaglin and Johnson
together on the commencement platform in front of the great
seal of the university. The story, however, implied considerably
more belligerence on Eaglin's part than seemed justified. The
paper mentioned only the boos and catcalls, not the applause
that greeted the event. It had Eaglin quoted as saying, "You
people are all under arrest for supporting a murderous war from
afar." It wasn't quite what the man had said.

Later, having dressed and shaved with an electric razor,
Charles Johnson sat down to breakfast. It was seven-thirty.
Jeanne Johnson was at the table with him. Karen was still in
bed. Kylene had stayed overnight with a friend. It was Mrs.
Johnson's overriding impression as she watched her husband at
the breakfast table that morning that the acting president had
weathered the storms of the year. It was as she'd hoped. Once
summer came, once the angry students had left the campus,
once the demands of the presidency had narrowed down to
matters containing lesser tensions and fewer confrontations,
he'd be his old self again. Even now he was beginning to gain a
new perspective of his role. He was beginning to see the reality
of the situation, the sheer impossibility of bringing every situation to a successful conclusion. Above all, Mrs. Johnson
sensed, he was cheerful. He had slept well. He was behaving
more like the old Chuck Johnson. He was even a little
talkative—talkative, at least, for the quiet kind of man she had
married twenty-seven years earlier.

He sat down to a breakfast of fruit, cereal, and coffee. He
adjusted his new trifocal glasses and looked out of the big
window of the dining room. It was a beautiful morning, a balmy
sixty-five degrees at seven-thirty. Then, after finishing his breakfast and a second cup of coffee, he leaned back in his chair, a
characteristic pose when he was about to announce something
important.

"Well," he said calmly, "I guess today is the day that I'm
going to have to go in and have a talk with Bill Blevins. I'm

going to have to tell Bill that there are some problems of this university that simply are not going to be solved."

She was glad to hear him say that.

Karen breezed through the dining room where he sat. "Hi, Dad. Going to work today?"

"Yeah."

"Are you going to let me take you to the office this morning?" asked Mrs. Johnson. She had been guarding the car keys ever since he disappeared that second time.

"Yeah," he said. He rose. "That was a good breakfast."

He walked to the bathroom that adjoined the master bedroom at the rear of the house. Several minutes elapsed. Karen returned to her room to write a letter. Jeanne Johnson entered and asked, "Where's your father?"

"I think he's in the den. I just heard the back door slam a couple of minutes ago."

"I just looked. He's not there. And the Volkswagen is gone."

"I thought you were going to drive him to the office."

"I was."

"Well, maybe he decided to go by himself." Karen returned to her letter. It was a few minutes after eight.

Alan Rinehart, cautiously guiding his thirty-six-ton truck down the highway, was somewhere in the vicinity of the tiny community of Nimrod on U.S. Highway 126, about twenty-seven miles east of Springfield. He was traveling west, making fair time, but being cautious. He was taking it nice and easy, and it looked as if things were going to be okay.

The tiny, cream-colored Volkswagen did not go to the university campus. It veered abruptly onto a route that led east from Eugene, bypassing the adjacent community of Springfield. The little car reached a junction with the McKenzie River Highway, U.S. 126. There it turned east, pulling out just ahead of a large truck carrying chemical supplies. The truck was also moving east, destined for central Oregon on the other side of the Cascade Mountains. Its driver, Harry V. Bedwell, followed the Volkswagen for several miles. He took particular note of it because the driver alternately slowed and speeded the car. His head kept turning left and right, as though taking in the sights.

An out-of-state tourist probably. That's what Bedwell thought. The Volkswagen would get a distance ahead of him and then slow down, permitting him to catch up. Then it would speed up again. The driver, Bedwell thought to himself, probably had never been in this part of the country before. He simply was enjoying the sights.

And why not? The McKenzie River country in June was rural America at its best. It was a kaleidoscope of gentle green scenery, of grassy meadows dotted with daisies, buttercups, and lupine, of sheep and cows and horses grazing on the lush grass. Everywhere groves of tall Douglas fir trees formed a backdrop. Sometimes the trees stood alone, giant sentinels silhouetted against the morning sun. The traffic was light going east, the direction the Volkswagen was taking, heavy going west. The westward traffic contained mostly log trucks, each thirty-six tons of logs and steel.

The Volkswagen was heading into the morning sun. A driver behind the Volkswagen, Gary Hiddleston, was bothered by the glare on the hood of his car. Hiddleston had pulled up ahead of the chemical truck and was now a few hundred yards behind the Volkswagen. The glare was so bad, Hiddleston found, that sometimes he had difficulty seeing ahead. Hiddleston was going fifty-five to sixty miles an hour, and he seemed to be gaining on the Volkswagen.

The wooden bridge was one of the most tantalizing bits of scenery on the whole McKenzie Highway, at least until one got up into the high mountain pass. A rustic wooden bridge with sides and a roof, it was built in 1912 when engineers designed bridges of wood. They put roofs on them as protection against the generous Oregon rain. Beneath the bridge flowed the clear, cold waters of the McKenzie River, reflecting the morning sun. The light danced and bounced off the water. Just before the bridge stood a yellow sign with a curved black arrow to indicate a right-hand curve. Beneath the sign was a smaller sign bearing the figure "45." That was the speed recommended by the highway engineers for the curve just beyond the bridge. A dangerous curve.

State highway patrolman Alfred M. Edwards, in his job of patrolling this section of highway, had driven that curve just about every day for four years. He tried it at various speeds and conditions. It had been his experience, substantially, that if a driver went into that curve and didn't start turning his steering wheel at precisely the right moment, he automatically would fly right straight over the centerline.

It was 8:20 a.m. Charles Ellicott Johnson, PhD, died instantly in a head-on collision with a thirty-six-ton Mack B-61 logging truck driven by Alan Rinehart, who reported:

I started around the corner, and I looked up around the corner and here he was in my lane. That's when I first saw him. He wasn't that far away. I don't know how far away he was when I first saw him. I just saw him, and when I stepped on the brake—when I saw him in my lane my first reaction was to step on the brake—it seemed like no more than the brakes started to take hold and he hit. He wasn't trying to get out of my way or anything. From the glance I got he was kind of bent over the steering wheel just kind of wiggling it a little bit. I don't know if he was trying to get out of the way or if there was something wrong with his car or what. It just happened so quick. It shocked me, really. It surprised me. I don't know where it came from. I know it seemed at the time that he was going awfully fast. I don't know, I can't say how fast he was going or anything. But when I first saw him, and the speed that I was going, it just seemed like he was going pretty fast. At first I didn't quite know what to do with myself. I got out of the truck and looked at the car, and I knew there wasn't any hope for anybody that was in it. And then, I don't know, I just kind of got ticked off that it happened. I wasn't really thinking straight, I guess. I walked over, and I was thinking about jumping into the river. I don't know if that's a normal reaction. I walked over and sat down at the guard rail. I started to feel kind of weak. Within a couple of minutes, I'd say, the State Police were there.[2]

This boy stated more or less in substance that he had been traveling west at approximately 40 miles an hour, and he was coming around this curve. He had looked ahead to see if there was anything coming—this is a bad curve. He didn't see anything. He said it was possible that when he looked the Volkswagen was behind the bridge. It other words, his line of sight was such that the Volkswagen would have been behind the bridge. He was staying on his own side of the road, was going around nice and easy, and all of a sudden he was right there. He said he hit his brakes, and it appeared to him that the Volkswagen was trying to get back into his lane—back into the eastbound lane, the direction the Volkswagen was going—and that he was swerving all over. [3]

[Notes of the police officer, Alfred M. Edwards of the Oregon State Police.]

Twenty-Two:
The Teacher

Perhaps in that last split second just prior to eternity, Charles Johnson had achieved his highest ambition of the moment. He was a teacher again. And the citizens of Oregon—the kids, the cops, the taxpayers, the alumni, the faculty—were his students. Surely there was a lesson to be learned from what came to be known as the "Tragedy of Charles E. Johnson." Johnson was, at the very least, asking an incisive question in that instant.

The use of the question had been among his favorite teaching techniques. It is a dramatic device in the hands of an accomplished teacher. It forces a student to try to find the answers on his own, in short, to *think*. The teacher can use the question to poke holes in pat answers, to penetrate through the emotional smog that so often accompanies controversial issues, and to explode specious theories. The teacher can thus help the student glimpse, if only for a fleeting moment, that ultimate Shangri-la of intellectualism, the truth. Sometimes the student, in his search for the answers, discovers that there are no answers, or at least no easy ones. That, too, is truth.

In that terrible instant just before the collision with the truck, Charles Johnson, teacher, was asking the most important and the most difficult question of all.

Why?

How does it happen that one of education's least violent men should die one of education's most violent deaths, leaving a body so crushed that even his closest associates could not identify it for sure?

He committed suicide, of course.

That's the easiest, most frequent, and least satisfactory explanation offered by citizens of Oregon. And how do they know he committed suicide?

"He was depressed."

"Everybody knows it."

"I heard it on the radio."

"Just ask anybody."

"He always took the easy way out. He always caved in to student demands. His suicide was just one more easy way out."

But look at the evidence. The death certificate, signed by the county medical investigator, said "accident." The investigating State Police officer said the crash occurred on what he'd come to recognize, in four years of patrolling that section of highway, as a tricky curve. The truck driver, the only witness, wasn't sure; at first he said it looked as if the Volkswagen was trying to get back into its own lane, though in subsequent accounts he declined to draw any conclusions. He just didn't know. Dr. Saslow, the psychiatrist, suggested that some campus problem might have triggered another "partial dissociation" or fugue state similar to the two previous ones. "Add to this his known low ability as a driver at high speeds, and little else is needed to make the most probable explanation of what happened . . . an accident and not a suicide attempt."[1] Could it be, then, that a more careful examination of the evidence, together with the application of logic and reason, might cast some doubt on suicide as the answer? It was the kind of question that ought to be asked. For up to now the citizens of Oregon have not treated Johnson with any greater dignity, compassion, or understanding in death than they had in the last year of his life.

True, they voiced all the requisite platitudes of sorrow: the promising career tragically cut short, the clear voice of compassion forever stilled, the far-sighted executive whose services the state could ill afford to lose, etc. These comments were on the public record. Their private comments were not. Privately, many citizens of Oregon ignored the complexities. Not only did they pronounce his death suicide, but many of them echoed the sentiments of a secretary in Monmouth, Oregon: "Now maybe somebody will come in and clean up the mess."

Question. Is it possible that the State of Oregon *was* the mess? That the impatient bigotry, the demands for blood, the intense emotional conflict over now trivial issues like grapes and hair and dirty words were just as symptomatic of a sick society as the most strident of revolutionary students on the campuses? The citizens decried obscenity and decaying morals on the campus. But no statewide turmoil has greeted the plethora of "skin shows" in Portland—the "naked cuties" on display at the strip joints, the "hard core action" movies, or the "adult book stores" and porno shops. And while citizens were quick, and inexplicably severe, in condemning the look of the shantytown on the campus, they have been awesomely lethargic in coping with the wretched aesthetics of Oregon's communities: the rotting urban cores, the neon and billboard-infested sprawls on the outskirts, and the polluting outpour of industrial waste into the rivers and the air. It is precisely this kind of hypocrisy that makes the young people uptight.

This is not to deny the genuine feelings of sorrow, remorse, and quite a bit of guilt felt by citizens of Oregon at the loss of the acting president. Those closest to him felt the loss most keenly. It was Ray Eaglin, the tough ex-Marine, ex-football player, who first thought of the flag. When he heard the news of Johnson's death he walked to the president's office three times. The first time, he walked into the outer office, looked around, and left without saying anything. The second time he asked, "Is it true?" "Yes." He turned and walked away. The third time he paused at the door, looking around. The secretaries thought they saw tears in his eyes. He turned and walked away, saying nothing.

He stopped a member of the university's coaching staff on the corner of Thirteenth and University streets.

"Hey, Coach, did you hear that the president got killed?"

"What president?"

"President Johnson."

"President *Johnson?*"

"University President Johnson."

"You mean Chuck? Chuck Johnson?"

"Yeah."

"My God."

The flag.

Eaglin sought out Bill Sanford, the operations manager of the Student Union.

"The flag," Eaglin said.

"What?"

"The flag. Somebody's got to lower the flag to half-mast."

"You're right. Why don't *you* do it?"

"Me?"

"Yes. Go on up and talk to Dick. I'm sure he'll say okay."

Eaglin climbed the steps to the mezzanine floor and entered the office of Dick Reynolds, the manager of the Student Union. Yes, Reynolds agreed, the flag should be lowered to half-mast in honor of the university's chief executive, and it would be altogether fitting if Ray Eaglin were to do it himself. Reynolds noticed tears streaming down Eaglin's face.

After he had lowered it to half-mast, Eaglin looked up at the flag, etched against a clear blue sky, stirring gently in a soft breeze. It was now a little after noon and warm, eighty-five degrees at least. It was going to be a hot day, like those he'd known in Texas.

Just as they were determined to pronounce the president's death suicide, many citizens of Oregon appeared certain that it was that last confrontation at commencement with "that big Negro guy" that tipped the balance of an already disturbed mind toward thoughts of self-destruction. It was all the boos and catcalls from the audience, they said, that caused the fatal emotional deterioration.[2] Eaglin began to get nasty phone calls and acerbic letters, though he claimed not to be bothered by them.

"It was business as usual for me," he told a journalist later:

I didn't mind the letters. All they meant to me was that somebody else liked the president, too. Don't you see? It just meant that they liked President Johnson, too, and if they wanted to take out their grief and anger on me, well, I guess that's all right. It wasn't anything personal.

What really bothered me were all those editorials and comments about how great a man President Johnson was. Well, black people already knew that. He was honest and open. He told us things that we could verify as facts. If people didn't see the significance of him when he was alive, it's almost a distortion to try to magnify his significance now that he's gone.

The significance of the "Tragedy of Charles E. Johnson" transcends the significance of the man himself, of course. He was the Colin Kelly of the campus wars. His fate symbolically documented the plight of all beleaguered college presidents. It fell to his lot to play the role of protagonist in a tragicomedy of monumental proportions. That the sequence of events was tragic scarcely needs elaboration. That it had elements of comedy, too, became evident largely in retrospect. Only Johnson, among all the players, saw the humor at the time, and then only briefly. To think that citizens could get so intensely and emotionally upset about a few dirty words in a flyer or about the length of somebody's hair or about a few tar-paper shacks temporarily adorning a campus lawn. That was pretty amusing.

And the marches, the demonstrations, the horrendous adenoidal cries of "Power to the people! . . . Strike! . . . Shut it down!" They, too, were good for a few laughs, at least in retrospect.

Johnson played his role well, a man of good cheer and high principle overwhelmed not only by the rampaging social forces over which he had little control, but by his own compulsive and perfectionistic self-identity. *He must not fail.* Another man with a different set of self-concepts perhaps would have played the role differently. But Johnson found himself racing forward on a freeway destined for annihilation with no off ramps in sight. It was, in short, a modern version of classical Greek tragedy.

It was Glenn Starlin, a speech professor, Johnson's longtime friend and colleague, who first drew that comparison at the First Congregational Church, located six blocks from the campus, during the Johnson memorial services. A floral display of fresh roses graced the scene. The roses came from Johnson's own garden. Though neglected by him during those last desperate weeks of the spring, the garden continued to produce flawless blooms. Starlin addressed more than 700 persons who overflowed the church:

> I know not of any oracle from Delphi with pronouncements or portents of evil which, in a classic Grecian way, dictated that the path was paved with tragic events. But the unrest, the change, the challenges, the questions, the confrontations in society in general and on university campuses in particular, are complex enough, controversial enough, important and powerful enough to have the stuff out of which modern tragedy is made.
>
> To set the scene: The classic purposes and goals of the university as an institution, led by a man of high purpose, intelligence, and stature—a royal figure being challenged by the changing forces of good and evil.
>
> This man, rising to the challenge in protecting his castle of learning through the forces of logic and reason as his convictions and ideals dictate.
>
> Action, conflict, doubt, decision, if not dramatic intrigue.
>
> A fatal flaw, which intervenes to destroy the hopes, the aims, and the desire of a noble man to accomplish a goal definitely and idealistically set. Such is the stuff tragedy is made of.
>
> Such was the fate of Charles Ellicott Johnson to be cast in the leading role. The tragic flaw here was not patterned after the dramatic examples of classic literature . . . vaulting ambition, jealousy, avarice, pride, revenge. This great, good, gentle man was cast in a more modern tragic mold—*he cared too much!* . . .
>
> He felt too deeply. . . . As time grew short, as fatigue moved in, as certain disappointments overshadowed his solid achievements, despair replaced hope. The battle was not yet won and he wanted it to be. He wondered *why*. He wondered *how* this university or any university today could be saved from the conflicting forces that prevail

upon it. . . . As he sought escape and time and solitude to reflect and reason, the tragic hand of fate moved in to steal away both time and place, and to still his thoughts for the future.

Johnson's death unleashed many public recriminations in the newspaper letter columns. Spencer W. Alpert, a law student at the university, wrote, "When a man has worked endlessly in the 'pursuit of excellence' . . . and he sees this institution heading on a path of pronounced mediocrity as a result of blind, self-righteous idealism on one side and an even blinder reaction on the other, and he can see no salvation in sight, his position is futile. This is the tragedy of Charles E. Johnson."

A professor of history, Edwin R. Bingham, wrote: "Perhaps all of us in this community and this state need to take a close look at ourselves—faculty and students (protesters and listless alike), legislators, members of the business community, farmers, all of us—to see if maybe we should give a little more quarter to leaders of Chuck Johnson's caliber; if perhaps we should be a little less certain of the rectitude of our position, a little more temperate in our demands, a trifle less corrosive in our criticism. Hell, what's the use? I suspect we shall go on practicing our particular brand of assassination, and the callous among us, the self-seeking and cynical, the carpers, the complacent and self-righteous, the play-it-safers, and the uncommitted will die in bed full of age and ashes."

Professor Bingham was right. Charles Johnson was no isolated example. Even so sparsely populated a state as Oregon has come close to destroying other college administrators. The casualty list of "walking wounded," as one administrator called them, contains the names of the state's leading educators.

There was James Jensen, of Oregon State, displaying the same haggard look and the same loss of weight as Johnson that spring of 1969. Then, during the Kent State-Cambodia demonstrations in May 1970, Robert D. Clark, Johnson's successor at the U. of O., began showing symptoms ominously similar: a haggard, preoccupied look combined with a seeming inability to recover fully from the flu.

At Portland State University, two administrators were literally carried from the battlefield during the Kent State-Cambodia paranoia. Gregory Wolfe, Portland State's president, suddenly collapsed in the middle of a crisis and was carried out of his office on a stretcher. He had been suffering from a serious ear infection and from "fatigue and exhaustion." A few days later, E. Dean Anderson, then Portland State's director of university relations, collapsed with a perforated ulcer and was rushed to a hospital by ambulance. He arrived barely in time to be saved from death due to severe internal hemorrhaging.

Meanwhile, no fewer than 11,000 of the citizens of Oregon let it be known through letters, petitions, and phone calls that they expected the wretched conditions at Portland State University and the University of Oregon to be cleaned up—and no funny business.

Charles Johnson was forgotten too soon.

Portland State's situation became so tense that Mark Howard, the president's assistant, suggested, tongue in cheek, a macabre monetary pool: "The next one of us to be carried out of the President's Office on a stretcher gets the money." His associates failed to see the humor. Perhaps Howard was using it in the manner prescribed by Johnson, to put things in perspective. With or without that perspective, the incidents at Oregon's universities through the years documented graphically the comment of Dr. George Saslow, the psychiatrist: "We learned one thing at Anzio during World War II—if you keep men exposed to combat long enough, you'll have 100 percent emotional casualties."

Combat fatigue.

There is an important analogy here. The term "combat fatigue" covers a variety of psychiatric disorders brought on by the severe distress of exposure to combat. The disorders can range from a wildly gyrating heartbeat or sudden outbursts of tears or anger to the most bizarre of symptoms: sudden inability to use an arm or a leg, to see, or even to remember—a mental blackout. Often these symptoms beset the most experienced and combat-hardened soldiers. They behaved in strange

314

ways they could not explain and because of which they often lost self-confidence and self-esteem. Military doctors have a name for it—the "old sergeant syndrome."

They simply had been in combat too long. After sufficient rest, their symptoms usually disappeared. It was this constant exposure to the perils of armed combat that caused even the coolest and most unflappable of men to behave strangely—in short, to break. How awesomely similar this is to the constant exposure of university presidents to the perils of combat. Keep a president in combat long enough and you'll have 100 percent emotional casualties.

The analogy is apt. There was a war on, and Johnson was one of the casualties. Johnson's "last flight," the one that resulted in his death, might be looked at in the same light. He was the "old sergeant," behaving in a strange, inexplicable way. The fugue state allowed the subconscious mind to take control and do the thing the conscious mind would consider too cowardly— to run. And so Johnson became like a soldier who, in the grip of a mental blackout, runs from the cover of the trench during a period of heavy bombardment. He runs through no-man's land and is cut down in the crossfire. That was suicidal, of course, but not suicide.

In Oregon, the public at large knew nothing of these peculiar psychiatric problems besetting Acting President Johnson. Some people hardly knew there was a war on. Oregon was the "vast suburb," as the late Robert Kennedy described it, far removed from the great social turmoils of the day. The problems in the urban ghettos, in the poverty belts, in the migrant labor camps were little more to a lot of Oregonians than distant rumbles on the television tube. Oregonians wished desperately to *continue* to be far removed from those issues. And when they saw the first symptoms of their approach—signs of turmoil at the University of Oregon—they reacted quite naturally. They demanded that the president do something about it. Many assumed that it was President Flemming who permitted their entry into Oregon in the first place.

It's not just Oregonians who don't know what to do with

their college presidents. Perceptive observers spoke as early as 1969 about the perils of college management on a national scale. One of them was John W. Gardner, the former secretary of Health, Education, and Welfare. Speaking at the inauguration of Kenneth Pitzer as president of Stanford in the spring of 1969, Gardner said:

> I call to your attention with some sorrow that a number of fine university presidents have had their careers destroyed by the conflict that has raged on our campuses. Looking back at those incidents, I do not think they reflect credit on any of us—the faculty, students, trustees, or alumni. We have now proven beyond argument that a university community can make life unlivable for a president. We can make him the scapegoat for every failure of the institution, every failure of society. We can use him as a target for all the hostility that is in us. We can fight so savagely among ourselves that he is clawed to ribbons in the process. We have yet to prove that we can provide the kind of atmosphere in which a good man can survive.

The words were prophetic. Pitzer, beset by impossible problems, lasted only eighteen months as president.

Also in 1969, Corbin Gwaltney, the editor of the trade paper, *Chronicle of Higher Education,* toured the nation interviewing college administrators. He returned shaken. Never before, he said, had he seen so many college executives preparing to commit "career suicide," shunting their careers away from administration and back into teaching or into other less demanding roles.

Out of such considerations comes the possible conclusion that the modern state university does not deserve the services at the presidential level of sensitive scholar-teachers like Johnson. What the modern state university deserves—and may very well get if the citizens, students, alumni, and faculty don't show more understanding and compassion for the men they place in leadership positions—is a combination of King Henry VIII and Mayor Richard Daley, the former for his ruthlessness, the latter for his machine efficiency. This would politicize the campus, as the revolutionary students wished to do. It might even give it a touch of relevance: if the university needed to cut back faculty personnel because of a budget squeeze, it could merely behead the Republicans.

In any event, even the strongest supporter of Charles Johnson's presidential tenure now concedes that he was the wrong man for the wrong job at the wrong time. Other men endured the turmoil in similar, sometimes worse, situations and survived. What was there about this man in this circumstance that turned a typically bad year at a state university into a modern version of tragedy?

Most of the answers lay within the man himself. There is nothing complex about the personal, internal forces that brought the year to its inevitable denouement.

That he "cared too much," as Glenn Starlin suggested, was certainly part of it. It was not entirely a selfless concern. The Johnson ego, his identity as a man, was inextricably linked with the tangible *thing* that stood as a monument to his accomplishment. It could be so small a thing as a medal for scholarship. It could be the master sergeant's stripes in the army, the textbooks he helped to write, the deanship of the largest segment of the university. It could be the presidency. It was important to him, no matter what. "By my accomplishments shall you know me," he seemed to be saying. He had not known failure since the frustrating days of childhood. His successes spoke so eloquently for him that he could even indulge in the luxury of downgrading himself with self-effacing humor.

Successful though he may have been, the bitter failures and frustrations of his childhood remained within him, like a caged monster, under control, but dangerous if unleashed. When circumstances conspired to drag him down—the flu, the criticisms, the indecisiveness, the disappointment, the depression—the monster escaped and began gnawing at him. But the monster, of course, was not the only trait to emerge from childhood. The characteristics that made him successful and compassionate also came from those early years.

His sensitivity and compassion were traits generally attributed to his mother and to his stepmother, both sensitive women beneath placid exteriors. Perhaps his mother's death and the two lonely, hungry years before his father's remarriage sharpened his feelings for people further. Yet he never learned to express his feelings in overt ways. He withdrew into himself, presenting a superficial façade of sunshine and cheer.

His other characteristics of note, the compulsive, perfectionistic personality, probably came from his father. Not only did Palmer Johnson behave that way himself, but he expected a lot of others as well. Charles, perhaps, viewed his father with a mixture of awe and affection: a strong authoritarian figure whose attention and praise meant a great deal to him. Palmer Johnson gave praise when it was due and withheld it when it wasn't. Perhaps the younger Johnson felt that he had failed to measure up to his father's expectations on any number of occasions, as in athletics, for example, or in defending himself against the neighborhood bullies. This caused him to strive harder and to continue to strive, setting goals for himself that may well have been quite beyond his father's expectations. It surely is more than a coincidence that all but one of his five letters to his parents during the presidential year contained a subtle look-what-I've-achieved-now theme.

This is a common motivation, and a powerful one. Equally powerful was the satisfaction Johnson obviously derived from the life of the mind, the academic setting which he chose as a way to pursue his compulsive-perfectionistic way of life. Having found recognition in the academic arena, and having been rewarded generously by it, he now felt compelled to move it forward and onward, and to defend it from new forces that threatened to harm it. He cared too much.

He cared too much in other ways. He detested leaving a job unfinished. Every column of figures had to be underscored by the double lines of the accountant. Even so minor a task as starting a fire at the beach with wet wood symbolized a challenge that must be successfully completed. But university life is singularly untidy under the best of conditions. And when the fortunes of the university began to decline, there wasn't much he could do about it except what he was doing: defend his castle of learning, absorb the blows, rise each time he fell, negotiate, explain, listen.

The decline had a personal impact. His ego was attacked. Then came the fatigue from the post-influenza period, the accompanying depression, the frantic attempts to keep pace, the haunting encroachment of old problems (the monster unleashed), and, ultimately the loss of his most important asset: his rationality.

Even the psychiatrists could offer only limited help. He rejected them just as he rejected doctors and medicine generally. He was fighting the monster. And with the monster eating at him from within, there seemed to be no solution.

Quit? Unthinkable. He couldn't give up.

Yet he couldn't make the necessary decisions.

And he couldn't give vent to his feelings. He hadn't learned to use but a few of the dozens of ways people employ to give release to emotions they don't really understand. He hadn't learned to yell, stomp, cuss, pound the table, or kick the dog. He was unflappable. Eventually the tears caught up with him. The crying caused him further loss of self-esteem in front of his wife: *I hate myself for doing this.*

And then, finally, the subconscious mind began to assume responsibility for its own defense. The beleaguered acting president uttered his last words of substance that morning. He planned to tell an associate that some problems of the university simply were not going to be solved.

Never leave a task unfinished.

Was this the trigger for that third and fatal dissociative reaction, the fugue state? Whatever the answer, it is clear that the battle-fatigued "old sergeant" acted in an irrational manner. He was, indeed, demonstrating some of the irrationality of the era, and that irrationality cost him his life. It was all very symbolic.

If the analogy with wartime battle fatigue fits, visiting the University of Oregon campus at this writing ranks with visiting the quiet, picturesque beaches at Normandy. It is spring, three years removed from that spring of despair of 1969. All's quiet on the campus.

True, one man is speaking at the Student Union Terrace, scene of countless strident confrontations in the past. He is what the students call a "Jesus freak," issuing a call to come forth and find God. The students pay him no attention. Inside the building, within earshot of the terrace, an oil portrait of Charles E. Johnson hangs at one end of a lounge. Beneath it is an inscription.

"There is no power greater than the power of a good idea."

Several groups of students worked together to buy it and present it to the university. The students, many of them, seemed haunted by the memory of Charles E. Johnson. They were not alone.

Elsewhere, too, people remembered Charles Johnson. A psychology professor, Norman Sundberg, could never rid his mind of what he perceived to be the awesome symbolism of the fatal accident: the tiny Volkswagen, representing free-wheeling intellectualism, colliding head-on with the massive, unyielding logging truck, representing the entrenched Establishment—the final confrontation.

The governor of Oregon also remained haunted. Once, during a taped interview with a journalist, Governor McCall was asked whether it was "fair to say that you were opposed to the candidacy of Johnson as permanent president?"

The governor paused, a little flustered.

"Well, I think it would be fair to say it," he said finally. "What I'm saying is that I *murdered*—"

The governor grew silent.

"Why do you say that?" the journalist asked.

"Because I think he had tremendous disillusionment and disappointment when he wasn't made the permanent president. I think he'd be alive today if he hadn't been disappointed—I mean, now what do you think?—if he'd had that vote of confidence by being selected president. . . . Well, I never conducted a campaign against Johnson, the kind where I would call every member of the board to say we've got to do this or that. I think I did suggest to Roy or Bud[3] that it wouldn't be in the public interest to have him, but—"

It was a common reaction.

Today the players in the drama of 1968-69 have dispersed. Most of the militant students and nonstudents have left. Some are running small businesses. Kip Morgan, the radical student-body president, opened a bookstore in Portland. Roy Bennett, the beret-hatted Che Guevara type, was, at this writing, serving time in the state penitentiary in connection with an attempted bombing of the Democratic party headquarters in Eugene in 1968. Arthur P. Litchman, author of the words, *a year of challenge and achievement,* died unexpectedly of a heart attack in a Portland hotel about a month after Johnson's death.

Robert D. Clark came to the university as president in August 1969 and proceeded to set up the kind of vice-presidential organization envisioned by Johnson. The incidental-fees question was settled largely on the students' terms, and some members of the Department of Athletics later professed to prefer the new system whereby students buy tickets to games at reduced prices. It allows the department to sell leftover student tickets at higher rates, thus accommodating more athletic fans and making more money. The California grape strike was settled largely on the terms asked by Cesar Chavez. The *Emerald* became independent of university control, relying for financing on advertising and circulation revenue, and its editor said he did *not* plan to use this new freedom to circulate four-letter words: obscenity is a false issue that detracts from the important matters, he explained. Radical-revolutionary students more or less agreed; they found that the obscenity had been counter-productive to their own ends, just as Johnson had predicted. Few people worried about the length of men's hair anymore. It peaked at about shoulder length in fall 1971, and appeared to be getting shorter as jobs became more scarce during a period of economic downturn. And a notoriously noisy radical student, sought out by the author for an interview, replied, "No way, man. I don't need any more publicity. What I need is a job."

In fall 1969, the University was invited to membership in the American Association of Universities, a select group (forty-eight members in 1969) of the nation's outstanding universities. The announcement, which caused scarcely a ripple of excitement in Oregon, dramatically supported Johnson's view that the university's prestige—viewed from outside the state—had never been higher.

Such has been the aftermath of the Johnson tragedy.

Many questions remained unanswered, perhaps even unasked. The answers may yet be found in the fiery crucible of rigorous debate, with ideas flowing freely, the good ones rising like cream to the top. They will certainly not come from authoritarian edicts of a president or a teacher. They will come from the students' own sense of discovery. That is the way an effective teacher operates; it was the way Charles Johnson operated.

And if the tragedy does cause a sense of discovery among the citizens of the state and nation, then Charles Johnson may yet affect eternity by bringing into dramatic focus a reality of college management: college presidents are not possessed of cast-iron stomachs and gnarled-oak minds, at least not yet. There are limits on human emotional endurance just as there are limits on physical endurances. A man's mind can be broken almost as easily as his back.

One could ask James Jensen, for instance. He was the retiring president of Oregon State University who told a journalist on the occasion of Johnson's death: "This is a terrible tragedy. I hope now the people of Oregon will understand—"

At that point he stopped abruptly. He said he'd better not go on.

Two years later the journalist asked him if he'd care to complete the statement. Just what was it that he hoped the people of Oregon would understand?

No, Jensen replied, he preferred to leave it exactly as is— forever unfinished.

By its brevity its meaning becomes clear to those who wish to understand. Those who require further enlargement are not going to understand anyway.

It's a fitting epitaph for the nation's only university president literally driven to his death by the stresses of his job during an era of unprecedented turmoil.

I hope now the people of Oregon will understand—

322

Appendix A.
Psychiatrist's Report

(Concluding Summary)

Summarizing comments. How is one to regard the fatal event? His history has indicated that as a result of the cumulative strain he was under and, in all probability, as a result of his insistence on attempting to work at his usual level while in a period of postinfluenzal asthenia, he could suddenly behave in a dissociated manner, and experience a fugue state which lasted a number of hours. He had never had such an experience before in all his life, and found it hard to understand what Dr. Straumfjord and I pointed out to him: the possibility that a capable person could lose rational control of his behavior when under sufficient strain. It appears that on a second occasion, he got himself into a situation which he could not predict and from which he needed his wife's help to extricate him.

An important possibility, then, is that on the morning of Tuesday, June 17, on entering his office[1] to continue some kind of work, he was reminded of a problem, or began working on a problem, that acted as a trigger to set off another state of partial dissociation with the capability of carrying out highly complex movements in an automatic but not fully rational manner, such as driving. Add to this his known low ability as a driver at high speeds, and little else is needed to make the most probable explanation of what happened to him—what might have happened to any other person who was a poor driver coming to this particular difficult curve in the road—to make him unable to bring his car into control in time when he found himself partly in the wrong lane or wholly in the wrong lane in the curve.

From the description given by the truck driver of Mr. Johnson's car as not moving sharply and suddenly into the wrong lane and so into a head-on collision, but rather as "drifting" into the lane, it is also most improbable that he made a deliberate or impulsive head-on collision to end his life.

My conclusion is that the probabilities are all in favor of an accident occurring as a result of the several circumstances I mentioned above, and that the accident was an accident in this sense and not a suicide attempt.

GEORGE SASLOW, M.D.
Dictated June 22, 1969

Appendix B.
Arnold's Chance,[1]
by Charles Johnson

Before Smallville knew what was happening, Littleburgh's right half had carried the ball over the goal for a touchdown!

A traveler going along in northern Wyoming by car would suddenly find himself swooping down a hill leading to a pretty village nestled in among hills. Trees thickly line the boulevards, and the houses are neat with many flowers. It is a pleasant sensation after coming off the dry plateau above. The greatest attraction according to the natives is a small brick high school in the east part of town. Though small, the high school is noted for its sports. It is situated on a lake and has water tournaments every summer. It has a fine baseball nine and a basketball team, but the sport that interests the citizens and the students most is football.

L. E. Freeman is the football coach and he sure knows his stuff, though he has learned lots of things through experience.

Freeman used to have a prejudice against negroes. A negro in his mind was way below "whites." Since, he has changed.

One year a big intelligent negro from Georgia named Arnold, came to Smallville. He was in his senior year high. That fall Freeman sized him up as a dandy fullback and found out he was, but because of his race wouldn't give him a chance. Smallville had run away with all her games so far and the only school barring her way to the championship was Littleburgh. Arnold had been on the bench all the time so far and had not played except in practice games and then it was on the second team. Littleburgh had beat Smallville every year that they had played and this year Smallville wanted to beat them very bad.

The Littleburgh eleven arrived in the morning of the day of the game and were escorted to the hotel.

That afternoon when the Littleburgh eleven trotted onto the field in their orange jerseys, coach Freeman saw that Smallville would have to play very hard to beat them. Several of their old stars were back and as they ran through several plays every thing went smoothly.

When the black jerseys of Smallville trotted out Arnold was on the bench as usual. Littleburgh won the toss and chose to receive. The refferees whistle blew and the game was on! Littleburgh immediately started plowing their way down the field and before Smallville knew it, on a wide end run, Littleburgh's right half had carried the ball over the goal for a touchdown making the score read Littleburgh *6* Smallville: *0.*

Smallville tightened up and untill the last quarter the ball was held in the middle of the field though Smallville did no scoring. In the last quarter with 2 min. to play, Reigland, Smallvilles fullback hurt his leg and had to go off the field. Arnold was looking at the water bucket and didn't notice the accident. He was startled at hearing Freemans voice saying, "Arnold, go in at full for Reigland. Arnold grabbed his helmet and was out in the field before Freeman had time to say anything else. He got into position and yelled out, "This teams no good, we can beat them." Tweeeeeet! Penilized 15 yards. Arnold felt twice as bad as the rest of the team. "I've got to make it up," he said, as he saw Freeman frown.

Arnold was called to take the ball for a center smash. He hit center like a ton of brick and made 6 yards but when he got up he was limping. Signals! He was to take the ball again. "Oh Lord," he whispered, "help me to make it." The ball snapped back and he started out limping. One of the players noticed it and yelled, "Give him a hand fellers. The whole Smallville eleven put all their strength into it. Blocking! Pushing! Putting all their strength into it. Arnold was trying to dodge and limping along. An orange jerseyd player caught up with Arnold and started to tackle him. Arnold gave a painfull leap and landed in a heap **** over the goal! Then everything went black and when he came to a lot of noise was from the grandstand and Freeman was leaning over him. "Did we win?" asked Arnold. "Yes," replied Freeman. "Pug kicked over the goal." "God answered my prayer," Arnold said joyfully. Coach Freeman had learned his lesson.

THE END

****

EDITORS NOTE

I sincerely hope you have enjoyed this
book and I thank you for your
kind attention.
Signed
Official Editor
Charles Johnson

Notes

CHAPTER THREE

1. In an interview in 1971 Flemming said: "In 1959 if anybody had told me that I'd be invited to occupy a position in Oregon I would have told him he was crazy. I had the impression that it wasn't even safe for me to go there as a visitor. While I was in Oregon representatives of the cranberry industry told me, 'You didn't render us a disservice; you rendered us a service. We knew we had people in the industry who were violating this regulation, and your decision forced us to clean house and to be more creative and imaginative in the marketing of our product.' "

2. Flemming had opposed Hall's appearance on campus when first approached by the student group wishing to sponsor him. He was persuaded, however, by faculty and administrative advisers to allow the speech. He ultimately wrote a strong endorsement of free speech as a principle worthy of a great university. If he were to make a list of undesirable characters, Flemming wrote, Gus Hall would be high on the list. But to prevent him from speaking because the university does not endorse his views would put the university in the untenable position of endorsing the views of those it *does* allow to speak. Flemming received an ovation when he announced at a faculty meeting that Hall would be allowed to speak. Later he won the Alexander Meiklejohn Award from the A.A.U.P. for his defense of free expression.

3. A passage from a poem written by Philip Whalen. Published in *Northwest Review*, Spring 1964.

4. About a year after Flemming's departure from Oregon, the date was quietly changed back to 1876.

5. Oregon's supposed complacency on social issues did not escape the attention of a prominent outsider, the late Robert F. Kennedy. When Kennedy lost the Oregon Democratic primary election in May 1968 to Eugene McCarthy, he concluded that Oregon was a "vast suburb," far removed from the social problems of the time. The interpretation was self-serving, of course. Oregon's political observers tended to attribute McCarthy's victory to his firm stand opposing the war in Vietnam. A more devious interpretation blamed Kennedy's defeat on Arthur Flemming. Kennedy talked in his campaign about many of the same social issues that Flemming had been discussing for years, and Oregonians were sick of hearing about them.

CHAPTER FOUR

1. The State System of Higher Education, formed in 1932 to consolidate the state-supported institutions of higher education, included the following units in 1968: the University of Oregon, Oregon State University, Portland State College, Southern Oregon College, Eastern Oregon College, Oregon College of Education, the University of Oregon Medical School, the University of Oregon Dental School, Oregon Technical Institute, and the Division of Continuing Education. The system was governed by a Board of Higher Education consisting of nine persons appointed by the governor.

CHAPTER FIVE

1. The administration building, Johnson Hall, was actually named for the university's first president, John Wesley Johnson, 1876-1893.

CHAPTER SEVEN

1. He had thus immortalized many, including his daughter, Kylene, of the "Kylenier Corporation," his friend and fellow accounting professor, Bob Jaedecke, who inspired "Mr. Jeda" and "Mr. Key" to form the "Jeda-Key Partnership," and his neighbor, Max Risinger, a music professor who, as head of the "Risinger Corporation," is beset by complex accounting problems.

2. Coach Arnold indicated this in an informal telephone conversation with the author, but he declined to submit to a formal interview.

CHAPTER NINE

1. The university comprised two major academic areas: the twenty departments of the College of Liberal Arts and nine professional schools. That totaled twenty-nine; the uncertain status of the remaining two departments was somehow symbolic of the unsettled times in 1969. One was Military Science, an orphan accepted neither as a liberal arts department nor as a professional school. The other was the Department of Fine Arts, once a part of the School of Architecture and Allied Arts, but which, as a result of an internecine war, secured a divorce and operated autonomously for a brief period before remarrying Architecture.

2. For inexplicable reasons, it infuriates Oregonians to hear their state's name pronounced in the slightly nasal twang of the eastern-seaboard aesthete: "Ore-GAWN" instead of its proper "OR-e-gun."

CHAPTER TEN

1. He was not nearly so guarded in a speech to a parents' group: "I don't think you can believe everything you read in the papers. They print what they think will sell papers, and they don't always worry about getting the facts straight or about waiting until a situation has been brought under control before they write about it and make it more difficult to control."

CHAPTER ELEVEN

1. The term, as applied to college presidents, was discussed by J. Kirk Sale, writing in the July-August 1970 issue of *Change* magazine. Among the presidents he described as men of "low profile": Dale Corson of Cornell, "a retiring man, low keyed to the point of apparent lethargy, quiet, rarely stirred to anger, soft-spoken, conservative."

2. The study, *Profiles of American College Presidents,* by Michael R. Ferrari, was published in 1970 by the Michigan State University press.

3. The U.O.'s Presidential Search Committee calculated its direct costs at $11,000, but no member has had the courage to calculate the indirect costs.

CHAPTER THIRTEEN

1. Comments of George White in a 1971 interview. Johnson referred to White in a 1968 speech: "I grew up living next door to a Negro family. The boy in that family was my best friend. I owe the fact that I can throw a somewhat wobbly pass with a football to his tutelage." White and Johnson were neighbors in Great Falls, Montana.

2. See Appendix B.

3. Ann Talcott, later Mrs. Keith Rohde, said the letters were preserved because of her mother's packrat habit of refusing to throw anything away. "I found letters in that trunk from boys I can't even remember."

4. For reasons he never explained, he always claimed Wyoming as his home state, rather than Montana.

CHAPTER FIFTEEN

1. McCall exaggerated slightly. A 1969 survey by Professor M. M. Chambers of Illinois State University showed Oregon ranking fifth in per capita support of higher education, behind Washington, Hawaii, Alaska, and Wyoming.

CHAPTER SIXTEEN

1. The author, serving in 1969 as editor of the alumni magazine, conducted this interview in the presence of Bill Blevins.

CHAPTER SEVENTEEN

1. And, indeed, even in 1972.

CHAPTER EIGHTEEN

1. The name has been changed here to a fictitious one.

CHAPTER NINETEEN

1. By "all three spheres," Dr. Straumfjord meant *time, place,* and *person:* he knew the date and time; he knew where he was and who he was.

2. Johnson was mistaken; he got the flu *eleven* weeks earlier.

CHAPTER TWENTY-ONE

1. From a tape-recorded interview with Alan Rinehart.

2. From a taped interview with Alan Rinehart, December 4, 1970.

3. From a taped interview with Alfred M. Edwards, Pfc., Oregon State Police, reading from notes made shortly after the accident occurred but before the identity of the deceased was known.

CHAPTER TWENTY-TWO

1. See Appendix A.

·2. Witnesses appeared to have selective memories. A tape recording of commencement reveals more applause than derision on that occasion.

3. Roy Lieuallen, chancellor, and J. W. ("Bud") Forrester, chairman, State Board of Higher Education.

APPENDIX A

1. It was thought, at first, that Johnson had gone to his office before the fatal trip on the McKenzie Highway. A telephone repairman reported seeing Johnson enter the administration building that morning. But he realized it was mistaken identity when he saw the man he *thought* was Johnson enter the building several days later.

APPENDIX B

1. "Published by Charles Johnson; copywrighted Aug. 25, 1933. Patent U.S. off."

Sources

A nonfiction book is only as good as its sources. I was fortunate to have from the beginning the most impeccable of sources, Charles Johnson himself. He had a habit of putting things in writing. He seldom shot from the hip. Even his most casual conversational remarks often found documentation in a letter or memo he'd written earlier. To discover such documents supporting one's hazy recollections of Johnson's oral comments was like finding gold in the vault to back up the paper currency.

On the theory that the faintest ink is better than the best of memories, I have relied heavily on these written sources. They include two four-drawer filing cabinets filled with presidential correspondence. They also include nineteen boxes of personal papers. And they include numerous childhood documents preserved by relatives and friends for as long as four decades.

The second major sources of information is my own memory aided by contemporary news accounts and public records. During the year recounted here, I served in a dual role as editor of the university's alumni magazine and executive secretary of the Presidential Search Committee. In these positions I saw Johnson in a variety of important and revealing circumstances. The notes I kept proved extremely useful later.

The third source of information is journalistic "footwork." I conducted 199 formal interviews, most of them tape recorded, plus perhaps another hundred informal conversations with professors and telephone repairmen and students and alumni and many others. It is impossible to list each person who contributed to this work, but some of them must be noted because I am extremely grateful for their help.

First is Jeanne Johnson, the president's widow, whose complete candor set the tone for the rest of the interviews. Other members of the family also proved immensely helpful: the children, Craig, Karen, and Kylene; the parents, Palmer and Cora Johnson; a sister, Phyllis Taylor, M.D.; an aunt, Bessie Johnson; a cousin, the late Vivian Johnson O'Neill.

I gratefully acknowledge the help of Governor Tom McCall and university President Robert D. Clark who allowed me access to state and university files and archives. I also received valuable assistance from archivist Barbara Fisher and secretaries Janice Medrano and Christine Leonard.

I also appreciate the help of the following:

Childhood friends: Ann Talcott Rohde, Burt Talcott, George White.

Presidents and former presidents of colleges and universities: Arthur S. Flemming of Oregon and Macalester, Robert Clark of Oregon, Branford Millar and Gregory Wolfe of Portland State, Dale Corson of Cornell, James Jensen of Oregon State, William C. Jones of Whittier and Oregon, Roy Lieuallen of the Oregon State System of Higher Education.

Faculty and administrative colleagues: Ray Hawk, Bill Blevins, Charles T. Duncan, John Hulteng, Chapin Clark, David Finlay, Norval Ritchey, Jerry Frei, Ivan Niven, Steve Belko, Ron Stratton, J. O. Lindstrom, Bob Findtner, Tom Ballinger, Morris Yarowsky, Lloyd Staples, Max Risinger, Mark Greene, Leona Tyler, Norman Sundberg, Clyde Patton, John Lallas, Larry Large, Jerry Kieffer, Don Schade, Glenn Starlin, Roland Bartel, Embert Fossum, Vernon Barkhurst, William Dunseth, Francis Reithel.

Former students: Ray Eaglin, Jesse Estrada, Kip Morgan,

David Gwyther, Roberta Hanna, Julie Keith, Ann Martin, Rose Noel, Wandalyn Rice, Rick Fitch, Gil Johnson, Larry Chadwick, Patty Thomas, Bill Muir, Neil Murray, Steve Neal, Larry Robertson, Tom English.

Members of the State Board of Higher Education: J. W. Forrester, Elizabeth Johnson, the late Charles Holloway.

Public officials: District Attorney John Leahy, legislators Robert G. Davis and Jason Boe, both members of a special 1969 legislative committee on higher education.

Medical doctors: Charles Williams, George Saslow, and A. A. Straumfjord.

Journalists: Lloyd Paseman and Jerry Uhrhammer of the *Register-Guard,* and Walli Schneider and Rolla Crick of the *Oregon Journal.*

Special thanks to Alan Rinehart for candor in recalling painful memories, to the U.O. budget office for tutoring me in the ways of campus fiscal management, and to the U.O. Development Fund for a travel grant.

Thanks must also go to two friends, Bob Bowlin and Lewis Goldberg, for encouraging me to undertake this project, to my colleague, Professor Dean Rea, for spurring me on through Chapter Fifteen, and to my wife, Betty Jane, for her nearly inexhaustible patience.

Printed in the United States
768300001B